"This book will make your hea[r]... [sim]ply on what it means to live and lo[ve] .... [o]ffer the chance to engage in dialogue, to collaborate, and ultimately to have the courage and wisdom to embrace the sea of possibilities within our schools."

— **Dame Alison Peacock**
chief executive officer of the Chartered College of Teaching, London

"In a world that wants to turn education into bureaucratic data management, information cramming, or ideological rectitude, we need every resource we can get that reminds us that at the heart of education lies the pursuit of the spiritual, ethical, intellectual, relational flourishing of students, teachers, and communities. This is that kind of resource, one that starts from questions about what is good rather than questions about who is right and addresses them with valuable research. Read it for fresh insight into how schools might flourish."

— **David I. Smith**
director of the Kuyers Institute for Christian Teaching
and Learning at Calvin University

"This is an exciting book. It is well researched. It has an international dimension that reveals common themes for educators, students, and schools everywhere. It has a wonderful vision of flourishing for all rooted in clear purpose, loving relationships, wise learning, high-quality resources, and total well-being. It deserves to be read by all in education—not only those who share the authors' Christian faith."

— **Paul Butler**
Bishop of Durham

"The Flourishing Schools model is essential for all schools, not just those of faith, to reflect on and commit to their purpose within education. It provides an essential basis from which an authentic culture develops. This book should be a handbook not only for school leaders but for all educators who wish to commit and connect in a deeper manner to their purpose."

— **Allana Gay**
head teacher at Vita et Pax Preparatory School
and cofounder of BAMEed Network

"*Flourishing Together* is a gift to Christian educators, students, and schools for these times. Winsomely written, it breathes peace, possibility, and practical and professional wisdom into our community life; please order a copy for your staffroom, every administrator's office, and every teacher's desk."

— **Beth Green**
provost and chief academic officer at Tyndale University

"In an age when fragmentation, isolation, and individualism abound within educational policy and practice, this optimistic and hope-filled book seeks to orient educators back to the importance of the core cultural elements that contribute to flourishing together within our school communities. In a refreshingly engaging tone, Swaner and Wolfe identify the key building blocks of what constitutes flourishing within our schooling ecosystems and seek to provide a reimagined sense of what authentic and life-enhancing flourishing looks like within contemporary educational contexts."

— **Darren Iselin**
director of research and innovation at Christian Schools Australia

"In *Flourishing Together*, Lynn Swaner and Andy Wolfe lift the eyes of Christian educators from the easily overwhelming responsibilities of their daily work to refocus on an inspiring portrayal of their Christian purpose. Bringing together insights from the USA and the UK, this unique book weaves together research themes, biblical insights, and reflective exercises to create a resource that can be used by individuals or as a staff professional development stimulus."

— **Trevor Cooling**
emeritus professor of Christian education
at Canterbury Christ Church University, UK

"A Christian vision for education is one that equips young people to live the abundant life Christ promises, to be and make disciples. But how can Christian schools be places that actually promote this vision for flourishing? Building on the groundbreaking Flourishing Schools research, Lynn Swaner and Andy Wolfe vividly detail a practical model and framework for what makes a Christian school truly *educate Christianly*, in such a manner that it is itself an act of worship."

— **Jay Ferguson**
board chair at the Association of Christian Schools International
and head of school at Grace Community School, Tyler, Texas

"What an energetic and inspiring work! This book is part education theory, part devotional, part case study, part visioning exercise, and part handbook. Swaner and Wolfe track the research, tackle the worldview questions, and try the practice. In short, this book is a multidimensional map to new frontiers of flourishing."

— **Michael Van Pelt**
president and CEO of Cardus

"When we read an excellent book, we often highlight sections, take notes, and share insights with others. *Flourishing Together* is that kind of book. Lynn Swaner and Andy Wolfe ignite our thinking, inspire our hearts for education, and engage the entire school with specific activities for each of the respective groups: teachers, students, administrators, and stakeholders. This book is an invaluable resource for schools to create vision, collaborate with one another, and construct a school culture where everyone flourishes together."

— **Jody Capehart**
author and founder of Christian and classical schools in Texas

FLOURISHING TOGETHER

A Christian Vision for Students, Educators, and Schools

Lynn E. Swaner and Andy Wolfe

WILLIAM B. EERDMANS PUBLISHING COMPANY
GRAND RAPIDS, MICHIGAN

Wm. B. Eerdmans Publishing Co.
4035 Park East Court SE, Grand Rapids, Michigan 49546
www.eerdmans.com

27 26 25 24 23 22 21   1 2 3 4 5 6 7

ISBN 978-0-8028-7957-8

Library of Congress Cataloging-in-Publication Data

A catalog record for this book is available from the Library of Congress.

Unless otherwise noted, Scripture quotations are taken from the English Standard Version.

Dedicated to Erik Ellefsen, a friend to many in Christian education,
who inspires us in living life to the fullest

Contents

CONTENTS

Foreword

In the story of creation, God looks at all that he has created, including humankind, and says, Yes! Meaning, "it is good." We're told that God made us one human race in his image, that he provided for us with a beautiful environment—the sea and everything in it, the different animals, the land with its trees and fruits and flowers, the natural resources all spread across the world. God wanted us all to flourish together.

God wanted us just to take what we needed. Remember the words of the Lord's Prayer? "Give us this day our daily bread." God wants us just to take what we need for each day so that we can flourish together.

Sadly, as humans, we have been selfish. We have taken much more than we needed, and in order to do this we have enslaved other human beings, and animals. We have told some people that they are not good enough, because of the color of their skin or because they are disabled. We created weapons of warfare, and we have destroyed our environment.

This is one of the reasons why millions of people are on the move, leaving the countries they were born in to try and get to another place where they can prosper and flourish with their families. We should never think that because we have food and drink, because we have a lovely home, because we have good clothes or we can get good medicine, that all is well. Only when everyone flourishes will we all truly flourish together.

So as we grow up, let us remember that we belong together—all who are made in God's image. We don't just get to choose the people who look like us or speak like us or the ones we like.

There is a Zulu word called *ubuntu*. It means "I am, because you are." In other words, we are a people together. We are interdependent. We do not exist by ourselves. No one really flourishes unless we flourish together. Black and white, young and old, rich and poor, with and without disability. We are all God's children.

We will flourish not on our own, but we will flourish when we are all together. And that's a wonderful message to remember and to think about as we go forward, daily living our lives. I am, because you are. Together we will flourish.

The Rt. Revd. Rose Hudson-Wilkin, Bishop of Dover CD, MBE
Address to Oak National Academy, July 2020

Preface

The genesis for *Flourishing Together* was the discovery that our organizations, schools, and leaders have a foundational question in common—namely, how do students, educators, and schools flourish? And particularly, how do they flourish in light of Jesus's claim that he came so we could have life, and have it abundantly?[1]

It may seem curious that two educators from opposite sides of the Atlantic—one from the Christian school context in the United States, and one from the Church of England school setting in the United Kingdom—would collaborate on a book exploring these questions. We first met as part of an international group of educators who traveled between the United States, the United Kingdom, Canada, and Australia, to visit each other's schools, speak with leaders and teachers, listen to students, and dialogue with university faculty (the group's learning around educational transformation and innovation is shared in a previous book, *MindShift: Catalyzing Change in Christian Education*[2]). It was through this journey of mutual learning that we discovered our common focus on educational flourishing.

In the United Kingdom, this focus is expressed in the following central question posed by the Statutory Inspection of Anglican and Methodist Schools (SIAMS) framework for school inspection, used by all Church of England and Methodist schools in the country: How effective is the school's distinctive Christian vision, established and promoted by leadership at all levels, in enabling pupils and adults to flourish?[3] And in the United States, the Flourishing Schools research initiative at the Association of Christian Schools International (ACSI) engaged over 15,000 Christian school leaders, teachers, staff, students, families, alumni, and trustees to answer a related question:

What elements of Christian school culture and community contribute to flourishing for students, educators, and the school itself?[4]

As we began to share what we learned from exploring these questions, along with the networking resources and data-driven tools our organizations were developing to help schools flourish, we hit upon a refrain that can be heard throughout this book: *anything that is worth building cannot be built alone*. Put simply, the flourishing of our schools is interconnected with that of our educators, students, and ourselves as leaders. This holds true even if classroom and office walls, school fences, geographic boundaries, and societal rifts divide us. And only by working together can we hope to overcome the resource scarcity, market competition, and accountability pressures that can constrain our schools and inhibit flourishing for all.

As Christian school educators, we see the importance of 'togetherness' foregrounded throughout Scripture. In his first letter to the church at Corinth, the apostle Paul writes: "The way God designed our bodies is a model for understanding our lives together . . . every part dependent on every other part. . . . If one part hurts, every other part is involved in the hurt, and in the healing. If one part flourishes, every other part enters into the exuberance."[5] We are also reminded of the words written by the Rev. Dr. Martin Luther King Jr. in his "Letter from a Birmingham Jail": "We are caught in an inescapable network of mutuality, tied in a single garment of destiny."[6]

A Christian vision for flourishing acknowledges our interdependence and considers the inherent implications for practices in schools. Accordingly, this book lays out a vision for educational flourishing grounded in shared purpose, committed relationships, mutual learning, abundance mindsets, and collective well-being. Although it is a hopeful vision, it is not Pollyannaish—rather, it is backed by research, grounded in a biblical worldview, and practiced every day by courageous leaders, who generously share their stories in these pages. We pray that, like us, readers will be inspired through this journey to imagine afresh how students, educators, schools, and communities can flourish together.

About Our Schools

We believe the educational vision shared in this book can be generative for schools and educators internationally. At the same time, it is important to acknowledge our own contexts, both by way of background, and because they of course inform the perspectives we bring to this work.

Church of England Schools

In 1811, a church leader in London, Joshua Watson, gathered together a group of like-minded individuals with a vision for their churches to create free educational institutions to serve the children of their parishes. At that point in time, there was no access to education for families who could not pay for it. Thus, the Church of England globally pioneered the provision of schooling for families of every socioeconomic background, by opening schools which grew quickly in size and popularity and spread across England through the Church of England's parish system. It was a culture-changing moment of social justice which would change the nation's approach to education and go on to influence educational provision on a global scale.

Over two hundred years later, the Church of England oversees just under five thousand schools in forty-one dioceses, each with its own bishop and educational team to provide support and governance for Church of England schools. In many rural areas, these schools—often called "village schools"— are the only educational option for families. In total, the Church of England educates over one million students, representing approximately 20 percent of the English education system—a quite remarkable engagement of church and state, and a pervasive opportunity for a Christian vision for education to impact the lives of young people.

Christian Schools in North America

The origin point for Christian schools in the United States and Canada is harder to identify as a singular event, though of course all educational institutions birthed this side of the Atlantic, some three or four centuries ago, would have been considered "Christian" at their inception. The modern Christian school in both countries owes much to Dutch immigrants who, corresponding with multiple waves of migration from Holland in the late nineteenth through the mid-twentieth centuries, founded schools and universities as part of their vision for Christian community.

Other Christian denominations, as well as independent churches and associations of like-minded families, founded Christian schools at an increasing rate through the latter half of the twentieth century. Many of these schools were formed out of explicit visions for education as part of Christ's call to discipleship and a desire to serve families in answering that call for their children. Some were founded in response to social change and upheaval that led to greater secularization of public schooling and reflected explicit efforts to further separate church and state. Still other schools in parts of the United States continue to grapple with painful histories, as they were founded in response to the desegregation of public schools during the civil rights movement. In more recent years, new Christian schools have been founded in urban areas to serve students in under-resourced communities, often thanks to availability of publicly funded school choice programs.

This uneven history is reflected in the tapestry of Christian schooling in North America today. Schools can be independent or church-sponsored. If church-sponsored, they can be Baptist, Reformed, Pentecostal, Presbyterian, Lutheran, Episcopal, Mennonite, affiliated with other denominations, or non-denominational. Some schools enroll students from any faith background or none, while others require that at least one of a student's parents affirm Christian beliefs. Several different Christian school associations serve schools throughout North America, with the largest being the Association of Christian Schools International (ACSI). With close to 2,300 member schools in the United States, along with another 25,000 affiliated schools in nearly a hundred countries, ACSI has a reach of over five million students worldwide.

Introduction

How do students, educators, and schools flourish together? We encourage you to pause for a moment to reflect on this question. What comes to mind when you imagine flourishing students? What do flourishing teachers and leaders look like? And what does it look like for an entire school to flourish?

These are the questions at the heart of this book. They are also questions we have asked thousands of educators in our own countries and across the world. And to a person, we have found that leaders and teachers know flourishing *when they see it*—in students who are exuberant in their learning and are growing socially, emotionally, physically, and spiritually; in educators who love their students and their craft, and who are ever improving as professionals and serving well together with colleagues; and in schools whose shared energy, creativity, authenticity, and hope overflows and blesses their communities. This reflects an important reality: flourishing is not an external ideal, or something that is completely foreign to us as educators. Instead, flourishing is something that we intuitively know ought to be the goal of education for students, the purpose of our lives as professionals, and something we desire ultimately for our schools.

And yet across much of education, flourishing is often far from the norm. In fact, it seems that many factors serve to inhibit flourishing in schools, whether financial pressures or limited resources, overworked teachers and leaders, students' struggles outside of school, or societal rifts related to inequality and injustice. Schools are also influenced by reductionist views of the purposes of education, reflected in shallow definitions and measures of success for which our societies have settled; thus while schools' mission statements may be loftily expansive, the daily experience of educators and students alike reflects a much narrower story about what can be accomplished in schools. We can witness the convergence of these realities in all-too-common educational "fallout," from student disengagement to teacher burnout to school closures.

Our goal in this book is to *call us back* to educational flourishing, in the hope that by doing so, we will find fresh vision and energy to reimagine our schools—and ourselves—as what we intuitively desire them to be. To this end, we agree with C. S. Lewis's assertion in *Mere Christianity*: "Really great moral teachers never do introduce new moralities. . . . The real job of every moral teacher is to keep on bringing us back, time after time, to the old simple principles which we are all so anxious not to see; like bringing a horse back and back to the fence it has refused to jump or bringing a child back and back to the bit in its lesson that it wants to shirk."[1] As Lewis suggests, the journey toward flourishing involves a journey back—back to the heart of education, and what it means to be an educator. And in fact, we believe that it is precisely in going back that we can discover generative ways of going forward.

While we desire deeply for all schools to embark on this journey, our starting point is the Christian education sector. This is not just because we work with Christian schools, although of course our day-to-day work is highly influential in our thinking. But rather, it is because we believe that a Christian vision has much to offer in terms of broadening the purpose, goals, and intended impact of education on flourishing. We take our cue from Jesus, who declares in the Gospel of John, "I came to give life—life in all its fullness."[2] If this was Jesus's purpose in his life and ministry and in the incarnation itself, we would reasonably expect that communities, organizations, and institutions bearing his name would reflect this abundant life. Where they do not, a Christian vision would suggest our own human tendencies toward fear, pride, selfishness, and exclusivity (to name a few) are at fault. But that same vision would encourage us with overflowing hope that transformation in our schools, our students, and ourselves is possible. And a Christian vision would fill us with the all-sufficient, enabling grace we need to rethink and reshape our practices such that they aim toward flourishing. Accordingly, the goal of this book is to lay out such a vision.

Flourishing is far from a new concept, and indeed many frames have been used to explore flourishing—perhaps beginning with the Aristotelian concept of *eudaimonia*, of human flourishing that is derived from "doing and living well." From psychology, the concept of flourishing has been used to redefine well-being as a holistic state, one that is greater than just the absence of illness.[3] Theologians from many different traditions have also deeply explored the question of human flourishing, and in fact, this book has been shaped by extensive conversation with some and draws upon the rich writing of many more.[4] Our primary orientation, however, is educational research and practice in Christian settings. As such, we have laid out the vision in this book—grounded in a biblical framework, informed by rigorous research, and enriched by actual practice in schools—so that it will be useful for school leaders and teachers, academics and researchers, and those who support Christian schools through organizational or ministry work. We also pray that educators in all sectors, and across the globe, might find something attractive in this vision for education, and thus might consider joining us in collaborative conversation about what educational flourishing could look like for all schools. We believe the offer of abundant life is available to all, freely given, and generous enough that—as the title of this book suggests—we can flourish together.

Called, Connected, Committed

Our Christian vision for educational flourishing rests upon three foundational principles—that we are *called* to flourish, we are *connected* to flourish, and we must be *committed* to flourishing in schools. While readers in the United Kingdom are likely to be familiar with the "3-Cs" language from the Church of England Foundation for Educational Leadership's *24 Leadership Practices for Education Leaders*,[5] we unpack how these principles relate to educational flourishing below.

Called to Flourish

We observed earlier that leaders and teachers intuitively know flourishing when they see it. We would suggest that, from a Christian perspective, this is because we have been *created* for flourishing. In line with the biblical narrative, a Christian vision for education views human beings as created in the image of God, as we are told in the first chapter of Genesis.[6] We also know from the Psalms that we are "fearfully and wonderfully made"[7] by a loving

Creator who delights in us. Moreover, we have been intentionally created as amazingly diverse, in a reflection of the dazzling imagination and creativity of the Creator.[8]

Even though the world we live in today is far removed from the beauty and simplicity of the creation, it was always—and still is—God's intention for us to flourish in the world he created explicitly for that purpose. While we still can enjoy the beauty and bounty of creation, we are called to work redemptively to address the pain, suffering, and injustice we now see in a hurting world. To this end, Paul's letter to the church at Ephesus makes it clear that we all have been given unique gifts by God, which enable us to do "good works, which God prepared beforehand, that we should walk in them."[9] Considered in this frame, our inherent goal as education professionals will be to build institutions that enable human flourishing. In other words, we are all *called to flourish*. We mean "called" in the sense of the word "vocation"—that there is a goal worthy of our life's work, one that is deeply meaningful and for which we are well-suited, and one that will produce fullness in our own lives as we pursue it. This is true for the children and young people who are our students, for us as leaders and teachers, and for our schools and communities.

This view toward flourishing allows us to again see students who—like teachers and school leaders—are whole human beings. It allows us to reenvision the holistic nature and process of education and to move beyond efforts to reform, improve, or otherwise change schools based on a narrow set of criteria. It permits us to reimagine our schools as places that are designed, organized, led, managed, evaluated, and known for flourishing together.

Connected to Flourish

In thinking about ways to describe flourishing together, we have found the natural world to be deeply instructive. As the Old Testament figure Job encourages us, "Just ask the animals, and they will teach you. Ask the birds of the sky, and they will tell you. Speak to the earth, and it will instruct you."[10] Specifically, we have found it helpful to consider schools as a kind of *ecosystem*. Ecosystems are complex biological environments that are defined not only in terms of all the living organisms that populate them, but also by those organisms' interactions with each other and with inanimate elements in the environment (such as topography or climate).

4

A poignant example of this interconnectedness can be observed over the last twenty-five years at Yellowstone National Park in the Western US.[11] After a seventy-year absence due to overhunting, wolves that had once been native to Yellowstone were reintroduced in 1995 in very small numbers. With the reintroduction of these apex predators, the overpopulation of elk—and their destructive overgrazing of the park—diminished. As native vegetation began to regrow in turn, species like beavers increased in numbers as well. Perhaps most remarkably, this process of revegetation and repopulation began to re-shape the actual topography of the park, including the shape and health of waterways. Twenty-five years later, the number of wolves has only grown to upward of sixty—but their impact on the ecosystem's health during that short period of time, even given their small number, demonstrates the "intricate web of relationships that is the power of nature."[12]

Similarly, schools are not simply collections of discrete programs and classrooms run by individuals who operate independently of each other. Rather, schools involve webs of relationships and reciprocal actions between leaders, teachers, staff, students, families, and others who engage with and in the school community. In this sense, we can say that we are all *connected to flourish*. We have already emphasized this concept earlier in the preface, specifically in the apostle Paul's description of our interdependence: "If one part hurts, every other part is involved in the hurt, and in the healing. If one part flourishes, every other part enters into the exuberance."[13]

And yet mutuality in flourishing is a radical notion when we consider how most students and educators experience schooling. The more common currency in school is competition: students and schools compete on the basis of academic achievement, and schools and individual teachers compete for resources. Certainly, healthy competition has its benefits and therefore has a place in schools and society. But competition alone makes a poor foundation for an entire system of education. This is because a key assumption of competition—that not all can win—is incompatible with a Christian view of educational flourishing, which again, is founded in Jesus's declaration that, for all people, "I came to give life—life in all its fullness."[14] Much like the various species of Yellowstone, the health of everyone in the educational ecosystem matters to the health of everyone else. Put simply, students, educators, and school communities flourish together, or not at all.

Committed to Flourish

We draw a final, instructive principle from the natural world regarding flourishing together: we are in need of a long horizon. In the example of Yellowstone, it took years to see positive impact of the reintroduction of wolves to the park. What if the park administrators had looked at the results after a few months—or the length of a single school year—and decided that their efforts simply were not working?

We already know intuitively that flourishing takes time. Most teachers, coaches, and parents would agree that children and young people develop at a unique—and definitely non-instantaneous—pace. Learning to read, return a tennis serve, play a violin concerto, and develop healthy friendships all take a considerable investment of time, which itself varies from student to student. Moreover, the journey to flourishing is often circuitous rather than direct—meaning that students may look very much like they may be "failing" at something, but if given the opportunity to grow through setbacks, they can acquire important skills like patience and build essential capacities like resilience.

It is crucial then to see flourishing not just as a state of being, but also as a process—one to which we must be fully *committed*. We can think of the "challenging" student who returns well after graduation to say something like, "I didn't appreciate it at the time, but what you taught me has helped me become the person I am today." Hearing these words in the future is predicated upon a daily, relational commitment to students' flourishing in the present. It requires walking alongside them through the ups and downs of their unique paths, not giving up on them—and just as importantly, not giving up on ourselves as educators or our schools as communities of learning. As Scripture informs us, and nature confirms, "For everything there is a season," and yet, a Christian vision promises we can be "like a tree planted by streams of water, which yields its fruit in season and whose leaf does not wither—whatever they do prospers."[15]

This is not to deny that external pressures and our own human limitations frequently tempt us to give up. Indeed, having a long horizon for flourishing is perhaps the biggest challenge to the way our educational systems are currently designed, as most prioritize immediate, observable results, as well as every identifiable efficiency to obtain those results. We see this from the packaging of standardized curricular content into discrete units to be mastered by students on a predetermined timeline, all the way to a linking of school budgets to improvement as measured by gains (or lack thereof) in yearly test performance. Often these realities reflect the demands òf our modern societies, themselves driven by market forces that reward what is ever better, ever faster.

The simple but inconvenient truth, however, is that human beings are not wired to immediately produce high-quality results on demand. This means than an ecological understanding of the time it takes for children and young people to learn and develop, as well as the uniqueness and unevenness of the process for every individual, will be essential to reimagining schools as sites for flourishing. This will require us to push beyond various illusions of the industrial and information revolutions, many of which have obscured very important realities about what it means to be human. And where those illusions have shaped our practice in schools, we will need to commit to questioning, dismantling, and reimagining those practices, so that our students, educators, and school communities can truly flourish together.

The Five Domains of Flourishing

In these principles—that we are *called*, *connected*, and *committed* to flourish—we see the emergence of a vision for flourishing together. For any vision to become actionable, it must allow for educators to put it into practice within their own school context. To this end, we draw upon findings from ACSI's Flourishing Schools research initiative, which engaged over 15,000 students, family members, alumni, leaders, teachers, staff, and board members in Christian schools in the United States, as well as at English-instruction international schools.[16] This research identified the following five domains, or broad areas, that are connected to flourishing outcomes for students, educators, and schools:

1. *Purpose.* A clear understanding of our shared purpose—*why* we are together at school—sets us on the path to flourishing. A common purpose helps us to be unified around clear goals and to work toward a "greater good" to which we aspire together.

2. *Relationships.* Our flourishing is dependent upon *who* we are with—together in community. As relational beings, the degree to which we value, honor,

and care for each other—students, teachers, leaders, and families alike—impacts our mutual flourishing. School communities that are characterized by a sense of belonging are places where all can flourish together.

3. *Learning.* Undoubtedly, learning is *what* students are supposed to do at school, and the quality of that learning is supremely important. At the same time, student learning is intricately linked to the learning of educators and the school itself as an organization. When we all learn together in what Étienne Wenger termed a "community of practice," as a group of people who "share a concern or passion for something they do and learn how to do it better as they interact regularly,"[17] we grow together.

4. *Resources.* Because schools are real places occupied by real people, *where* we meet together matters. Our campuses are shaped by our access to physical, technological, and human resources, which in turn shapes our experiences at school—students, educators, and families alike. However, simply "having" enough is not really "enough." Instead, practicing good stewardship and generosity when it comes to our resources contributes to flourishing, whereas competition and scarcity-mindedness inhibits it.

5. *Well-being.* The physical and emotional heath of students, characterized by healthy habits and developing resilience, is critical to whether—and *how*—students flourish. The same holds true for teachers and leaders. Those in helping professions like education can only help others effectively when they are doing so out of a place of abundance; otherwise, the results will be educator burnout and poorly educated students. For this reason, flourishing schools prioritize the well-being of their communities.

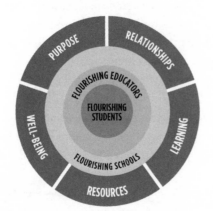

The Flourishing School Culture Model (FSCM). © 2019. Association of Christian Schools International. All rights reserved. Reprinted by permission.

These domains provide the structure for the five parts of this book—"Purpose" (Part 1); "Relationships" (Part 2); "Learning" (Part 3); "Resources" (Part 4); and "Well-Being" (Part 5). Each part consists of three chapters, which are sequenced to take us progressively deeper into each domain. The first chapter in each explores the research related to that domain; the second deepens our understanding of the domain through the lens of Scripture; and the third helps us to reimagine our practice through individual reflection and collaborative discussion with our teams. We may think of this progression as shaping our minds, hearts, and hands for flourishing.

Exploring the Research

In the first chapter for each domain, we examine the findings of the Flourishing Schools research, with a specific view toward the dynamics, dispositions, and actions in schools that have been shown to contribute to flourishing outcomes. Each of these chapters begins by considering the research findings for schools—as the larger ecosystem in which flourishing occurs—and goes on to discuss findings for educators and students. In this way, this first chapter for each domain helps us to develop the mind—meaning the understanding, and frequently the mindset—necessary for flourishing together.

We also draw upon additional research, as well as collective practice in schools, to unpack the implications for educational strategy and leadership in these chapters. As Lee Bolman and Terrence Deal have famously said in their book *Reframing Organizations*, "A vision without a strategy remains an illusion."[18] And as Richard Rumelt explains in *Good Strategy, Bad Strategy: The Difference and Why It Matters*, strategy is the opposite of a "big-picture overall direction"; rather, it "is about *how* an organization will move forward."[19] Leadership is of course key to that process, in at least two ways: leaders not only guide and implement strategy, but also shape overall school cultures that are conducive to flourishing. In other words, leaders—both those in formal roles and those in more informal or unstructured roles—help to plant the seeds for flourishing through strategy, and then till and water the soil of school culture, so that flourishing can emerge.

Deepening Our Understanding

A vision "is a clear mental picture of what *could* be, fueled by the conviction that it *should* be."[20] We hope that once readers have developed a clear picture of educational flourishing through the first chapter of each domain, the second chapter will inspire the conviction—and the heart—to take action in their schools.

To do this, we explore the ways in which a deeply Christian narrative shapes and characterizes our understanding of flourishing in each domain. We have selected five theological lenses, as follows:

- *Zoē*—a Greek word in the New Testament meaning "life," for the Purpose domain;
- *Abide*—a core theological concept in John's gospel with deep relational implications, for the Relationships domain;
- *Questions*—one of Jesus's primary pedagogical methods, for the Learning domain;
- *Bread*—one of the most valued physical and symbolic resources in the Bible, for the Resources domain; and
- *Jars of clay*—one of Paul's richest metaphors for human flourishing under pressure, for the Well-Being domain.

These five lenses are of course not exhaustive and there are many other sources of theological reflection in each of these spaces. Yet, we offer these as a starting point for going deeper—not simply in our knowledge of the Christian narrative, but especially in our sense of calling to our roles in education. We close each of these chapters with a case story from one of our schools, selected for its embrace of each theological lens and the profound ways in which its practice has been reshaped for flourishing.

Reimagining Our Practice

When it comes to considering our practice in light of a Christian vision for educational flourishing, we are reminded of the words popularly attributed to Antoine de Saint-Exupéry: "If you want to build a ship, don't drum up [workers] to gather wood, divide the work, and give orders. Instead, teach them to yearn for the vast and endless sea." Accordingly, the third chapter for each domain aims to lift our eyes to the sea of possibilities when it comes to flourishing together in schools.

To this end, we offer a series of reflections that provide "word pictures" of flourishing for students, educators, and schools themselves. In contrast to the first two chapters, this third chapter for each domain is not meant to be read in one sitting. Rather, we encourage you to read these reflections slowly and thoughtfully—even imagining a real student, educator, or school that you know, and using their names (or your own!) as you read. To encourage dialogue and collaboration, these pieces are interspersed with development activities for leadership teams (ideal for team meetings) as well as ideas that can springboard schoolwide discussion (perhaps during professional development days or strategic planning sessions).

Finally, these third chapters are ordered in reverse fashion from the first chapter for each domain—meaning that we start here with student-centered reflections, then move to educators, and close with schools. This reordering is intentional and primarily meant to demonstrate the interconnected (versus unidirectional) nature of our flourishing together. But we also hope to overcome the very natural challenges of perspective that we educators may face, thanks not only to the number of years since we were students ourselves, but also to the fact that we are usually the ones holding the authority and power in schools. By beginning these reflections with the students, as opposed to adult vistas of education, we prompt ourselves to consider deeply how students actually experience schooling—and how their voices might open up new pathways for us to flourish together.

As with anything important in life, a journey toward flourishing in schools will require that our minds, hearts, and hands work in tandem. These final chapters in each part of the book spark our imagination for what *could be*, if we allow our vision to reshape the collective work of our hands. As we travel together over the coming pages, we pray for hope, courage, and conviction to reimagine our schools as places where we experience "life in all its fullness"—together.

1

PURPOSE

1

Our Shared Calling

Education is not an end in itself; it is a *means to develop a response to our calling in life*. Consequently, when we discuss a purpose for education, it must be related to an adequate purpose for living.

—Donovan Graham, *Teaching Redemptively*[1]

Three bricklayers are asked: "What are you doing?"
The first says, "I am laying bricks."
The second says, "I am building a church."
And the third says, "I am building the house of God."
The first bricklayer has a job. The second has a career.
The third has a calling.

—Angela Duckworth, *Grit*[2]

The question of purpose is a question of story. As Steven Garber explains in *Visions of Vocation: Common Grace for the Common Good*, "Human beings are story-shaped people, stretched between what ought to be and what will be. In our imaginings, our longings, at our best and at our worst, we are people whose identities are formed by a narrative that begins at the beginning and ends at the ending."[3] Accordingly, every school has its own story—with a beginning, focused on why our schools were founded, how they were founded, and by whom; a middle, which centers on what we do every day as leaders, teachers, and students; and an aspirational end, which identifies what we aim to achieve for our school, for our graduates, for ourselves as educators, and for our communities and societies.

Most schools internationally have attempted to articulate their organizational purpose through mission or vision statements, which point directly to the story that schools desire to tell about themselves. In Christian schools these words may have an explicit or implicit biblical underpinning, or links to particular theological perspectives and local church traditions. The purpose statement for many Christian schools in North America is often grounded in what is referred to as a "biblical worldview," while for Church of England schools the terms "Christian vision" or "Christian ethos" may be more familiar. Regardless of our preference for a specific term or the intellectual and ecclesiastical history from which it arises, our statements of purpose point fundamentally to the story in which Christian schools locate themselves.

If we are to understand the purpose of our schools, we must understand this story. While in some ways it may appear similar to that of other types of schools, the principal difference is that Christian schools ground their story in the biblical narrative of the Old and New Testaments. In *Restoring All Things: God's Audacious Plan to Change the World through Everyday People*, Warren Cole Smith and John Stonestreet explain,

> The Bible is not, or not merely, a book about how to have a better life or how to handle life's problems. It is a book that explains the universe and how God is in the process of redeeming and restoring it to its original good, true, and beautiful state. . . . He created it good and loves it still, despite its brokenness and frustration. He has plans for it yet and invites the redeemed to live redemptively, for its good and our flourishing.[4]

A Christian vision of education offers this narrative as a framework for students and educators alike to see a path toward a purpose-filled life, which necessarily includes understanding the pain, difficulty, and doubts in their lives and in the world around them, as well as thinking of themselves and their unique passions and talents as "gifts" for the lifelong restorative work to which people are called. As Garber explains:

> When we see all of life as sacramental, as the graceful twining together of heaven and earth, then we begin to understand the meaning of vocation. . . .

We can begin to see that all of life, the complexity of our relationships and responsibilities—of family and friendships, of neighbors near and far, of work and citizenship, from the most personal to the most public—indeed, everything is woven together into the callings that are ours, the callings that make us *us*.[5]

We are reminded of the apostle Paul's words in his letter to the church at Ephesus, referencing the biblical narrative and our calling within it: "For we are God's handiwork, created in Christ Jesus to do good works, which God prepared in advance for us to do."[6]

While the stories of our schools may vary in their attractiveness, hopefulness, and effectiveness, all of us, together, collectively inhabit these stories. They shape how we believe and behave as individuals, how we interact with one another, and how we gauge whether and to what degree we are successful. At the same time, each of us helps to shape our school's story—and, if we work together, we can even be so bold as to *reshape* the story, in ways that lead to greater flourishing for schools, educators, and students.

Flourishing Schools

When we think about how an articulation of purpose comes to be held in common across a school community, right away we find that our metaphors around shared vision are unhelpful. Words like "casting" and "catching" vision give the impression not only that vision is something external, but also that it is something leaders toss to constituents—who in turn, may or may not "get" it. Unfortunately, this is sometimes what we find in schools; there is a huge variety in stakeholder engagement, with notions around purpose sometimes conceived by a charismatic individual school leader bringing personal vision to bear, or sometimes by an external organization (educational or ecclesiastical) imposing a set of values that may or may not be shared locally.

In contrast, flourishing together in Christian schools requires that our school's purpose be truly and authentically shared across the school community. This begins with an honest appraisal of why our schools exist and what we are trying to accomplish together. Smith and Stonestreet identify "visionary leaders" in education as those who "ask not only what makes a 'quality education' according to the standards of education experts. They also ask the question 'Why?' Why are we educating ourselves and our children? To what end?"[7] Asking "why" enables schools and teams to focus on what truly "matters." In *The Answer to How Is Yes: Acting on What Matters*, Peter Block defines the question "why" as "shorthand for our capacity to dream, to reclaim our freedom, to be idealistic, and to give our lives to those things which are vague, hard to measure, and invisible."[8] With our "why" questions and answers in full view, we move toward a shared calling in schools that both unifies us and enables us to work toward the "greater good" to which we aspire together.

Along these lines, the Flourishing Schools research found that flourishing outcomes were positively linked with everyone within the school—from trustees to administrators to teachers to staff members—having a shared sense of *responsibility*.[9] Responsibility implies much more than agreement or even buy-in, but rather involves leaders and educators interpreting purpose in and through their daily lives and work. Rather than being dictated, shared responsibility must be cultivated through collective dialogue and reflection. In *Mission Drift: The Unspoken Crisis Facing Leaders, Charities, and Churches*, Peter Greer and Chris Horst also cite the need to "intentionally craft the culture" of organizations through "traditions and practices"[10] which can either promote or inhibit the flourishing of those who engage in them. Professional development, board meetings, and schoolwide community meetings provide opportunities for intentional engagement, through reflection and dialogue, around the school's purpose. Care must also be given to the orientation or training that is commonly provided for new trustees and employees; often this induction experience focuses on role-related tasks and responsibilities, but it also presents a ripe opportunity for substantial engagement with the school's purpose.

The Flourishing Schools research also found that a school's purpose must extend beyond the school walls—involving more than a calling held just by those who work in the school—to a genuine *partnership* with school families.[11] The research showed that when families feel they are a part of the school's mission, and that their involvement with the school is truly valued, there is a positive link with greater flourishing outcomes. The emphasis in this finding is that families *feel* there is a genuine partnership. This means that understanding families' perspectives is essential, as is realizing that our actions and interactions as leaders can be perceived by others in very different ways than we intend. This means cultivating partnership with families must go beyond a suggestion box or even a parent volunteer organization, to gathering in-depth feedback, involving families in decision making, and resolving conflict in healthy ways.

Importantly, we need to also broaden the circle of families we typically invite to engage and include those who are on the margins of our school community—whether because of background, socioeconomic status, geography, work schedule, or other factors that may inhibit their meaningful involvement in the daily life of the school. To this end, it is helpful to ask ourselves "Who is missing?" and "Who are we leaving out?" when we plan school events or send out communication to families. Forging genuine partnerships requires showing hospitality and care as part of the biblical command to "love each other deeply."[12] It also requires that we be willing to change long-standing practices to remove barriers to engagement with families, and to take the time and effort needed to develop trusting relationships (something we address further in Part 2, "Relationships").

On a final note, even if our school's purpose is widely shared among staff and is manifested in genuine partnership with families, it must necessarily impact our practice in the school in tangible ways. The Flourishing Schools research found that *integrated purpose*[13]—when our biblical worldview or Christian ethos fully shapes how we educate—is linked positively with flourishing outcomes. Other research has similarly identified constructs like "coherence," or "consistency, coordination, integration, and alignment" of vision with practice as "essential beams supporting the correlates of highly productive schools."[14] A school's purpose is translated into action through our decision making, in our schedules and budgets, and frequently in how we address our most challenging circumstances. With this in mind, we turn to consider the centrality of educators—leaders, teachers, staff, as well as trustees—in translating our school's purpose into action.

Flourishing Educators

As Angela Duckworth's "parable of the bricklayers" suggests, while holding a job or having a career is an individual pursuit, fulfilling a *calling* binds us to something larger than ourselves. Whether a cathedral or a school, anything that is worth building cannot be built alone. This is because a calling imparts a sense of collective "why" that not only motivates professional work, but also provides deep meaning to that work. This in turn engenders character, excellence, and an abiding commitment. Educators who are *"called . . .* demonstrate this through their words, actions and decision making, exemplifying a strong moral purpose, confident vision, and ambitious trajectory of improvement," the outgrowth of which is a "deep sense of resilience" exhibited during seasons of challenge and change.[15]

Since most educators have little free time beyond their current workload to develop new activities and routines, the key to living out the school's purpose lies in what we are *already doing.* This necessarily begins with a realistic assessment, both personally and collectively, of how integrated our purpose is with our daily practices. This is no easy feat, given our human tendency to become entrenched in our habits of work without thinking back to how they connect to the "why." In *On Christian Teaching: Practicing Faith in the Classroom,* David Smith of Calvin University recalls a moment of revelation in this regard:

> It became viscerally clear to me how powerfully my subconscious self was scripted by particular narratives of what a teacher was supposed to look like, and that I had not consciously chosen these. Much of my teaching is shaped not so much by a clear-sighted evaluation of what will lead to the most learning at any given instant, or by my carefully honed articulations of my beliefs about God and the world, but by what I have done before, what I have seen others do, and what I assume others expect from me.[16]

If we are honest and humble, we can see ourselves clearly in the mirror of this confession. Our challenge in schools becomes to recognize where we have elevated our practices—or the things we do—above their purpose, or why we do them in the first place.

We are reminded of Jesus's statement—aimed at the religious leaders of the day, who often criticized him for healing and engaging in other life-giving ministry on the Sabbath—that the *"Sabbath was made for man, not man for the Sabbath."*[17] Since the word "sabbath" derives from the Hebrew word that means to "rest from labor,"[18] Jesus is saying the Sabbath was created to bring life to people, and not the other way around (people were not created to bring life to the Sabbath!) We can apply this principle in education by asking, for example, if our teachers and students are "made" for the master schedule—as something that dictates their day, regardless of the resulting quality of life and learning—or if the master schedule is something that is "made" for our teachers and students, to *support them* in their work in schools. The same can be asked of our curricula, budgets, assessments, and so forth: Do our practices in these areas exist for the life of our school community, or have we fallen into a mindless trap of existing for our practices?

Smith goes on to encourage us that, rather than engaging in a super-human effort to "weigh every choice, to focus on intentionally getting each one right . . . [we] need sustaining stories, habits, routines, patterns of practice out of which to live and teach."[19] In this regard, Smith highlights the relationship between practice and imagination: where our practice falls short of our purpose, imagination can reinvigorate our practices so they become "an implicit invitation for grace to give form in our lives to the vision of which it has persuaded us."[20] Similarly, Walter Brueggemann charges, "Our culture is competent to implement almost anything and imagine almost nothing. It is our vocation to keep alive the ministry of imagination."[21] Particularly in schools whose purpose arises from a biblical worldview or Christian ethos, educators can be more attuned to the capacity for boundless imagination with which we have been created, as well as to God himself, who the apostle Paul says "is able to do immeasurably more than all we ask or imagine, according to his power that is at work within us."[22]

If imagination provides a bridge between our school's purpose and educational practice, then cultivating imagination for educators becomes leaders' key priority. This can include, for example, a reorientation of professional development from acquiring skills and improving task performance to asking deeper questions about our work, embarking on pedagogical experiments, engaging the school community in creative "rethink" or "redesign" projects for programs and spaces, and inclusion and celebration of the creative arts within collective worship events and chapels. When these and similar efforts begin with a reorientation to the school's purpose, followed by an open invitation to imagine the possible, we can re-create our practices in ways that bring us closer to our collective purpose.

Flourishing Students

As educators connect their practice with their purpose in meaningful ways, they help shape a school culture where students can do likewise. We have articulated previously the symbiotic relationship between educators' and students' experiences within the school ecosystem, and this relationship is easily evident in the domain of purpose. For example, a teacher whose creativity in the classroom inspires students to explore their passions, individually as well as collectively, is less likely to hear dreaded phrases like, "Why are we learning this?" "How will we ever use this?" or "Just tell us what will be on the test!"

Along these lines, the Flourishing Schools research identified *holistic learning* as a key construct linked to student flourishing, which entails "teaching the heart and soul, as well as the mind."[23] In other words, holistic learning involves students' spiritual and emotional growth and development, in addition to cognitive learning. Most educators recognize that students are complex individuals who think, feel, act, and relate to others, and faith-based schools have often led the way in attending to students' spiritual formation and character development. People today are still engaged in creating, cultivating, developing, growing, and learning, all of which can be viewed through the lens of creation in the biblical narrative—and certainly an education that prioritizes flourishing would also prioritize these human activities through holistic learning experiences.

Even so, Christian schools may struggle against the tide of a near-exclusive focus on academic learning that drives many educational systems across the world. In these systems, high stakes testing often forces schools and teachers to design their curriculum backward to enable students to perform on tests; in turn, teacher supervision and evaluation prioritizes competencies that contribute directly to academic achievement. And for most schools, regardless of sector, programs and personnel that are deemed "non-academic" are usually the first to be reduced or cut when financial pressures are exerted.

A Christian vision for educational flourishing holds that an education which does not attend to all dimensions of human experience is "impoverished," because it fails to serve the holistic educational needs of students.[24] It is also anemic, in that it cannot adequately nurture students or those who teach them. An incomplete education can have little hope of making a significant and positive contribution to wholeness of mind, body, emotions, and relationships that contribute to flourishing. We can see this reflected, at least in part, in increasing stress and anxiety among students and in high degrees of teacher burnout and attrition. There are glimmers of hope, however; across all educational sectors, the growing emphasis on social and emotional learning and trauma-informed instruction in recent years, as well as an increasing focus on teacher well-being, is heartening.[25] But deeper conversations are needed to ask how we can structure schools and classrooms as places for holistic learning, up to and including how we measure educational success for students, teachers, and schools.

If history and current conditions are reliable indicators, our schools may need to initiate these conversations instead of waiting for external encouragement or official permission. We can start by asking our students purpose-focused questions, such as:

- "What does 'school' mean to you?"
- "What do you hope to get out of being here at school?"
- "What about our school brings you joy?"
- "What is missing from your experiences at this school?"
- "What makes you feel demotivated at school?"
- "What are your biggest hopes and dreams, and how do your experiences at this school fit—or not fit—into them?"

These questions can offer a diagnostic of how well students are flourishing in their minds, spirits, emotions, and relationships—in other words, in the wholeness of human experience. We have a lot to learn from individual and collective responses to these and similar questions, as we consider how to provide a more holistic education for our students.

Among the various dimensions of holistic learning, the Flourishing Schools research identified *spiritual formation* as especially linked with flourishing outcomes for current students as well as graduates.[26] As the word "formation" suggests, the research showed that spiritual formation is an iterative journey, rather than a one-time affirmation of belief or sign-off on a doctrinal statement. For example, the research found that students frequently asked questions about what they believed, wrestled with doubts about faith, noted a lack of time for engaging in spiritual disciplines, and grappled with what we might call "religiosity"—the proclivity of faith communities, and indeed all communities, to be judgmental of those who differ from or do not live up fully to the community standard.[27] Simultaneously, the research found that flourishing outcomes were positively linked to students seeing themselves as part of *God's story*—where students believed they were part of a bigger plan, and that they could be used by God to make a difference in the world.[28] We see in this juxtaposition that quite often students' spiritual formation involves ups and downs, and steps forward and back.

Perhaps most importantly for Christian schools, a vision of educational flourishing recognizes and normalizes these realities of spiritual formation, as well as offers a recentering of individual experience within a collective and shared journey—that is, the "bigger plan" students identified in the research. As we have emphasized at the start of this chapter, human beings are meaning-makers; the stories within which we find ourselves—and by which we are shaped—are all-important to how we understand and interact with the world. From the perspective of a biblical worldview or Christian vision, the story arc in Scripture provides a narrative framework for students to understand the brokenness they see in the world and the redemptive role they can play in response. Although our students may not articulate it in quite the same way, we can hear an echo of this in the research when they expressed a desire to "make a difference." At the writing of this book, we see an international groundswell of young people turning to activism, volunteerism, and community outreach around environmental issues, racial injustice, economic disparity, and gun violence. Regardless of whether we as educators may agree with their efforts either in approach or focus, students naturally perceive the brokenness in their world and their potential for effecting change—even without much or any prompting from us.

How might a Christian vision of educational flourishing help to nurture this sense of purpose intentionally? In *Teaching Redemptively: Bringing Grace and Truth into Your Classroom*, Donovan Graham pinpoints the need for students to learn to "act in that creation and toward others in ways that bring healing and restoration [as] a tangible demonstration of God's character. . . . God Himself identified with His people and came to them to live in their presence. The incarnation is a marvelous lesson in how we are meant to live out the image of God in the current age."[29] This collective work of restoration into which we can invite students, according to Graham, includes:

- bringing *healing* by addressing "the economic conditions that produce suffering [and] the social conditions that produce isolation and loneliness";
- being agents of *renewal* by "taking something that already exists and making something better of it ... [like] renewal in our cities, housing projects, corrupt governments, and industry that has so little concern for its workers. ... We are called to build something better that reflects the glory of God in its completion and operation just as the new heaven and new earth will";
- working for *deliverance* of others, as "redemptive activity should remove us and others from the bondage prevailing in the kingdom of darkness ... [like] poverty, drugs, sexual immorality, racial oppression ... to break the rule that such things have over the lives of people in our world";
- advocating for *justice* to "right those wrongs precipitated by the fall, especially those we inflict on one another" wherever we may find them, whether in the legal system, unethical business practice, or elsewhere; and
- seeking God's *peace*, or *shalom*, that "reflects the wholeness and togetherness God intended," whether in caring for the environment as part of God's creation or caring for others around us.[30]

In the coming chapters on relationships, learning, resources, and well-being, we drill down into educational practices that engage students in this work across these domains of flourishing. Not only will we need to examine our practices, but we will also need to think critically about our metrics—the way we measure success—as some will fall short of gauging our attainment of the broader aims of flourishing.

But for now, we return to the questions that framed the beginning of this chapter—"Why?" "Why are we educating ourselves and our children?" "To what end?"[31] A Christian vision for education responds to these questions by inviting students, as well as ourselves and our communities, to see our shared purpose through the richness of the biblical narrative. In doing so, we may come to glimpse, desire, and strive toward the promise of flourishing together.

2

Fullness of Life

"I came to give life—life in all its fullness."

—John 10:10b (NCV)

We have suggested that flourishing together begins with defining purpose—the "why," and not merely the "what, how, when, and who" of education. As purpose underpins vision, it becomes our orientation, passion, energy, compass, scales, light, reason, driver, safety, comfort, and wisdom. Where purpose exists—sometimes articulated in words, but always actually proved by actions, decision making, budgets, and schedules—it gives students and educators the potential to flourish together by drawing them toward abundant life. Where purpose is absent, confused, crowded out by external pressures, or silenced by fears within, progress becomes stilted, priorities are forgotten, and communities grow fatigued and fragmented. Purpose can never be reduced to a slick mission statement or a well-shot corporate film; rather, it is revealed in the ups and downs, twists and turns, joys and pains, and the order and the chaos of life itself.

It is no wonder therefore that Jesus spent so much of his time talking about purpose through the kind of abundant life to which we are called, as well as demonstrating tangibly just what that purposeful life could look like in miracle and mystery, in signs and stories, in relationships and rest. In John's gospel, we find Jesus boldly declaring: "I came to give life—life in all its fullness."[1] The Greek word used for "life" here is *zoē*, which is employed repeatedly by John (thirty-two times, compared to only sixteen across the other three gospels combined). *Zoē* contrasts with two other possible Greek words for life: *bios*, meaning literal "life," including breath, pulse, and physical ability, from which we draw the word "biology"; and *psyche*, meaning the mind, emotion, and will, from which we draw the word "psychology." By employing the word *zoē*, John's gospel communicates the absolute fullness of life—eternal, moral, ethical, social, cultural—in all breadth and depth of experience. Hence, "life in all its fullness." John's gospel repeatedly points us to the "real and eternal life [*zoē*] in the way he [Jesus] personally revealed it."[2] In other words, Jesus's life and ministry modeled for the disciples—and for us—what life in all its fullness looks, feels, and acts like.

In the early narrative exchanges of John's gospel when the disciples first encounter Jesus, the very first question Jesus asks may be one of the most crucial questions for any individual, community, school, team, or society: "*What do you want?*"[3] These four very simple words are ones we might ask after greeting a student who enters our office, or when we take a coffee order for a colleague. Yet at the same time, these words may well be key to unlocking a deeper understanding of how our students and we ourselves flourish, as it uncovers our motivations, vulnerabilities, hopes, fears, and needs.

This question works to frame the gospel narrative as an *education of desire*—a journey on which we as readers embark, through the stories and characters we encounter, which point to the possibility of abundance in every part of our lives. Using this lens, purpose does not simply mean our mission statement, motto, or policy documentation, but rather, our purpose says something about the formation of shared desire together—a communal will for something to happen within and because of our community. In answering the question "What do you want?" *zoē* educates our desires to be deep and broad, expressed as an ambitious and holistic purpose for flourishing together.

For students and educators alike, *zoē* invites abundance in our relationships, learning, resources, and well-being. *Zoē* is manifest when we show compassion and support, reflecting life-giving relationships that are nurtured between staff and students. It is seen when we celebrate each other's progress and success, resulting from a view of learning as a shared endeavor rather than an individual competition. *Zoē* is evidenced when our most precious commodity—time—is given freely, and students and staff alike know they are valued and loved. And it is on display when our schools take measures that prioritize health and wellness and mitigate stress and burnout, building toward an overall ecology in which students and educators alike can flourish together.

In short, *zoē* calls us back to the richest vision of education we could imagine. We say "calls us back" intentionally, because *zoē* stands as a clear counterpoint to many of the reductionist narratives that can dominate our educational culture. It challenges the narrow (and ultimately short-term) definitions of success, which constrict the purpose of education into an economic good. When the larger culture redefines "life in its fullness" as a proposition where there are clear winners and losers, it creates a zero-sum game for our relationships and interactions with one another. It also results in schools jammed into systems and structures that are based on competition and the market forces that drive it (which also frequently underpin accreditation, inspection, and assessment methodologies). Of course, the ironic statistical reality is that only half of our schools can ever be "above average."

The call to *zoē* reroutes us from this path, and while never leading us to settle for mediocrity, rather energizes us toward a broader, deeper, longer-term flourishing that will far outlast our and our students' years in our institutions. Thus, *zoē* reeducates our desires—from a narrow vision for which we have often been forced to settle, to the fullness of flourishing for which schools could aim. And as we continue on in John's gospel, we see that *zoē* calls us to *abundance*, calls us *together*, and calls us *to love*.

Called to Abundance

As the gospel narrative unfolds, John shares stories of abundance, extravagance, and generosity. Jesus's first recorded miracle is seen at the wedding at Cana, where his first sign of water changed into wine is in many ways beautiful, hospitable, and lavish.[4] In other ways, it can seem almost unnecessary and unwise (with sensible and prudent resource managers regarding it as irresponsible and unjustifiable). Later, Jesus promises the woman at a well "a spring of water welling up to eternal life," and a vast crowd gathers up a staggering twelve leftover baskets in the feeding of the five thousand.[5] Even in the detail of the breakfast Jesus shares with his disciples after his resurrection, we are told meticulously the extent of the abundance of the fishermen's catch: "It was full of large fish, 153, but even with so many the net was not torn."[6] In all of these cases, flourishing appears to be reflected in abundance in very real terms—in going well beyond what is simply "necessary."

Abundance does not happen automatically, however. By definition, abundance requires that there be a giver. In each example of abundance in John's gospel, we see that Jesus was never self-serving, but rather invited people in and drew communities together. Flourishing together is a generous activity that removes overly individualized perspectives, whereby we see our own fulfillment as justification for our actions. Instead, flourishing together prefers others in our decision making. This might lead, for example, to our students being more interested in the success of their peers over their own journey, or to our schools giving away to other schools precious expertise, time, and resources (a theme which we discuss in Part 4, "Resources").

In fact, the life of Jesus himself—culminating in the passion narrative of the crucifixion—shows that giving away, manifested in and through a willingness to suffer, is integral to abundant life. We love to use the word "passion" in leadership; it conjures up motivational speeches, energy, and joy. However, the word's root—from the Latin *passio*, meaning suffering—shows us that passion is tied to a willingness to suffer for another, as well as to *com*-passion, a willingness to suffer with another. As recorded toward the end of John's gospel, Jesus tells his disciples during their final meal together, "In the world you will have tribulation. But take heart; I have overcome the world."[7] Thus while there appears to be no promise that *zoē* will remove challenges, pain, suffering, and doubt, it does help us understand these difficult parts of our journeys and reframe them as part of a bigger story. The *zoē* life that Jesus offers enables abundance in the midst of inevitable difficulty and challenge.

Finally, *zoē* life entails a story of ongoing faithfulness versus a finalized destination. *Zoē* offers freedom to create and choose—shown in the passage in John's gospel about the gate through which the sheep "will come in and go out, and find pasture"[8]—and faithfulness to act on the familiar voice of the shepherd, whose "sheep follow him because they know his voice."[9] In this way, we are invited to go deeper into flourishing, beyond passing achievements and rose-tinted platitudes, toward a lifelong journey of learning (or discipleship) that is never finished. Flourishing is not an item to be crossed out from our to-do lists. This is very much what education is—an inherently incomplete, though richly purposeful, business. Although our systems are often focused on examinations and testing, which commonly serve as gateways to the next phase of formal learning, the reality is these are never the sole end in themselves. Instead, flourishing together is about our reflecting joy amid the very real hardships and a call to sacrifice that accompanies our pursuit of abundant life together.

Called Together

Jesus's life and ministry, as depicted in the Gospel of John, provides foundational insight into what it means to flourish *together*—beginning again with Jesus's turning water into wine at the wedding in Cana.[10] Why start with this as Jesus's first recorded miracle, his "opening act" as Messiah? What does this tell us about Jesus's mission to bring *zoē* or "life in its fullness"? In this sign, we see a theme that echoes throughout the rest of Jesus's ministry—namely, there were no conditions placed on who the wine was for, but rather, all those gathered at the wedding were invited to partake.

The vision of an abundant, purposeful life appears to be offered generously to everyone in John's gospel, regardless of their backgrounds or qualifications. In fact, the gospel narrative portrays a seemingly disproportionate number of marginalized people as the ones who take up Jesus's offer, such as the Samaritan woman at the well and a woman caught in adultery.[11] This does not happen by accident; Jesus seems to go out of his way to call out, visit, and eat with people from all walks of life, particularly those on the margins—including the segregated (Samaritans), the outcast (lepers), the powerless (widows), and the despised (Roman soldiers and colluding bureaucrats). John's gospel makes clear that *zoē* is not just reserved for the pious or privileged, but rather is on offer to those who are outsiders, vulnerable, lost, lonely, or hurting.

The widening trajectory of inclusion is seen in Jesus's claims regarding his purpose and backed up by his actions in seeking and saving the lost, setting free the oppressed, healing the sick, and helping the poor.[12] This has implications for what it might mean to flourish together in schools. If we consider whether and how our schools offer *zoē* as inclusively as Jesus does in the biblical narrative, we may be provoked to deep reflection and questioning. For example, when we think of educational flourishing, who gets to flourish? Who are our schools for? Who are they *not* for? Invariably, our answers to these questions will be reflected in our practices related to admissions, retention, and finances, to name a few. These questions will appear as a refrain throughout this book, because Jesus's words and actions suggest the centrality of inclusion for flourishing together. Asking these questions in light of *zoē* can help us better bring about the healing, renewal, and change required to move from flourishing apart—which, as we have already posited, is not truly flourishing—to flourishing together.

We can take inspiration from Christians throughout previous centuries and indeed millennia, who acted sacrificially upon this vision to found places of refuge, hospitals, and even schools that welcome all, regardless of background. At the same time, we can find ourselves grappling with the tendency that religious communities have had throughout time (including the Pharisees of Jesus's day) to gather around self-interest, often with the result that our visions for flourishing are more delimited than God's heart. We see this heralded in perhaps the most well-quoted statement of God's purpose—also found in the Gospel of John—that "God so loved the world that he gave his one and only Son, that whoever believes in him shall not perish but have eternal life [*zoē*]."[13] And it is to this connection between *zoē* and love that we now turn.

Called to Love

We began this chapter with Jesus's very first question to his disciples: "*What do you want?*" The call to *zoē* asks each of us and our schools this same question. But as we have seen, the gospel narrative does not end there. Rather, it goes on to shape and realign our desires within the context of a purpose worthy of *zoē*: love. Like *zoē*, the central concept of love is more prevalent in John compared to the other gospels, with the word being used fifty-seven times in John's gospel—more than the other three gospels combined.

From the outset, the word's usage is relentless, defining for example the relationship between God and the world and between the Father and the Son.[14] Toward the end of the narrative, it appears in the singular, repeated question that Jesus asks Peter—"*Do you love me?*"[15] And though one might imagine the gospel writer seeking to outline a wide range of teaching points and doctrinal structures, there is simplicity and precision in perfect balance when Jesus reveals his key central command: "A new command I give you:

Love one another. As I have loved you, so you must love one another. By this everyone will know that you are my disciples, if you love one another."[16]

Love one another: it is remarkably simple, yet its implications ripple out across all areas of our schools, as we consider how to enact our purpose in terms of curriculum, funding, personnel, student behavior, inclusion, networks, and professional development. This is because love is not just an abstract concept; rather, Scripture makes clear that love compels us to action—"it always protects, always trusts, always hopes, always perseveres. Love never fails."[17] Where our school routines and structures do not align with love—and quite often they may not—we need to rethink them carefully and deliberately.

What Does Love Require?

To this end, we would commend to you the simple (yet radical!) exercise used by the staff at Halton Hills Christian School outside of Toronto. For an entire year, all the educators and students at the school asked a single question of every encounter, action, and decision: *"What does love require?"*[18] This question forced a collective examination of all that happened in the school in light of Jesus's call to serve others, motivated by a desire for them to flourish and born out of sacrificial love. After a full year of applying this question—to every lesson, every book, every assembly, every interaction with parents and families, every student behavior, and every choice made from professional development to classroom design—the staff and students reported a radical transformation in their daily practice. According to principal Marianne Vangoor,

> Answering the question of "What does love require?" is not easy, and the more we asked the question at our school, the more areas we saw its application. It is a risky, demanding question but it has a simple answer—go and love in My name, or love *"Everybody, Always,"* as penned by Bob Goff in his book of the same name. This means doing things that may be hard and uncomfortable. When we as school staff struggled in this discomfort, we would remind ourselves that dying on the cross for the sins of the world was harder than anything asked of us. . . . As we've worked to answer the question "What does love require," we are excited to find that our desire and capacity to love others in our community is growing. Small steps are turning into bigger steps.[19]

As Vangoor notes, the transformation occurring within the walls of the school overflowed into how the school related to the broader community. For example, after a white supremacist shot and killed fifty-one people at two mosques in Christchurch, New Zealand, on March 15, 2019, staff and students responded to the news reports with shock and grief—and then began to ask the by-then reflexive question, "What does love require?" Their response was to host students and staff from a nearby Muslim school for a day of discussion, games, and play, in order to build relational and cultural bridges, foster understanding, and develop friendships between the school communities. Similarly, a project-based learning exercise—in which students were developing a newcomer's guide to Canada for refugees—led to students planning fundraisers to sponsor a refugee from Eritrea in his immigration journey. The students were there to greet him at the airport when he arrived in Ontario two years later, even though the project was long over.

By asking the simple yet profound question "What does love require?" for a year, engagement, empathy, care, and creativity sprung to the surface and overflowed in the lives of students and teachers, ultimately leading to a reshaping of the school culture. Not surprisingly, school leadership had a significant part to play in this transformation. As Vangoor explains,

> School leaders too have to ask the question "What does love require?" We need to ask, Am I being bold and courageous in my leadership and empowering those who work in my school to see students as capable and passionate difference makers? Am I willing to have difficult conversations that challenge perceptions or practices? Asking what love requires in your school setting will help you overcome barriers as you follow the command of Christ to love everybody always, even when it is hard.[20]

Halton Hills Christian School has been transformed by the question of what love requires—and not just for that single year. Now, some years later, Vangoor reports that it remains a constant refrain at the school, through ongoing professional development, investment of resources, and communication at all levels. As Vangoor explains, "Loving everybody always is challenging and complex work—and it is not a one-and-done."[21]

This has continued at the school even after Vangoor passed the leadership torch to a new principal, Angie Bonvanie, who explains, "Leading with love continues to be the heart of Halton Hills Christian School. Intentional succession planning has paved the way for the vision and mission to be carried on quite seamlessly. Feeling a deep sense of conviction for why we, as a school, lead with love, influences the direction of leadership and each decision that is made. It is simply part of the fabric of who we are."[22] It started off as an exercise involving a single but powerful question. Now loving others has not only become the school's purpose, but also the mechanism by which *zoē* has been more fully released in the lives of students and educators. And ultimately, it has overflowed as a blessing to the larger community.

Our exploration of "life in all its fullness" has taken us through the Gospel of John, where we see *zoē* depicted in the extravagance of the water turned to wine, the multiplication of the bread and fish, the inclusion of anyone and everyone, and the multiple depths through which this abundant life is displayed in Jesus's life and ministry. We have seen that a *zoē*-oriented purpose contributes to the flourishing of school communities, which sometimes celebrate together, at other times suffer together, and at all times are called to love together. As we continually reframe purpose in these ways, we rise to the challenge issued by the apostle Paul to Timothy, a young leader, and by extension to us—to "take hold of the life [*zoē*] which is truly life [*zoē*]."[23]

3

Reimagining Purpose

We become educators through the notion of a *calling*. . . . It might be the joy in seeing people learn; it might be a commitment to help-ing to shape the future or a passion for contributing to a learning community. . . . Making moves to improve the quality of learning for the present-day learner ignites the joy and is essential to progress.

—Heidi Hayes Jacobs and Marie Hubley Alcock,
Bold Moves for Schools[1]

What we'll meet around one bend will bring a smile to the depths of our souls while others will create a sting of conviction that will send us straight to our knees. Either way, the prize of abundant living will make the trip well worth it.

—Priscilla Shirer,
One in a Million: Journey to Your Promised Land[2]

As we reflect on the importance of purpose and the deeper calling to the *zoē* life we have explored in the first two chapters, we turn now to consider what this might actually look like in our students, educators, and schools. In shaping a series of short reflections, we hope to offer some lenses through which to see your own context afresh and inspire you to imagine what flourishing to-gether might look like. We invite you to read the six reflections in this chapter slowly (see the figure on p. 36), and keep in mind that, much like a journal or devotional, this chapter may be most helpful if read in multiple sittings.

You are building a cathedral—you may never see the outcome you're working towards.

You know the seasons—you are patient for things to change.

flourishing **educators**

schools *flourishing*

educators flourishing

We choose life every morning—life in all its fullness.

We lead with a passion for the possible—we choose to stick around.

flourishing **students** *flourishing*

I am excited about the journey ahead—I don't always need to understand the destination.

I am watching you as a role model—my character shapes my achievement.

We also invite you to engage others in collaborative discussion through the activities interspersed in the chapter.

During the compulsory schooling years, children and young people may have little choice about being on an educational journey, yet the orientation of students (and groups of students together) is fundamental to their flourishing. Students' sense of discovery, momentum, energy, and direction all shape their progress, as does their perception of the adult role models with whom they engage during their education. Reflecting on the relationship between character and achievement provides a more holistic view of a student; this is because flourishing students may well succeed in the comparative competition of the test, race, or performance, but inhibited character development may undermine any other measure of success they may attain.

For educators who are overwhelmed, under immense pressure, and are working seemingly endless hours each week, a deep and long-term perspective regarding their roles will be essential. We offer a metaphor of "cathedral building"—considering the breadth and ambition such architecture demands, as well as the investment that will last long beyond an educator's years of service. We then explore together what it might mean to notice and understand the seasons of our work and lives more accurately, so that we can develop the purpose-filled and hope-oriented resilience we need for the long haul—as well as to encourage our fellow educators in their journeys.

Finally, our reflections on flourishing schools serve to unpack the role of our purpose in our ability to "stick around" and provide the consistency and dependability that students deeply need. We explore together what hope might look like and the extent to which we might expect *zoē* life in our schools. While there are no rose-tinted solutions, a vision of flourishing together can increase our "life expectancy" in our schools, by reshaping our schedules, emails, action plans, budgets, teaching, curricula, resources, relationships, and partnerships. Only when our vision for flourishing is enacted fully in our practice can we truly say it is our vision.

"I am excited at the journey ahead—I don't always need to understand the destination."

Flourishing is not a thing you do one day and then it is done (as in "I have flourished"); rather, it is an ongoing journey. *The grammar of flourishing is the present continuous tense.*

While it is observable in the present, it is in many ways evidenced by an orientation toward the future. A student's understanding or concept of what the next steps hold is fundamental to their present flourishing. The joy of the present leads to the pursuit of the future—whether that future is known or unknown. Given that education is in many ways an inherently incomplete journey (despite the signposts of examinations along the way), a student's understanding of the path ahead has a significant impact on their motivation and engagement in the present. Flourishing longs for further growth.

This is often more chaotic than our curriculum structures may be set up to support. While subject disciplines are of course important for coherence in the curriculum, the interdisciplinary borderlands are frequently the location of the most interesting questions from students.

While our systems can often force quite linear learning journeys, the reality of most roads in life is that one cannot see far down a path that is not straight. There are inclines to ascend and descend, obstacles to go around, false summits to be overcome, pitfalls to be avoided, sights not to be missed, and a horizon to give perspective. There are changes of terrain, weather, light, and heat, and even different modes of transport to use. The different elements of the journey build wisdom for the next stage, and overcoming the challenging parts of the path gives energy for that which is to come. Flourishing students are excited about the journey itself, and recognize the necessary twists and turns it may take. Flourishing provides the momentum that enables the putting down of the left foot, then the right, even when a student can't see everything that is to come.

While there is a beauty and peace and solace to be found in walking alone, the vast majority of us find journeys easier to take when we walk together. There is companionship and help when we stumble, feel tired, consider quitting, and endure elements of the journey that may be boring but necessary. When forks in the road come, we make better decisions if we make them together—especially when uncertainty is present.

Some of our best learning decisions allow uncertainty to creep in: Will we make it? Is it too steep? Do we have enough to sustain us? What if we take the wrong turn? Flourishing students do not always need to know the full answers in order to put their best foot forward.

It would be so much easier if everyone needed to go to the same destination and walked together at the same speed. Yet the flourishing of students can be stifled by the imposition of a single or preferred route (either by the system, or by educators interpreting the system) which is often quite traditional and fixed. While generally well-intentioned, this does not always create the conditions for flourishing holistically.

Some destinations (college, formal professions) seem particularly valued by our societies, and this can create a hierarchy of vocation. However, our vision for flourishing together must be as broad as the society that we serve. Educators need to be wary about overhyping certain destinations to which a significant proportion of students may not wish (or need) to travel.

Equally, some of the key resources that students need to flourish on their journey may not come from qualifications alone, so wise educators seek to equip students to develop *creativity, resilience, passion, care, joy,* and *interdependence*—all needed for the journey ahead, and all necessary for life well beyond formal education.

Finally, a note on journeys of faith. Although it may be easier to categorize students (and adults for that matter) in binary or linear ways, faith development is far more dynamic and unpredictable. Acknowledging such journeys allows space and time for students to develop at their own pace and in their own way. Meaning-making is interdependent, and frequently energized by questions (which imply a journey) rather than answers (which imply arrival). Such narratives are rarely defined by a classic "beginning-middle-end" notion of storytelling, but are often chaotic, unpredictable, intertwined, or without simple resolution. While this may offer a challenge to our admissions policies, worship activities, and Bible or religious education classes, the flourishing of students' faith requires an iterative journey, one that they must be motivated and inspired to take themselves.

Questions for Further Reflection

1. How do your students feel when they start the year with you? How does their motivation increase or decrease throughout the year?

2. What difference does it make to students to know that they are on a journey with others rather than alone?

3. To what extent can our educational systems reinforce a hierarchy of vocation?

4. Have you ever shared your learning journey with your students? What impact might that have?

"I am watching you as a role model—my character shapes my achievement."

When adults reflect back on their own time in school or college, they can frequently remember teachers who had an incredibly positive or negative influence on them (and interestingly, they often find the negative influencers easier to call to mind). However, when a second question is considered—"What was it about them . . . ?"—there is often relatively little reflection on teaching techniques, classroom management, or curriculum structures.

Rather, the majority of recall appears to focus on the character or attributes of that teacher, as in, "She was so patient with me when . . ." "He was someone I could really rely on during . . ." "They seemed to have time for everyone who . . ." "They really believed in me as . . ."

This is not to say of course that pedagogical techniques, planning, grading, feedback, and the craft of teaching are not important. However, it highlights that *the character of teachers is foundational to the flourishing of students.*

A student's character is developing all the time and it is difficult to pin down or measure exactly how and through whom this happens. This is sometimes caricatured in the debate of whether character is *"taught or caught"*—whereby instruction, wisdom, coaching, and character education curriculum are held in tension with the relationships and role-modeling that students experience.

There is an "osmotic" quality to character development; young people absorb lessons about character from the educators (and peers) with whom they interact. Flourishing students are acquiring understanding of character all the time through the intentionally life-giving interactions they have every day, with both the words and the actions of the educators in their schools. The character of an educator—modeled in patience, passion, persistence, integrity, and humility—matters intensely to the learning and progress of flourishing students.

And character development has a more integral relationship with achievement than we might automatically think.

Sir Clive Woodward, the celebrated World Cup–winning coach of England's rugby team, adapted many principles to develop and enable his team to perform at the highest level. One of these is called "TCUP," Thinking Correctly Under Pressure, and was built on the realization that however frequently and successfully skills were practiced and perfected in training, the ability of his players to think under pressure was central to their chances of success. This is highly resonant with most educational assessment systems, where young people are generally given one shot on a fixed date to achieve a set of numbers that will define the next steps of their journeys.

Under pressure in these conditions, our training and practice routines are crucial of course, but two key moments require character above all. The first is the moment of panic when a question is posed and the answer is not certain, when the choice to attempt an answer rather than pass over the question demands resilience and self-belief. In the second moment, the choice to keep going when tired, bored, demotivated, or fearful—even though the test is far from complete—requires tenacity and endurance.

Character, perhaps more than cognitive recall or practice, is often what enables students to rise to challenges, whether during high stakes performance moments or periods of longer "tests" in life. Character does not determine academic achievement or sporting success in a simplistic or causal way, but it nonetheless shapes such success significantly and is thus integral to the genuine flourishing of students.

Character is also frequently formed most deeply in the most challenging experiences, which need to be noted, discussed, and worked through together. The longer-term flourishing of students has as much to do with the character that develops in them as it does the academic achievement with which they emerge from school. It involves a "both-and" tension that can be harnessed in schools to build the capacity for long-term, purpose-filled flourishing.

Questions for Further Reflection

1. To what extent do you think character makes a difference to academic achievement? Tell a story of a student you know to illustrate your point.

2. What factors make your students give up under pressure? What could you do to invest in their resilience?

3. To what extent do you think character is "taught" or "caught"?

4. What kinds of experiences have the biggest impact on the development of students' character?

ACTIVITY: COMING ALONGSIDE STUDENTS

Which voices are the loudest?

Students have so many voices vying for their attention. For most, their sense of purpose will be indelibly shaped by the voices they perceive to be the loudest. Which voices have the most influence? Which propel students forward? Which hold them back?

In this activity, call to mind a student, or group of students, that you teach or with whom you work. Develop a list of "voices" that you imagine they are listening to as they make their learning journey. Which do you think are currently the loudest or most influential? There are many ways to arrange these—a list showing hierarchy, a mind map showing connection, a painting showing images, a story explaining characters (or try an online word cloud generator, as shown below). In reviewing your list, think about how you might be able to help students interpret those voices as well as improve students' sense of agency as they make the journey.

Consider using this as a classroom or pastoral activity with students to help them think through the cultural forces that may be shaping them. Encourage them to be creative. Reflect together on how this multiplicity of voices shapes each student's perspective and discuss how students need encouragement for the journey.

"You are building a cathedral—you may never see the outcome you're working toward."

There are some beautiful places of worship across our planet—some small and intimate, some vast and imposing, some modern and efficient, some timeless and spanning multiple centuries. All of them required vision, purpose, resources, skills, and energy to create.

In the small city of Durham in the northeast of England, one of the world's great cathedrals stands visible from miles around. It has provided a center point for worship and prayer for nearly nine hundred years, on a site where Christians met to pray for many hundreds of years before the building even came about.

It is a vast entity—cavernous, stretching to the heavens, steeped in history, and made possible by unfathomable construction skills. The ambition and imagination of the eleventh-century architect is simply mind-bending.

One of the many challenges of such an occupation was the inherent problem of the architect's lifespan—namely, that having poured a lifetime of creative work into one of the world's most astonishing architectural endeavors, the architect would be highly unlikely to ever see the building completed.

They knew they would most likely never see it finished, yet they still chose to build the cathedral.

Angela Duckworth relates the "parable of the bricklayers" in *Grit*:[3]

> Three bricklayers are asked: "What are you doing?"
> The first says, "I am laying bricks."
> The second says, "I am building a church."
> And the third says, "I am building the house of God."
> The first bricklayer has a job. The second has a career.
> The third has a calling.

The flourishing of educators needs a deeper purpose and more ambitiously expansive vision of education to really bring it to life.

Very few of us can really survive for long by simply pursuing narrow measures of productivity or utilitarian progress metrics. In fact, it can be deeply damaging on a personal level to be reduced to the effectiveness of particular performance measures, some of which may not always be within our control.

Flourishing together demands that we lift our eyes and pursue broader, deeper, and wider outcomes for students and their communities, even though we may never get to see the result ourselves.

Our success now is important, but understanding that we are contributing to a future we will never see stands at the heart of our interactions in every classroom and with every group of graduates that leaves our institutions. The time they are with us, before they're gone, is infinitely significant.

Though it can be difficult to admit, for most of us, we are just passing through and playing our part in a cathedral being built. In fact, this can often lead to disappointment, as sometimes it turns out that the next person wants to build a different kind of cathedral.

Ultimately, though, no one really *needs* a cathedral.

There are lots of more functional ways of achieving the same thing—ways that are more utilitarian, sensible, and economical. But in choosing this way, we reflect something of the creativity, beauty, and extravagance of God.

Flourishing together means that educators, students, and communities come together to develop bold ambition and expansive plans for a "cathedral"—and we choose to invest in it, though we may personally never see it completed.

Questions for Further Reflection

1. What kind of cathedral do you dream of building? What is helping you to see that kind of future?

2. What holds back your imagination?

3. Tell a story of a student whose journey you played a part in—how did you feel as they grew up?

4. How can colleagues encourage one another in your school to focus on the bigger picture amid all the daily pressures?

"You know the seasons—you are patient for things to change."

There are very few plants that are constantly in flower, and for the vast majority, the variety of the seasons is crucial to their survival and flourishing. It is not always summer, and every season brings something necessary, even though it may be hidden.

While there are examples throughout nature of many plants that grow fairly quickly, the vast majority of species are there for the long term—frequently taking much longer to establish than we might like.

Flourishing educators know the seasons and adjust their expectations, behaviors, and practices to suit the season. This may feel contrary to the expectations within our sector, wherein one can feel the pressure to be constantly flourishing—in every lesson and every class, with every student, with no exceptions or excuses.

Our expected rate of change is usually as frantic, with high pressure for things to turn around quickly and an urgency that can quickly morph into a sense of panic.

On the contrary, in nature very little is rushed, and in fact when things are forced (as with genetically modified foods or factory farming) we instinctively know that the attractiveness of the speed of process is outweighed by ethical and sustainability considerations—and very often, leads to diminished quality. In education, we may need to develop patience for flourishing. As the writer of Ecclesiastes puts it in the great poem on seasons: "He has made everything beautiful in its time."[4]

However, flourishing educators are not simply laissez-faire, hoping for the sun to come out. They work wisely and appropriately in the seasons, playing for the long-term flourishing of their communities over and against short-term proxy measures of success.

Love is patient. The story often does not progress as quickly as we would want, and rarely resolves in the way we might have imagined. This sense of patience is more than an individual or corporate decision to take things more slowly.

Patience needs roots. Those who would flourish need to be planted in the right place and at the right time. The prophet Jeremiah paints a compelling picture of flourishing through the seasons: "They will be like a tree planted by the water that sends out its roots by the stream. It does not fear when heat comes; its leaves are always green. It has no worries in a year of drought and never fails to bear fruit."[5]

There is a beautiful realism to this picture, as it assumes there will be times of intense heat and predicts the year of drought. This will happen, and to you.

Patience can become our orientation in relationship with students and colleagues. It helps us to build compelling, attractive, and reliable communities to which others are drawn.

Flourishing educators know that challenge is coming. Patience often underlies endurance or perseverance, both of which can connote suffering or hanging in there. Amid the challenge, flourishing educators hold one another to a clear vision, and are not swayed by short-term changes of policy or procedure. *Flourishing educators have developed the wisdom to reframe the storm.*

An understanding of the seasons will help our teams learn from the simplicity of planting, harvesting, rest, and jubilee, all deepening our appreciation of a life cycle that invests in a future that cannot yet be seen. Whether it is February or August for our team, there is beauty and wonder in each, and yet things will change—we can be certain of that.

Flourishing educators patiently invest time in deepening those roots, not just focusing on what is happening visibly above ground. They know that in a changing world, it is our roots that will ultimately secure our purpose.

Questions for Further Reflection

1. What habits and practices might help you grow deeper roots? Who might help you develop these, perhaps through coaching or mentoring?

2. Who asks you difficult questions?

3. For what might you need to become more patient, allowing it to become "beautiful in its time"?

4. What does it mean to reframe your understanding of the storm, in light of a long-range view of flourishing?

LEADERSHIP DEVELOPMENT **ACTIVITY**: DESIGNING A CHRISTIAN HOSPITAL

When we work together in a specific sector (such as education) and a specific kind of institution within that sector (such as Christian schools), we can easily get caught in the details, jargon, and assumptions that are unique to our settings. It can be hard to "get outside of ourselves" to consider important questions about what we do and why we do it.

This exercise is for a leadership team to change their frame of reference for a few minutes, from education to the health care sector. The purpose of thinking in this way is not to push you toward an alternative career! Rather, it is to provide a different lens for thinking about the core purposes in education in general—and Christian schools in particular—and what matters for flourishing together.

Your team's assignment is to design the vision for a new Christian hospital. Once you have developed your vision collaboratively, ask what lessons you can apply when thinking about purpose in your school. Some questions to help get you started:

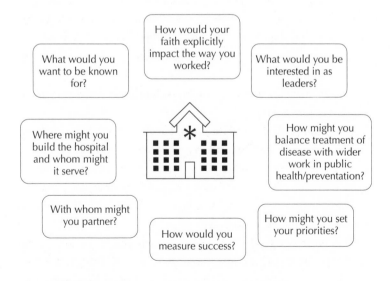

"We choose life every morning—life in all its fullness."

What is the life expectancy of your school?
This question asks not literally how long your school will last (or how long you will last)—but rather what is the *expectancy of life* in your school. In other words, what kind of life are we seeking, choosing, prioritizing, and valuing as we seek to flourish together?

This begins with a deeper understanding of what kind of life we are actually talking about, as Paul writes to his protégé Timothy, "so that they may take hold of the *life* that is truly *life*" (1 Timothy 6:19, NIV). This is the Greek word *zoë* that we have explored in Chapter 2.

This *zoë* life is the full, abundant, broad, deep, rich sense of living together through all the ups and downs, twists and turns, joy, pain, elation, depression, dancing, weeping, singing, and mourning.

Choosing life each day rarely amounts to students and educators skipping into school, high-fiving each other as they descend the bus steps or jump off their bikes. Rather, it means choosing fullness of life first and then together ordering our days toward the pursuit of the very fullest existence.

This life includes both pain and joy—*and those in flourishing schools choose to face both together.*

Flourishing schools never miss an opportunity to celebrate, to thank, to rejoice, to gather together, and to praise—in the big moments and in the minute-by-minute glimmers of progress in every classroom. They are relentless in their gratitude, for their people and their actions, and they establish routines, rhythms, and rituals that enshrine celebration in their institutional habits and procedures.

They notice the good, cheer it on, and teach students to do the same. They recognize the unique role that students have in validating and encouraging their peers, and they regard this as central to the growth of character as well as to the social, moral, and spiritual flourishing of each student.

Equally important, flourishing schools are not places where everything goes well at all times. The choice of life amid the challenge or crisis is different, and arguably more important, than at other times. Flourishing schools build resilience for the long term, and their communities understand that it is not simply about working harder and doing more.

A Christian understanding of resilience involves more than simply bouncing back or displaying grit or toughness. In our most challenging or painful times, God is at work in us, both as individuals and as teams—guiding, strengthening, refining and refocusing us—as the Holy Spirit helps us to build our character, to be filled with hope, and thus to bounce back stronger.

Embracing this fullness of life is crucial in a school, because it teaches students how to approach their own lives—in the whole blurry mess of pain and joy, trauma and attachment, fear and courage.

This presentation of "life in all its fullness" is far less about what is written on our walls than it is about our students' daily experiences in our school communities—the very expectation of life, or the life expectancy that we seek to offer to the students in our care, as well as to ourselves.

Questions for Further Reflection

1. How do schools corporately choose to face pain and joy together?

2. How has your expectancy of life changed through your time working in your current context? What factors improve or deteriorate this?

3. What habits and practices might your school community need to help all its members choose life every morning?

4. How might the journey of your school community reflect something of the faithfulness of God?

"We lead with a passion for the possible—we choose to stick around."

*H*ope is one of the key characteristics of flourishing schools—it is a driving force for leaders and is highly motivating for students. Flourishing schools led by flourishing leaders often acquire their momentum through the imagination of a future that others cannot yet see.

The first task of the leader in thinking about the future is to define reality accurately—however uncomfortable that reality may seem—even if this may make the situation seem initially hope-*less*. If we are serious about pursuing flourishing for our schools, we have to start with the facts and conditions. After all, what gardener or farmer would seek to plant before knowing the full details, and calculating what is actually possible given the circumstances? Cultivating a flourishing garden requires the accurate and wise definition of conditions of the soil, sun, and water needed for growth. It is imperative that we improve or change analogous conditions to release flourishing across our organizations.

Flourishing together happens when we define possible goals and pursue them with wise allocation of resources, thereby creating the right conditions for the people in our care to flourish. The onus is on schools committed to flourishing to plan the conditions wisely, including the complexities of assessing the current team and its potential to enact strategies that lead to flourishing.

Despite dominant superleader paradigms, ultimately the gardener has to allow the plants to grow themselves according to who they are and the particular conditions they need to flourish. True flourishing cannot be forced.

Hope also means sticking around.

This is true even though sticking around is rarely glamorized in our leadership thinking. The longevity of flourishing relies in large part on great leaders and great teams being around for the long run. This is what communities of students need—consistency and dependability, assurance and reliability.

Unless the flourishing of schools is for the long term, the goal is perhaps rather limited, not least because new leadership teams are so often expected to bring a fresh vision rather than build on the old.

While there is something exciting (and at times very necessary) about new green shoots and dynamic new plants, ultimately we long for the oak tree in schools—the final result of the dependability of the long term and the patience needed for the very best outcomes.

This is seen countless times in nature, and it helps us each to understand our small (important, but small nonetheless) part in a much bigger story.

A passion for the possible does not ignore the need for rapid change in some situations, but it recognizes that the system change that flourishing schools are pursuing can only be achieved over the long term—which therefore requires that leaders put their roots down and stick around.

So let us note the visionaries and creators in our teams, but let us also praise and thank the implementers, the detail people, the spreadsheet and action plan writers, the long-term thinkers who can turn the initial vision of flourishing into something that actually works now—and, more importantly, into something that will still be around in ten, twenty-five, or fifty years' time, long after we have concluded our contribution.

Questions for Further Reflection

1. Together as a school community, how do you define what is actually possible? How do you involve all school constituents in this?

2. What is the difference between creating vision and communicating strategy? How would you describe the balance in your organization?

3. To what extent is your school a place where leaders "allow the plants to grow themselves"?

4. What do you hope is true for your school in twenty-five or fifty years? How might that vision affect your current perspective?

A shared story

I f you ask a hundred people connected with your school—students, parents, employees, or community members—to define the core values of
your institution, very few would reach for your mission statement or website. They would likely share a story out of their daily experience in and
with the school, regardless of whatever is written down. This is because
stories are powerful; they help us to understand where we have come from,
where we are presently, and where we are going.

This activity is designed to help your school constituents tell the
school's story as a way of uncovering their understanding of their and the
school's purpose.[6] Gather a group of diverse constituents and divide them
into teams of four or five people. Have them use the prompts below to tell
the story of the school and then share it with the full group. They can even
be creative and illustrate the story on larger sheets of paper or act it out as a
group. Then, use the results of this activity as a springboard for discussion
around the school's purpose—past, present, and future.

*Once upon a time there was a school that*_____
_____.

*Every day at the school*_____
_____.

*Then, one day*_____
_____.

*Because of that*_____
_____.

And because of that _____
_____ .

And ever since _____
_____ .

2

RELATIONSHIPS

4

Flourishing Relationships

We know that educators are tasked with immeasurable work and incredibly challenging situations. . . . But let us not forget that educators also have the amazing opportunity to come to school and celebrate and experience joy with students—and to practice and teach kindness, love, and compassion.

—Julie Causton and Kate MacLeod,
From Behaving to Belonging[1]

Faithful presence means that we are to be fully present to each other . . . we imitate our creator and redeemer: we pursue each other, identify with each other, and direct our lives toward the flourishing of each other through sacrificial love.

—James Davison Hunter, *To Change the World*[2]

Ecosystems are complex biological environments that are defined not only in terms of all the living organisms that populate them, but also by those organisms' interactions with each other. Similarly, schools are not just an assortment of discrete classrooms and buildings, populated by individual leaders, teachers, and students who function in isolation one from another. Like an ecosystem, a school's culture is made up of many moving "parts" that are in constant contact—and often friction—with one another. Although our interconnectedness in schools can be seen in all domains of flourishing, it is perhaps the most pronounced in the Relationships domain.

Every school—Christian or otherwise—would cite positive relationships among its various constituents as important. However, in many schools, the subtext of relational work is "transactional," whether conscious or not. For example, positive interactions between leaders and teachers can be viewed as important primarily for efficient school management, while good relationships with families can be seen as a vehicle for reinforcing the work of teachers in the classroom. And families and students themselves may have a transactional view of relationships with teachers, as solely providing a product or service that increases students' social capital (that is, leading to acceptance at a good college and eventually a well-paying career).

All of these outcomes are certainly related to flourishing, but a Christian vision for education does not view them as ends that are justified by relational means. Rather, such a vision flips this narrative by framing the goals of education as *entirely* relational. Human relationships are not a means to an impersonal end, but the ends themselves are human—specifically, flourishing humans. As James Davison Hunter underscores in *To Change the World*, God "does not pursue us for instrumental purposes" and therefore we should "imitate our creator and redeemer: we pursue each other, identify with each other, and direct our lives toward the flourishing of each other through sacrificial love."[3]

As we consider how to build school relationships on this foundation, our interconnectedness in flourishing is brought to the forefront. It is difficult to pull apart the threads in the web of thousands of relationships that comprise a school, let alone examine each on its own. But in considering research and its implications, we can look to three coequal tiers of relationships—for the school, for educators, and for students—that are interconnected for flourishing.

Flourishing Schools

We tend to think of relationships as between individuals or groups of people, so it may seem strange to begin with schools themselves. However, in a very real sense, individuals in the community experience most of their interactions with school staff (as well as with students) in terms of an overarching relationship with the school, as an entity. One need look no further than schools' marketing materials and websites for evidence; these are often carefully crafted to portray a "type" of school that is hopefully attractive to prospective students and their families.

There is a common leadership saying attributed to Peter Drucker, that "culture eats strategy for breakfast." The relational culture at a given school may not trump the one-on-one relationships within that school, but it certainly has a shaping impact. For example, consider whether a school's primary relationship with families and students is conceived as one between consumers and a product or service provider, versus a collaborative partnership that holds common vision and goals. Whichever the paradigm in a given school, there will be profound implications for decision making and priority setting, from the curricula and scheduling, to the sports teams and activities on offer, all the way to school uniform policies. And as often is the case, differing perceptions of which paradigm ought to prevail can lead to relational conflict.

The Flourishing Schools research points to the importance of proactively building positive relationships with the community immediately connected to the school, beginning by *engaging families* of students.[4] The research found this involves teachers getting to know parents, guardians, or other significant adults in students' lives through frequent and effective communication. Leaders can promote positive school-family relationships by creating a vision together, through collaborative development of a written partnership policy or other document, that articulates a philosophy and expectations for those relationships.[5] The extent to which this vision is then lived out in the everyday experiences of school families is a reflection of the authenticity of our relationships.

Building personal relationships that foster trust is key to achieving such a vision, and will necessitate intentional and sustained work by leaders. For families, this means ensuring that they feel their input and participation is valued not only in their students' learning but also in the overall life of the school. Of key importance is not just increasing engagement between the school and families, but also doing so meaningfully. This will require involving parents and guardians beyond the traditional parent-teacher conferences and back-to-school nights, which "sometimes put parents in a passive role, unwittingly distancing the very people we most want to include."[6] One proven strategy for meaningful engagement is to involve families in school decision making.[7] Often schools will make sporadic attempts at this involvement, with leaders becoming discouraged by the relational energy and time required. While impasses may arise, fear of disagreement does not relieve us of our Christian responsibility to, "as far as it depends on you, live at peace with everyone."[8] Schools, like individuals, should live by the same principle in their engagement.

We can telescope out from school families to consider relationships with the larger communities in which our schools are situated. In North America, the imagery often used to describe Christian schools was that of a "three-legged stool," the three legs of which were the family, the church, and the school. This image was meant to depict a collaborative partnership between these three entities to ensure a cohesive educational experience for the student (who, presumably, is the one who sits on the stool). However, as our societies have diversified and the world has grown smaller due to technology and globalization, we propose a "four-legged table" of school, family, church, and community as a more suitable metaphor. While only one person can sit on a stool, many people—students, educators, family, clergy, and community members—can fit at a table. This new image encourages schools to become places where we can all meet together and break bread.

The Flourishing Schools research found evidence that community engagement of this kind is linked with flourishing outcomes.[9] Specifically, the research identified positive linkages when leaders engaged with the surrounding community by regularly tapping into community resources, including networking and resource-sharing with other schools. Interestingly, the research found that community engagement was positively linked with students' spiritual formation, including long-term outcomes as reported by alumni. While not necessarily causal, this suggests that schools that engage the community may help students learn to love their neighbors, which has a lasting impact into adulthood. Other research has identified positive outcomes linked to school engagement with parents, community agencies, and organizations, in terms of school improvement and student achievement.[10]

We would assert that, most importantly, this view of the Christian school is biblically faithful. The Old Testament prophet Jeremiah instructs the exiles in Babylon, "Make yourselves at home there and work for the country's welfare."[11] In *Educating for Shalom*, Nicholas Wolterstorff asserts that "Christian community exists not for its own sake but for the sake of all people."[12] The good news about a table, versus a stool, is we can seat as many people as we like simply by extending it. The gospels are clear that extending our tables in this way invites miracles of abundance and multiplication, as seen in Jesus's feeding of the five thousand (which we discuss further in Part 4, "Resources").

If we are to invite others to join us, however, we must also find ways to remove the obstacles that hinder them from accepting our invitation. This means schools should actively and purposefully remove barriers to community engagement.[13] Like all human institutions, schools are often places that practice exclusion, due to limitations such as classroom size, geographical location, admissions requirements, available resources, or tuition cost. Put simply, not every student has access to every school. Christian schools must do the hard work of squaring this unavoidable reality with the fact that Jesus's ministry was inclusive and engaging—sometimes scandalously so (as discussed in Part 1, "Purpose"). Jesus told his disciples, "Let the little children come to me, and do not hinder them, for the kingdom of heaven belongs to such as these";[14] likewise, a Christian vision for education seeks to remove barriers to access and engagement in our schools.

In terms of improving educational access, the Flourishing Schools research found that diversity in the student body is linked positively to flourishing outcomes. This confirms that diversity is not just a good idea in principle, but that flourishing together in schools is related to the degree to which our "together" is inclusive. The research also clearly showed, however, that diversity remains a challenge for many schools. For this reason, schools need to be intentional in recruitment and admissions processes, as well as ensure that the school environment is welcoming and inclusive of students from varying backgrounds when they matriculate and throughout their school experience. To this end, leaders should ask themselves and their staff, students, and families these key questions:

- Are we aware of our school and community demographics?
- Do we actively seek to recruit and retain a diverse student body, faculty, and leaders that are reflective of those demographics?
- Does our school celebrate diversity in our practices, from marketing materials to school events to curricula?
- Is healthy dialogue around diversity encouraged and facilitated between students, faculty and staff, families, and the community?

- Have we built enough relational trust among school constituents that we can engage together well—and if not, how do we build that trust?
- How do we repair trust and restore relationships between and with diverse school constituents, where needed?

If discussed collaboratively and regularly with school constituents, leaders can use these and similar questions to develop proactive (versus reactive) strategies when it comes to removing diversity-related barriers to access.

In terms of engagement with the community, schools need strategies not only to break down silos but also to replace them with what Daniel Pampuch and Darren Iselin call "*shalom* in action."[15] Nicholas Wolterstorff defines *shalom* as a "vision of what constitutes human flourishing," at the heart of which lie "right relationships to God, to one's fellow human beings, to nature, and to oneself."[16] In sharing their findings from Christian schools in Australia, Pampuch and Iselin describe a combination of strategies and structures that allow relational *shalom* into everyday experience in schools. First, schools must consciously ask and answer the question, "Who is my neighbor?" Based on the answer, schools intentionally "come into orbit"—or develop proximity—with those with whom they do not normally associate or cooperate. This can involve showing up at community events or serving needs in the community as well as hosting events and offering resources to community members.[17] The goal should be a long-term strategy to "move into the neighborhood"—much like Jesus became flesh and dwelled among us—and ultimately for schools to demonstrate over time what James Davison Hunter calls "faithful presence" in their communities.[18]

Several mindset changes need to occur to break down relational silos. Schools must overcome the impulses to shield students from brokenness in the world and to disengage from their larger communities (the Flourishing Schools research identified these as negatively correlated with flourishing outcomes, along with a lack of diversity in the student body).[19] As proximity is established, schools need to actively remove the suspicion of the "other" and replace it with a network of the "known." This may involve developing new and more inclusive language, which will help transition from an "us versus them" mindset to one of "you and us, together." And schools encourage *shalom*-seeking when they introduce students to issues in the world in developmentally appropriate ways, when they provide a safe environment for wrestling with those issues, and when they prepare students to confidently engage with those issues from a place of maturity and empathy. Through these approaches, we can shape a school culture characterized by engagement and redemptive work.

Flourishing Educators

As we move from considering the relationships between the school and the community, we turn to look at relationships *within* schools. Rob Loe, director of the Relational Schools Foundation, describes "relational" schools as those which both "nurture relationships and approach the design of a school with relationships as an intentional, values-based priority."[20] Arguably, positive relationships among school staff members provide the bedrock upon which other types of relationships—whether with students, families, or the community—can be built.

When it comes to the relationship among educators within a school, the Flourishing Schools research identified *collective leadership* as linked to flourishing outcomes.[21] Other research has consistently shown that a collective model of leadership leads to greater leader and teacher efficacy, including as measured by improved student outcomes.[22] As Jonathan Eckert of Baylor University observes in *Leading Together: Teachers and Administrators Improving Student Outcomes*, regarding collective leadership, "Viewing leadership as being about the work instead of the individual, position, or personal characteristics seems to be liberating and empowering. Educators seem more likely to do the leadership work that best serves their students when they are focused on the work and not their own inadequacy or the limitations of a position."[23]

The Flourishing Schools research identified two main strategies for building collective leadership within a school, the first of which is to cultivate *leadership interdependence*.[24] All leaders, including the board of trustees, can move toward interdependence when they come from diverse backgrounds, are transparent about their weaknesses, and rely on others to offset those weaknesses. Second, collective leadership also relies on building relational trust between leaders. Specifically, the research found that *supportive leadership*—evidenced by all staff members agreeing that leaders are trusted and "have their backs" and that they empower staff to make decisions—was positively linked with flourishing outcomes.[25]

These strategies share the common denominator of leading with humility. Leading in this way enables us to prefer others over ourselves, to lay down any selfish ambition or motives we may harbor, and to focus on the flourishing of the community and the individuals within it. As the apostle Paul writes to the church in Corinth, "I appeal to you, brothers and sisters, in the name of our Lord Jesus Christ, that all of you agree with one another in what you say and that there be no divisions among you, but that you be perfectly united in mind and thought."[26] Without humble leadership, we have little hope of achieving the unity to which we are biblically called in schools. Humble leadership—exercised collectively, interdependently, and supportively—may help flourishing schools to achieve the unity that we all desire but often find elusive in practice.

The next type of educator relationships that we can consider are those between teachers. The Flourishing Schools research found that *collaboration* between teachers was correlated with positive outcomes for flourishing.[27] Collaboration was defined as teachers' belief that learning from, and with, other teachers inspires and propels them to grow and become better in their craft. Other research has shown that collaboration on how to teach what students need to learn—in activities like unpacking standards, mapping curriculum designing lessons, constructing assessments that measure mastery of lessons— is correlated with academic improvement.[28] Similarly, collaborative work to support students who have learning difficulties is linked to successful inclusion of those students within schools.[29] And a commitment to collaborative planning activity on the part of teachers is linked with sustained improvement within schools.[30]

Collaboration is a necessary condition for creating what Étienne Wenger describes as "communities of practice," or groups of people who "share a concern or passion for something they do and learn how to do it better as they interact" by developing a shared language, working toward common goals, and committing to supportive relationships with each other.[31] Leaders set expectations and create the necessary conditions for this collaboration to occur, which include school practices and structures like co-teaching, team teaching, and professional learning communities.[32] By collaborating with colleagues, educators can, as Peter Senge articulates, "continually expand their capacity to create the results they truly desire, where new and expansive patterns of thinking are nurtured, where collective aspiration is set free, and where people are continually learning how to learn together."[33]

This same principle also applies to educators' relationships with their peers at other schools, though opportunities for cross-school collaboration can often be undermined by a stance of competition that precludes meaningful engagement. As Amanda Keddie notes in her examination of school collaborations within the English education system, "When schools are concerned with demands such as competing with each other for their 'market share' of students and generating income, genuine collaboration can be undermined, as can a focus on students and learning."[34] One example of cross-school collaborations that can break down these barriers to shared learning are networked improvement communities, or NICs, which have made their way into education from other fields like healthcare and technology in recent years. Anthony Bryk and colleagues note in *Learning to Improve* that successful NICs are marked by common and explicitly stated aims, a shared understanding of problems, the use of improvement research to inform interventions, and a nimble structure for widespread dissemination of findings to practitioners across the network.[35]

Such cross-school engagement is especially fitting for Christian schools, given the kingdom-mindedness of their faith foundation. As the Church of England Foundation for Educational Leadership's Peer Support Network notes, "the marketization of education creates a dynamic where schools are supposed to perform and outdo each other, in a zero-sum game. The problem of course is that a competition-based approach isn't in line with the economy of God's kingdom. More commensurate with that kingdom is an approach focused on community-building."[36] Over one thousand schools participating in this network have found that collaboration across schools bolsters educators' knowledge base, feelings of professional camaraderie, and an overall sense that they are working toward a greater purpose. And as we have learned in our work together and with colleagues from around the world, international collaboration holds great promise as we spend time with—and learn from—one another.

Flourishing Students

Not surprisingly, research shows that students "are highly sensitive to the emotional rapport they establish with adults in school settings."[37] The Relational Schools Foundation found that when schools prioritize supportive relationships, students experience gains in academic outcomes, reduced bullying levels, and greater physical health; moreover, strong relationships in schools can even have a remedying effect for students who have disadvantage (economic, social, or otherwise) in their backgrounds.[38]

When it comes to student-teacher relationships, the Flourishing Schools research linked flourishing with teachers demonstrating Christ-like love and kindness, as well as caring for students individually and being concerned about their spiritual development.[39] This includes positive outcomes in the area of spiritual formation for alumni, which suggests that the teacher-student relationship is not only crucial for students during the school years, but also has a lasting impact far beyond. Similarly, the *mentoring role* of support staff—such as coaches, aides, cafeteria staff, and office personnel—was identified as positively linked with flourishing outcomes. This role includes pointing out talent in each student, being aware of students' struggles at school or home, and truly coming to know students on a personal level.[40] These findings underscore the importance of including *all* school staff—both instructional and support—in vision-related school meetings and schoolwide professional development.

While relationships are crucial for the flourishing of all students, they are absolutely critical for our most vulnerable students. Rob Loe puts this simply: "You cannot learn well if you are frightened, unhappy, or if you feel you don't belong in a classroom."[41] Along these lines, the Flourishing Schools research found that a caring environment, in which students feel safe and are protected, is positively linked with flourishing outcomes.[42] This is especially true in the case of adverse childhood experiences—such as trauma, loss, abuse, or neglect—which can result in insecure attachments for students, often manifesting in schools as behavior issues or failure to progress. Louise Bombèr's work on trauma-informed education underscores the need to understand each student with these experiences on a personal level and, on the basis of that relational knowledge, adjust how we teach and care for each one.[43]

A caring environment must also prevent and protect students from bullying, which is a common source of trauma *in* schools. Bullying is typically not an isolated incident between two people, but rather "a dynamic social relationship problem" that requires a broader, school-level approach in addition to an interventional approach with individual students.[44] On this point, the Relational Schools Foundation found that where healthy relational systems and processes are intentionally put into place at a school, bullying levels are lower and student well-being is higher.[45]

Finally, the ways in which schools work toward inclusion for students with disabilities is correlated with flourishing. Specifically, the Flourishing Schools research found a positive link between flourishing outcomes and a school's responsiveness to the needs of students with disabilities—defined as teaching staff working together to support students appropriately, aided by processes and resources for identifying and responding to students' needs. Interestingly, the research also found that schools' responsiveness in these areas is correlated not only with increases in academic outcomes, but also with positive gains in spiritual formation, including that of alumni (regardless of disability status). This would suggest that successful inclusion promotes flourishing outcomes for all members of the school community.

In his extensive research with youth with disabilities and their families, Erik Carter of Vanderbilt University found that to "be present, invited, welcomed, known, accepted, supported, cared for, befriended, needed, and loved—all were identified by participants as aspects of what it means to be truly included in a community of faith."[46] Because of the compelling nature of these "dimensions of belonging" in Carter's work, we present them in further detail below:

- *To be present.* When it comes to human experience, disability is a natural part; thus, when students with disabilities are not present in our schools, we are excluding individuals who are part of society.
- *To be invited.* There is a qualitative difference between having students with disabilities be present and actually inviting them into our school communities.
- *To be welcomed.* Welcoming students with disabilities goes a step further than presence and invitation to the school community; extending hospitality is a first step in overcoming the reluctance, uncertainty, and avoidance that some may feel toward students with disabilities.
- *To be known.* As Carter points out, "Although Christians are called to welcome the stranger, the stranger should not remain one for very long."[47] A sense of belonging for students with disabilities arises from deeper connections with others, facilitated by sustained conversation and sharing our lives together.

- *To be accepted.* Acceptance of students with disabilities requires that we address stereotypes and prejudices around disability. Awareness efforts (such as special days or weeks, seminars, and so on) are positive, but even better is personal engagement with students with disabilities.
- *To be supported.* Students with disabilities need the same support as all students within the community, and at the same time may have individualized support needs. Of key importance is for leaders to listen to and consider students' voices when thinking through supports.
- *To be cared for.* Like all students, those with disabilities need care in order to feel they belong at school. However, educators need to both care *and* be careful at the same time, because what "feels like care to one person can be perceived as paternalism by another person ... a preferred posture is to find out firsthand what people want for their lives."[48]
- *To be befriended.* It falls on teachers and school families to help students learn to befriend others who may be different from them. This is made all the more important in light of research, which shows that "the friendships so fundamental to human flourishing remain elusive for far too many children and adults" with disabilities.[49] Birthday parties and other social events are important for all students in building friendships outside of the school context; educators can encourage school families and students to include students with disabilities in these and other gatherings and activities.
- *To be needed.* As mentioned earlier, schools may often adopt a position of viewing students with disabilities as individuals who have needs that must be met. But belonging in community involves mutuality, in which every person plays the role of both giver and receiver. Leaders should consider what the school and its constituents "gain by encountering the gifts individuals with disabilities and their families have to bring" and help the school community to view "itself as incomplete without their presence and participation."[50]
- *To be loved.* Finally, as we have emphasized for all school relationships, love is the firmest foundation for real belonging. The apostle John writes, "Dear friends, let us love one another, for love comes from God";[51] the love of God, flowing through our teachers and nurtured in community, should be extended to and experienced by all students at the school.

Although Carter's findings are specific to students with disabilities, we believe his work provides a compelling model of belonging in schools for all students. For those who have worked extensively with students with disabilities, this will come as no surprise: in education, often the work we do for inclusion can have tremendous benefits for all students. To this end, and following Carter's model, we can engage teachers, leaders, students, and families in discussion around questions of belonging in our schools. For example:

- Who is missing from our school? In what ways are we "losing out" because they are absent?
- How can we intentionally invite those students and families to our school?
- How do we "set the educational table" for students from all backgrounds, so they feel welcomed?
- How do we address stereotypes, not just through awareness efforts, but by fostering personal relationships—in which we get to know and learn how to befriend those who are different from ourselves?
- How do we ask students about their needs, and then truly listen and respond—in ways that not only meet those needs, but also communicate that students have been heard, are cared for, and are valued?
- How do we genuinely value the contribution of every student to the school community, and not just those that "excel" in "normative" ways? (Note that truly discovering and honoring each student's unique contribution is the exact opposite of "trophyism," where everyone gets the same award for simply showing up.)
- How would everything at our school (schedules, curricula) change if we based decisions on whether students feel they belong and have value in God's diverse kingdom—and therefore in our schools—including, and perhaps especially, those who have traditionally felt marginalized?

As we seek to answer these questions, we can consider how Christian schools offer unique opportunities to nurture a relational sense of belonging for students—specifically through the spiritual practices of Christian community. In *Real Kids, Real Faith: Practices for Nurturing Children's Spiritual Lives*, Karen Marie Yust lists a number of these practices, including thanksgiving, showing hospitality, and celebrating community. Spiritual disciplines like silence, stillness, reflection, and listening to God can help to envoke a thoughtful religious curiosity in students. And storytelling helps students hear others and learn to share their experiences through speaking aloud.[52]

Importantly, students not only engage in such practices, but in doing so also come to learn the language of the school's faith tradition (similar to the process of learning any language). For the Christian school, this includes the language of *shalom*—loving one another as Jesus loved us, and showing kindness, gentleness, and respect to others. As students learn to speak that language, they can practice it through opportunities to reach out to others who are different from themselves, which in turn helps to nurture students' care and respect for others. As leaders and teachers work together to build these practices into the life of the classroom and the school, the experiences of Christian community can powerfully shape students' lives—and the lives of educators as well—toward flourishing together.

5

Abiding Together

They said to him, "Rabbi, where are you staying [abiding]?" He said
to them, "Come and see."

—John 1:38–39 (NCV)

Abide in me, and I in you. As the branch cannot bear fruit by itself,
unless it abides in the vine, neither can you, unless you abide in me.
I am the vine; you are the branches. Whoever abides in me and I in
him, he it is that bears much fruit, because apart from me you can
do nothing.

—John 15:4–5

School communities are made up of thousands of relationships and interactions each day—educator to educator, educator to student, and student
to student—alongside relationships with the wider community of parents,
families, churches, and other groups. As we have explored in the preceding
chapter, our flourishing together is in so many ways dependent upon those
with whom we share the journey. Flourishing schools are characterized by a
sense of inclusion, belonging, and togetherness—values lived out in relationships that can support, encourage, heal, forgive, question, correct, inspire,
and reassure.

The entire arc of Scripture can be understood in terms of relationships—
from creation, where human beings were made in God's image and built for

relationship with God and one another; to the fall, where relationship with God, others, and creation was broken; to redemption, where Jesus's life, death, and resurrection paved the way for healing these relationships; to restoration, where God's people engage in loving and living well together. Undergirding this entire arc is love. Whether we are rejoicing in success or dealing with failure, our relationships should be defined by love, around which everything turns and toward which everything should be drawn. As we explored in Chapter 2, this love is fundamental to the *zoē* "life in all its fullness" we are called to lead.

We learn throughout the Bible that God *is* love, that God loves the world, and that all are welcomed and valued by this love.[1] Jesus instructs us that the greatest commandment of all is to love God with everything within us, and then to love our neighbors as ourselves.[2] When asked, "Who is my neighbor?" Jesus leaves no doubt as to who qualifies—*everyone*.[3] Knowing our human tendency toward self-interest (which often manifests in human communities through bias and exclusion), Jesus calls special attention to our responsibility to love those who are different from us, and in doing so, to build diverse communities where our collective flourishing is enriched. Jesus's instructions echo in the apostles' words throughout the New Testament as they urge us to live out God's love, by demonstrating compassion, kindness, humility, gentleness, patience, forgiveness, and respect for all.[4]

The word *meno*, used extensively in John's gospel, exemplifies the kind of relationships that we should pursue and live out. *Meno* is usually translated with a quite old-fashioned but very meaningful word: to *abide*. This Greek verb has beautiful implications for our relationships, carrying the sense of "to remain, to stay, to endure." Like *zoē*, it is a concept particularly used by John (thirty-three times, versus nine in all the other three gospels combined). *Meno* is sometimes used very literally, where the implication is clearly about accommodation choices—"Rabbi, where are you staying?"[5]—and also with much deeper meaning, most intensely throughout John 15, where the long-term relationship between Jesus and his disciples is explained through the metaphor of the branches (the disciples) abiding in the vine (Jesus). This divergence in the word's use may shine a light on what can be a healthy tension between the practicalities of our relationships and their deeper meanings. When we think about the implications of *meno* for a wider ecology of flourishing together, the kinds of relationships to which schools, educators, and students are called

76

together are *enduring, interdependent, inclusive,* and *serving*—all building toward a school community characterized by *shalom.*

Enduring Relationships

The educational systems in which we work can often demand much by way
of short-term change and success. Yet the call in *meno* relationship is for the
long-term, not the short. To abide, remaining in relationship with an individual, group, or school, implies sticking around for a reasonably long period
of time. One might think of the teacher's joy of journeying with the same
cohort of students right through their whole time in a school—welcoming
them as nervous, energetic children, and then sending them out as confident,
world-changing young adults.

In today's throwaway culture frequently fueled by personal ambition, it
may feel overly passive and wholly undesirable to stay in the same place for
many years. But the flourishing of students is dependent on the reliability
of educators who make the choice to abide with them. Having such adults
stick around is life-giving to students, as it unlocks learning and development
from a starting point of safety and trust. The same can be true with enduring
relationships between colleagues; while much can happen in the short term,
there is a deep joy and meaning in looking back over a long period of time of
serving together—through all the twists and turns, highs and lows, joys and
pains—and recognizing that we stuck together. Abiding for the long term
provides the time and space for flourishing to happen, for just like a well-
tended garden or a well-lived life, so little of it can ever be short-term. While
many of our educational planning cycles are jammed into short-term thinking
because of rapid policy or resourcing changes, a longer-term commitment
to abide together leads to richer, deeper, and more meaningful experiences.
John's vine metaphor helps us think about simply staying with one another
as a key action that can lead to flourishing together.

Such *meno* commitment also permits and expects things to go wrong in
our relationships. When we enter into a *meno* relationship with one another,
we do so acknowledging that we will make mistakes, let each other down, and
cause one another pain. The choice to abide *regardless* of that disappointment
shows grace at the heart of our connection, where we prioritize the relationship
over the day-to-day success or failure. The vine imagery echoes in the prophet

Jeremiah's description of a tree planted by the water, which "does not fear when heat comes . . . it has no worries in a year of drought."[6] The year of drought is not a fear, but rather an expectation—we will certainly encounter challenge, and yet we are able to meet those challenges with collective grace. As we commit to walk the path together for the longer term, we find a permanence through which our collective flourishing is released across every season.

This is also true *between* schools, not just within a single school. For all the excitement and energy of short-term collaborations and project-based approaches, the longer-term commitment to a relationship is always much more life-giving. Enduring relationships between institutions remove our fears that others are motivated by self-interest or may soon betray our trust (as in, "We can play nicely together so long as it remains clearly in our own interests, but if that changes, we're out"). Long-term relationships also give genuine change a chance. We learn more from one another when unexpected opportunities for growth emerge, as they often do when seasons change.

Interdependent Relationships

Our educational systems are often driven by competition rather than collaboration, emphasizing individuality over togetherness. In contrast, *meno* relationships are defined by collective growth and development. In John 15, branches that abide in the vine do not simply remain as they are—they grow in the context of their interdependence and organic interaction. The passage is full of both enriching positive imagery and darker consequential language, contrasting the prospect of the healthy branch, connected to the main part of the vine—growing and bearing much fruit—with the withering branch, disconnected and fruitless. Jesus puts it simply: "No branch can bear fruit by itself; it must remain in the vine."[7]

Sometimes our relationships in schools can feel very hierarchical, from trustees and governors, to senior leaders, to teachers, and finally to students. While the impact of leadership on a community's potential to flourish—creating the conditions, setting the culture, organizing resources and relationships—is essential, the mutual ecology of flourishing together is interdependent and multidirectional. Most educators will cite their most energizing and sustaining moments as coming directly from interaction with students and colleagues, far beyond success in paperwork, data charts, inspections, and class test scores. Likewise, students will long recall engagement with an encouraging teacher, demanding coach, or supportive peer as life-giving, far beyond any grades or completion of a project that may seem all-consuming at the time. Relationships in schools are so critical to flourishing together that hardly any extant research identifies other factors as more correlated with positive outcomes, whether for students (in relationship with their teachers) or teachers (in relationship with their principals).

Yet, paradoxically, teaching and leading in schools can be lonely, regardless of the quantity of people in the buildings. Teachers spend so much of their day apart from adult colleagues, often only touching base in the corridors. Leaders may rush from one meeting to the next, addressing action plans and deliverables, rarely stopping just to be with one another. Focusing on sustaining relationships is not a call to task avoidance, but rather to an essential of flourishing together. Given the busyness of schools, it becomes possible only if we deliberately spend time with one another relating—not just producing. If relationships are fundamental to flourishing, then each of us needs to take care to establish deliberate rhythms and routines with people we trust to guarantee we stay grounded.

This is inclusive of relationships *outside* our institutional "bubbles"—extending between schools, where our commitment can grow toward investing in one another's flourishing. This can occur at very personal levels, where leaders find peers with whom they can simply be honest in the journey. Equally, more strategic relationships between schools can release the efficiencies and economies of scale of working collaboratively together. These relationships can inspire us with fresh vision, reassure us we are asking good questions, give us patience for a season to pass, and correct us when we might have made better choices. Collaboration requires trust and exchange, but it also requires courage and vulnerability with one another and begins with the choice to give. As Paul encourages his readers in Corinth, with a particular challenge to those to whom much is given: "But since you excel in everything—in faith, in speech, in knowledge, in complete earnestness and in the love we have kindled in you—see that you also excel in this grace of giving."[8] As many of our school systems incentivize the opposite (that is, a market notion of "winning" within our local context), generously looking outward can be a particular challenge. Yet, these are the kinds of *meno* relationships in which we can grow—asking not what we can gain, but what we can give.

Inclusive Relationships

Throughout the gospel narrative, John repeatedly demonstrates the centrality of inclusion in the way Jesus spends his time and through the people with whom he chooses to connect and share life. History tells a sometimes-painful story of religion being abused with tragic consequences, frequently focused on the mistreatment of minority groups. Yet for Christians, the life of Jesus appears to portray the exact opposite: the desire and will to connect deeply with people of all backgrounds. In many cases, these connections upended expectations related to class, occupational status, ethnicity, nationality, gender, age, health, moral standing, and even religion—that is, Jesus engaged the poor; Nazarene fishermen; Samaritans; Roman occupiers; women; children and the aged; people with leprosy; the sexually outcast (the woman at the well, the woman caught in adultery) and the unethical (tax collectors); and the polytheistic centurion, at whom Jesus "marveled and said to those who followed him, 'Truly, I tell you, with no one in Israel have I found such faith.'"[9]

In fact, Jesus's life was so inclusive that the religious authorities of the day were utterly scandalized. Instead of inquiring about the miraculous provision and healing on display for all to see through Jesus's ministry, the authorities focused on the type of people with whom Jesus engaged, asking his disciples, "Why does your teacher eat with tax collectors and sinners?" Jesus's response, "Go and learn what this means: 'I desire mercy, not sacrifice,'"[10] is as applicable for us as fallible humans today as it was two millennia ago. There is a sense that we too must "go and learn"—or be highly intentional—about placing love of and engagement with the "other" ("mercy") above our own standing and reputation (religiously acceptable "sacrifice"). Our learning process may be different depending on the histories and current state of our societies, communities, institutions, and individual backgrounds. But if we are to genuinely pursue flourishing together, we need to first acknowledge our shortcomings— where and whom we have excluded rather than included—and then actively turn by doing the hard work of reconciliation and, where needed, restoration and renewal.[11]

We should again take our cue from Jesus, to begin by eating, talking, and dwelling with the "other." These are all actions implying significantly deeper commitment in first-century Judea than they do in much of our current world, and as such imply getting to know, understand, and commune with those who are (or whom we perceive as) different. This in turn helps us to break down our fear, stereotypes, and pride in the process and, though it will surely require hard work, we can hope and expect flourishing on the scale of what we might see in nature—ecosystems made strong and vibrant through a diversity of flora and fauna, standing in stark contrast to industrialized horticulture, rendered constantly susceptible to disease and blight by monoculture.

Serving Relationships

When flourishing is reduced to narrower definitions of individual success, there is the potential to miss out one of the most crucial aspects of flourishing relationships—service. Sacrificing one's personal agenda and aggrandizement to choose to serve others may not always be a natural instinct, but it is an essential pathway to flourishing together. Jesus shows the way throughout his ministry, including the famous story of the leader washing his disciples' feet in John 13. The actions and words Jesus uses are shocking to his friends around the table, so much so that they provoke an outcry by Peter: "You shall never wash my feet."[12] Jesus replies that such acts of service are fundamental to their relationships together, by responding, "Now that I, your Lord and Teacher, have washed your feet, you also should wash one another's feet. I have set you an example that you should do as I have done for you."[13]

Such practical service is central to our interdependent model of flourishing between students, educators, and schools. On one level, the call of the gospel is clearly to imitate and seek opportunities to do the same in our relationships, whatever their power structures and hierarchies. Yet the implication for our relationships is not simply that we copy this action, but that we should faithfully improvise on this model in creative and generous acts of service which, taken together, can come to define our communities. Given the sheer volume of work and expectation in our roles, it can seem unthinkable to consider how we could serve someone else today—yet consistently choosing service can cause ripples of flourishing through practical actions that put others first. Service brings joy and creates energy in the classroom, where each student's flourishing matters to every other student in the room. It can also change the culture and posture of an institution, as educators realize that their service toward one another is not another task to be completed but rather a foundation for relationships that are joyful, creative, and appealing to those looking on.

Faithful service together is a demonstration that we are abiding in *meno* relationships. The call is for the simple decision to put another first, to commit for the longer term, to seek out, invite, and welcome a stranger. These are actions that contribute to flourishing regardless of age, from an early elementary school child all the way to a late-career trustee. It can begin in small ways—and like every flourishing plant, it probably must. Our acts of service need not always be extravagant, or even seen; the call is simply to faithfulness demonstrated by the choice to serve.

Educating for *Shalom*

Thinking about relationships can sometimes lead us to an unrealistic vision of complete harmony and total elimination of pain, doubt, and difficulty. While a vision for living well together is attractive, some of our challenges may not be simply resolved and many of our questions of each other may not be easily answered. Things can go wrong, people may make mistakes, and our relationships may not yet be all that we want them to be. However, relationships that foster flourishing together are particularly forged through our commitment to endure, depend on, include, and serve one another over difficult roads. Even when traversing rough terrain, we can still be encouraged by the direction of travel and the companions with whom we are making the journey.

Some theologians describe this journey toward the restoration of relationship with God, self, others, and creation as pursuing *shalom*. Communities that reflect *shalom* impart a sense of peace, wholeness, health, safety, and permanence. They permit contrition and release forgiveness. They communicate that we belong together; that we place each other's needs before our own; and that we choose patience over disappointment, permanence over pain, attachment over isolation, and connection over competition. When it comes to Christian education, Nicholas Wolterstorff explains that "Christian community exists not for its own sake but for the sake of all people . . . in the modern world, if the Christian community is to share in God's work of renewal by being witness, servant, and evidence, its young members will need an education pointed toward equipping them to contribute to that calling" of *shalom*.[14] We turn now to share a story of a school that is deeply committed to, and highly engaged in, bringing *shalom* in the lives of students, staff, families, and the larger community which it serves.

With three campuses located in Philadelphia, The City School names *shalom* as one of its core commitments in serving a diverse student population and providing a quality Christian urban education. This commitment centers on the biblical injunction to "seek the peace and prosperity of the city to which I have carried you into exile. Pray to the LORD for it, because if it prospers, you too will prosper."[15] According to school leader Joel Gaines,

> Everyone wants to see a wholeness and completeness. I can show you a visual of one neighborhood that has all this devastation and destruction, and then another neighborhood where things are thriving and growing. Flourishing is what everyone wants, whether you are in a rural setting or an urban space. *Shalom* is that pursuit of something aspirational and bigger, even in the midst of challenges. Yes, it is a destination. But it is also a journey. It is messy, and it's not perfection, because things in our world will continue to be broken. But *shalom* provides a hope of what could be.[16]

The pursuit of *shalom* is fully integrated into the curriculum at The City School. For example, in one assignment, high school students are instructed to take pictures of where they see *shalom* either manifested or needed in their communities. Of one student who took a picture of a rose growing out from a crack in concrete, Gaines explains, "They were saying in the midst of challenges that are all around, you are still able to see the beauty of God's creation within a broken structure." Another student submitted a picture of a public bus—and, when asked what it meant, said it showed the need to bring *shalom* "in my coming and going."[17] Shortly after that, Gaines received an email from a public transportation rider expressing admiration for a student (recognizable by his school uniform) who had given up his seat for an older gentleman who needed one.

Students at The City School are also taking the initiative to apply lessons they learn about *shalom* in school in their own communities. For example, a high school senior began to consider how she might address pervasive gun violence in her neighborhood. She teamed up with Mighty Writers, a community organization that provides free writing workshops to area youth, in conducting and promoting anti-violence forums.[18] She also wrote an opinion piece featured in a local newspaper, which called for city leaders to provide more funding for extracurriculars for city youth, to convene community members and other groups for dialogue, and to meet people "where they are at," by attending events and engaging with residents within their community contexts.[19] As Gaines remarks, "She felt this was what God was calling her to, even though not many people might listen to a high school senior. But it was a true pursuit of *shalom* for her neighborhood, in which everyone wants to see human flourishing."

The importance of *shalom* also grounds the work of school staff members who have found that, in particular, the "idea of *shalom* is significant in talking about race, ethnicity, and culture in many Christian school communities because of the cognitive dissonance, discomfort, or pain that accompany such topics."[20] Ongoing professional development focuses on issues of justice, in a recognition that—as Wolterstorff explains—there "can be no *shalom* without justice. Justice is the ground floor of *shalom*."[21] At The City School, the dialogue around justice considers implications for teaching students, connecting with families and the community, and relating with colleagues. As Wolterstorff writes, and as the staff has found, by building collective "courage to seek *shalom* in others . . . the school community moves beyond diversity and begins to answer the Micah 6:8 calling to 'do justice, love mercy, and walk humbly before our God.'"[22] It is hard work that requires commitment that endures over time—in other words, *meno* abiding. As Gaines explains, "Challenges around racial justice are so deeply rooted in the fabric of this country. You're left with what feels like this sense of despair. But the pursuit of *shalom* is the very thing that ignites you to say, 'I can't give up.' This is ongoing work. This is work that I may not even see the benefit of in my lifetime. But I am still actively called to pursue it for the sake of those who come behind me."

Shalom demonstrates the *meno* choice to abide—to live in committed interdependent, inclusive, servant-hearted relationships. And indeed, *shalom* is the very promise that Jesus leaves his disciples with at the end of the gospel narrative: "Peace [*shalom*] I leave with you, my peace [*shalom*] I give you."[23]

And then after his resurrection, three times Jesus greets his disciples with "*shalom.*"[24] *Shalom* is the social evidence in a community that the vision for flourishing that Jesus offered is alive and well. *Shalom* is relational, communal, and plural. It is the collective peace that comes from knowing that while we may not have reached our destination, relationally or otherwise, we are choosing to abide together on the journey toward flourishing.

6

Reimagining Relationships

Our commitment to being a community has been and continues to be the most essential thing about us. . . . [C]ompromising community means compromising our essence. If this happens, we would not have much of value to offer to others.

—Ruth Haley Barton,
Pursuing God's Will Together[1]

The community that shares a common experience of moving toward the mess, serving together . . . becomes less self-centered and more missional. It gains clarity about a crucial fact: Christian community is never an end in itself.

—John Hambrick, *Move Toward the Mess*[2]

It's all about relationships. This is true whether in our classrooms, corridors, staff rooms, or board rooms. We can design any action plan, scheme of learning, budget trajectory, or staffing structure—but ultimately our flourishing together is defined by our relationships with one another. As we have seen, the kind of relationships that Jesus seems to have in mind are enduring, interdependent, inclusive, and servant-hearted, all converging in the pursuit of *shalom*.

In this chapter we explore six further reflections on what this might look like for students, educators, and schools, as shown below:

You give courage to others—you catch your colleagues before they fall.

You show us how to live well together—you celebrate diversity.

schools flourishing educators flourishing students flourishing

We seek to learn from other traditions—we don't need to win arguments.

We seek to bless all—we practice hospitality.

I know someone will walk alongside me—I know my unique story matters to you.

I have a voice that matters—and truly listening to me will change how you teach.

The very nature of this diagram shows the interconnectedness between students and educators, as well as the school overall, for flourishing. Rather than a hierarchy, this reflects interdependence—reminding us of the beautiful Zulu word introduced earlier in the foreword, *ubuntu*, meaning "I am because you are."

We begin our reflections and activities in this chapter with flourishing students, by delving deeply into the importance of recognizing and celebrating their individual stories as a necessary way into learning. Students know there are many stories in their classroom but need to somehow feel that theirs is crucial to the teacher—to feel that they are known and loved. This signals the importance of listening to the voice of students in our relationships. Flourishing students have a voice that is heard.

Our interconnectedness leads us to reflect next on the nature of relationships for educators and how central they are to the flourishing of our teams. This includes the giving (or taking away) of courage and compassion, as we share life together. We then further explore a key orientation for every educator—embracing diversity and recognizing the importance of listening to (and acting upon) voices that are different from our own. When we are bold in opening up challenging conversations, we are always the richer for it—no matter how contrite and humble our posture may need to be. It is the shared table that confirms and nurtures the relationship.

Finally, we turn again to the flourishing of the school as a whole, by exploring the call to look outward—to extend the table and to remove barriers to flourishing together. There are tough questions for us all about the nature of our relationships, and the difficult choices we each need to make if we are to reshape the culture which has for so long reinforced difference rather than celebrated diversity. Rather than checking a box or attending a training event, a long-term commitment to each other—abiding in relationship—is what is needed.

As in other "Reimagining Our Practice" chapters, we encourage you to read slowly and reflectively. We also invite you to connect with students and colleagues to engage the activities throughout the chapter. As you do, may you find inspiration for flourishing together in current relationships, in seasoned or broken relationships that need mending or repair, and in the new ones waiting to be sought out.

"I know someone will walk alongside me—I know my unique story matters to you."

However individualized our progress measurements become, education is fundamentally a social experience. Flourishing together is *lived out in relationships.*

Sometimes these relationships can make learning incredibly enriching, inspiring, enjoyable, and life-giving; and other times they can make it deeply depressing, fear-filled, isolating, and crushing. The social conditions and relationships needed for learning are foundational to students' daily experience, as well as to their perspective on how school is "going."

It seems much less likely that students would flourish alone. They instinctively crave the validation and love of their peers and adults. They long to be known by name—and then develop something deeper, securing a connection that shows the teacher understands and empathizes with them (even in the frequent cases when the teacher's own story is quite different from their own). Our students need to feel safe, secure, precious, and loved, knowing that someone is walking alongside them.

The more vulnerable or wounded our students are to begin with, the more they need this straightforward companionship and reassurance of presence. Students need reliability and predictability in a world that has taught them the exact opposite.

Walking together builds shared memories and develops the credibility built on shared experiences which reinforce the "together-ness" of learning. The seasons of life seem to be less surprising when we walk them together—we mind the searing heat of the sun or the bitter cold of winter far less, when we walk alongside one another.

Walking is patient; running is not.

Walking together gives time for conversation and exchange, while running does not. Pace is important—flourishing students sometimes need the adults to slow down and walk.

While walking together, we can discuss, debate, joke, and lament as we tell and exchange stories. Flourishing students feel like their unique story is the most important in the world to the teacher—and that it really matters. Even though there are of course many more students in the same room, they each long for their story to be known and understood. This cultivates empathy in teaching and the celebration of the many facets of each student's story.

Institutional life tends to force us into putting things in boxes, rather than listening to stories.

Stories are dynamic—they have a beginning, middle, and end—a past, present, and future. They are unpredictable (even when a teacher thinks they have taught someone "just like this" before—or worse still, an elder sibling!) Stories need to be learned in our own language and listened to well. Like learning a new language, listening to different stories will take time but will be paid back many times over in good times and in crises—simply because quality relationships stand at the heart of great teaching and pastoral care.

When a student's story is unknown, devalued, misrepresented, or oversimplified, the challenging pastoral or academic situation will often be made much worse. If the relationship is secure because we walk together, we can be confident that whatever challenge presents itself today, we still have the relational foundation we need to flourish together.

Questions for Further Reflection

1. If your students had to describe the relationships they experience in school, what would you *hope* they would say? What might they *actually* say?

2. How does it feel when someone listens to your story carefully? What happens to your relationship as a result?

3. How might we slow down the pace of our educational experience to allow time for students' voices to be heard?

4. What does it mean to walk alongside a student for the longer term? Think of a time when you have experienced this and the difference it made—in both the student's life and yours.

*"I have a voice that matters—and truly listening to me
will change how you teach."*

Every generation in human history has felt that the next generation is different from itself and frequently can become quite disparaging about those growing up behind it. It is easy to misunderstand those who come after us, not least because as adults we have not lived in their world.

In many ways it is of course the same world—some of the same geography, history, economics, and social functions—yet a ten-year-old has a viewpoint that is inherently different from that of a school leader in their forties (or beyond). This can lead to institutional hierarchies whereby leaders at the top make the majority of the decisions and may end up only paying lip service to the voices of students and young people.

As American philosopher Nel Noddings explains, "Traditional moral philosophy has overlooked the contributions of the cared-for"; she cites the student-teacher relationship as one which is "not equal or symmetric" but in which "the cared-for makes a distinctive contribution to the relation[ship] and establishes it as caring."³ Education has often overlooked this fact—no doubt restricted by the requirements and specifications of external examinations or high stakes testing.

Prioritizing the contributions of students and their voices to the teaching relationship is not just a pedagogical matter but an ethical one.

Flourishing together also means valuing one another's voices especially when they are different from our own. Spending a day as a student, walking a mile in their shoes, and trying to see the school through their eyes might be a start to develop that mutual appreciation of different perspectives. And our students need to learn to do the same for one another.

Flourishing students need to know and experience that their voice matters. As adults, we know our voice matters when it appears to make a difference—when things change because of what we say. Likewise, if the student's voice matters, lessons may go in a different direction.

Great teachers already know this, and they instinctively incorporate student voices through their relational pedagogy.

If students' voices are brought into the pedagogical heart of the school, such as through inquiry-based learning, projects may be reshaped, learning experiences may be redesigned, and physical spaces may be adapted. Courageous leaders welcome and enable student voices because they know they are indicators of engagement and ownership, which can then be harnessed across the curricula for deep and meaningful learning.

Students may only have the confidence or courage to speak up once, and so the teacher's response is crucial—the student will clearly learn quickly whether to speak up again. Equally, many students may not feel ready or willing or empowered to speak, so schools need to build in a range of opportunities for every voice to be encouraged and heard.

It is a risk, because the voices of students may not always fit within or reinforce the views inside educators' echo chambers—but nonetheless listening and acting upon their voices is central to flourishing together.

Questions for Further Reflection

1. What do you see as the main differences between the students you teach and your own generation? How might this affect your relationships?

2. How does it feel when your voice actually matters?

3. What kinds of structures could be set up to ensure that students' voices make a difference?

4. To what extent do you see giving students a voice as a risk to your school?

ACTIVITY: COMING ALONGSIDE STUDENTS

"Our Story" project

Many schools with a Christian ethos will seek to measure ways in which that ethos changes people, affects learning, and transforms the community. Some metrics can be useful and some tools can help. However, our activity here is simple—the telling of stories. My story is as important as yours (regardless of my age, or whether you are my teacher or leader), even though it is one story. Yet when we collect, read, and listen to the many stories within our community together, this collection of apparently singular stories becomes an "Our Story" project.

Gather a group of students—perhaps ten to fifteen to start—and ask them to tell a story about some aspect of their flourishing (perhaps their faith journey, cultural development, or formation of relationships). Document these students' stories in some way—perhaps two-paragraph written descriptions, two-minute films, or short audio recordings. Celebrate each story and encourage students to listen deeply, ask good questions, and respond courageously to the stories of others.

Then gather the stories—which are sure to be unique, and potentially disparate—into a simple collection. This could be through a book that contains them all and can be shared with the rest of the class or larger student body. It could be a montage of the films or a blending of the recordings, which can then be shared as an "Our Story" with the wider school community (of course, complying with permissions and safeguarding procedures).

Centralizing the personal narrative of each individual gives the school great evidence of the impact of some aspects of its work, but more importantly, through making the artifact, the school communicates to the

94

rest of the community that each person's individual story matters to all. The intertwining and interaction of all of these stories as "Our Story" is what really tells us about the identity of the school. While we can debate mission statements or lists of values, very few people can argue with a compelling story.

*"You give courage to others—you catch your colleagues
before they fall."*

Leading a flourishing school requires courage. Courage is the choice
to do something that seems uncertain, sometimes unwise—at least
untested—in the pursuit of a bigger picture, a future that cannot yet be
seen. Courage is only really ever known in action, never just on paper. And
educators know that Brené Brown, author of *Dare to Lead*, is right when
she asserts, "Courage is contagious."[4]

We can give each other courage through the celebration of one another's stories. Courageous stories often tend to highlight sustenance
through adversity. Remembering and celebrating them gives courage to
those who hear them, whether they were part of those stories or not.

These stories confirm our calling together. This sense of shared narrative is thus often underpinned by clear habits of gratitude and rhythms
of prayer.

Flourishing educators know that there is no success without succession. For this reason, leaders give courage to others to grow; they do not
simply seek to be the heroes on which everything focuses.

In fact, courage is often associated with passion, a word whose meaning goes beyond high energy, activity, and pace, drawing from its Latin
root *passio*—to suffer. While we may not seek suffering for ourselves or
our teams, courageous leaders know that their flourishing will involve suffering. They even extend this to the notion of "com-passion"—literally,
"suffering together." Flourishing leaders courageously share the suffering
of others as they empathize with and care for their teams. This "walking-
with" gives courage to others and can release their flourishing, as well as
the consequent shared joy this brings.

In the certainty of things going wrong, flourishing educators recognize that there is an art to building a culture in which those who fall are
instinctively helped up.

There are resources for forgiveness, healing, renewal and repair, and leaders know how to access them. Leaders share good news regularly, make routine deposits in their colleagues' emotional bank accounts, clear blockages in relationships, and make their teams' jobs easier.

Flourishing educators *systematize support*—they notice the wobble of the spinning plate and are proactive in their response, not waiting for the plate to fall.

To expect nothing to go wrong in a school would be like seeking to cultivate a great garden without expecting storm, drought, pestilence, or weeds. In fact, the greater the challenges educators face, the greater the opportunities for unearthing resources to help the community move forward. They recognize that flourishing in schools is not a solo performance, but an ensemble held together by mutual investment, care, and value. To the flourishing school, each educator is precious and inherently valued.

This is rarely shown through policies, mission statements, or motivational posters; rather, it is given definition in sustained, abiding relationships characterized by the normalization of acts of loving-kindness.

Questions for Further Reflection

1. Who gives you courage in your role?

2. How long can you survive in an organization without encouragement from others?

3. What might it mean to suffer together in a school context? What difference does this make to team dynamics and relationships?

4. How do we build a culture together in which "those that fall are instinctively helped up"?

"You show us how to live well together—you celebrate diversity."

The call to flourishing together can sometimes paint a picture of relationships which rarely go wrong, and communities that live in perfect harmony—smiling people in prospectuses, and school promotional films where permanently happy students achieve in every scene.

While this might be an attractive proposition toward which we are instinctively drawn, the reality is quite different for all institutions. If you put one hundred, five hundred, or a thousand people in a building together five days a week, things are going to go wrong—*and this is completely normal.*

There are just too many variables across so many relationships.

Arguments, disappointments, misunderstandings, isolation, intensity, pressure—these are all part of a normal school environment. While we may not seek such experiences, and they rarely feature in our school action plans, perfect relationships are not always possible in imperfect communities. Flourishing educators take note of this truth daily to make a range of wise decisions, thereby enabling the community to live well together.

Living well together means seeking first to understand the other; finding alternative angles in a disagreement; taking time to empathize; and pausing our hectic schedules just to sit and listen before diving into action.

It means proactively thanking colleagues and students; building a culture of encouragement; demonstrating relationships that begin by building up the other; giving time and space where needed; and remembering that each person is more than a job title. It means adopting a posture of service and generosity toward colleagues and students while demonstrating compassion and patience.

Living well together means making time and space to talk together about our relationships and communities—what is going well, and what we might need the courage to change. It means pausing, breathing, forgiving, and creating new starts; it means choosing to think the best of others, assuming positive intentions, walking together, working together, learning together, arguing together, grieving together, and celebrating together.

Living well together also means building teams of staff and students in a way that prioritizes diversity and inclusion at every opportunity. This is not just because it is the *correct* thing to do, but also because we think, lead, teach, and learn better because of our diversity.

School leaders recognize that the checkered history of our societies (from which, painfully, faith groups are not always exempt) may necessitate particular attention to schools' ethos, pedagogy, curricula, hiring, and use of resources in order to counter a lack of representation, stereotypes, discrimination, and unconscious bias, wherever and however they may be found. Living well together calls us to a diversity that embraces difference. Diverse religious communities that reflect the broader community also reflect the heart and nature of our creative God.

We do not have to look far to see the beauty of diversity and how living well together leads to our collective flourishing. There are ready-made lessons available for us in most gardens and ecosystems, where beauty and longevity come not from uniformity and singularity, but rather from the variety of many different plants and trees interacting with one another— all different sizes, shapes, functions, colors, ages, fragrances.

The diversity of the garden as a whole makes each plant itself more beautiful because of this relational context, often set up by a wise gardener who knows that, through interaction together, each individual can become something even more wonderful when it flourishes as part of a greater whole.

Questions for Further Reflection

1. What does "living well together" actually look like in your school? What happens when conflict and disagreement arise?

2. How can we find the personal resources to "seek first to understand" before diving in?

3.   What is your school's approach to issues related to diversity?

4.   How might we prioritize "living well together" at every opportunity?

LEADERSHIP DEVELOPMENT **ACTIVITY**

"En"-couragement

The word "courage" derives from the same Latin word from which the French word *le coeur* comes, meaning, of course, "heart." Courage is therefore the ability to "have heart" in a situation. *En*-couragement is the giving of courage to another—literally "to put heart into them." As we have seen, encouragement must be foundational to our relationships if we are to flourish together. The reverse is also true—*dis*-couragement means, literally, "to take heart out of."

In this exercise, we invite you to reflect on the "typical" lived experience of your team through a given day or week. There are twists and turns, ups and downs—but which factors cause this seesaw to tip toward encouragement or discouragement in your team's experience? Jot down some factors in the boxes below.

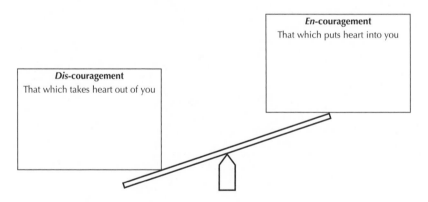

After you've written some words in the boxes above, consider:

- What habits and practices could you embed within your team to ensure your relationships are primarily *en*-couraging?

- How might your team become "known" for giving courage?

- What might happen as a result of the courage you give and receive from each other?

- How might a culture of encouragement spread from your team to others in the school, including students?

"We seek to learn from other traditions—we don't need to win arguments."

Faith-based communities historically have not always been known for dialogue, mutual understanding, and respectful interaction—rather, there has been (and still is) a danger that confidence and assurance in faith can lead to potentially combative language between traditions and communities.

This rarely leads to a greater depth of flourishing for anyone involved, and in fact living well together in an increasingly pluralistic society relies on a posture of dignity, respect, dialogue, and learning. Even where our communities may still reflect a historical homogeneity, this is highly un-likely to be the reality of the future toward which our institutions and societies are headed.

Flourishing schools acknowledge the ways in which their postures in the past may have contributed to explicit social division and exclusion, or the ways in which they may have harbored unconscious bias on a more subtle level.

Seeking to learn from others is quite different from attempting to convince others that we are right. This change in orientation need not be seen as a dilution of conviction, but rather a deepening and expand-ing of our love for neighbor—enriching and life-giving as we simply sit down together.

Sometimes we can be too eager to emphasize our differences and dis-tinctions, rather than our relationships and commitments with those dif-ferent from ourselves. Flourishing schools dismantle an "I'm right, you're wrong" posture, rather seeking to engage in dialogue with traditions that are "neighbors" to our own.

We don't need more arguments—we need more meals together.

Debates rarely change hearts and minds. Flourishing together begins with asking questions that we share and around which we can gather, followed by listening and responding with dignity.

Flourishing schools seek this for the people inside their institutions, and they create opportunities for students and educators alike to learn from and reason with others, including those beginning from a different starting point.

For schools in locations where this may be more practically difficult (because we all may look, sound, speak, and dress to some extent the same) we need to create opportunities to take ourselves and our students outside our immediate communities, to seek first to understand. Respect and care are grown in relationship; leaders need to be proactive to achieve this in many cases, so our students will be well-equipped for the global village in which we now all live.

Flourishing together leads us to wise dialogue, practical kindness, and loving inter-connectedness, where we expand our horizon beyond our own self-preservation, and seek the *shalom* of the wider community and world of which we are all a part.

Questions for Further Reflection

1. How might have religion contributed to explicit social division and exclusion in our communities?

2. All of us know what it feels like to be left out. Are there any who might feel left out—either in our schools, or in the broader community?

3. Based on your answer to question 2, who might you need to invite for a meal?

4. How could our school become known for a posture of learning from others, particularly those different from ourselves?

"We seek to bless all—we practice hospitality."

A school can become one of the most intense, enriching, inspiring, and encouraging communities in our society—where hundreds or thousands of students and educators live their daytime lives together, in all the beauty and complexity of thousands or even millions of relationships in one building. (In fact, it would make an interesting math problem to calculate the exact number!)

Such a community can offer love, encouragement, safety, security, growth, empathy, compassion, support, development, humor, fun, happiness, and joy. Relationships help its members grow through challenge, uncertainty, fear, pain, confusion, loss, loneliness, doubt, and division.

A flourishing school is one of those genuinely beautiful parts of society; *its community looks to it and thrives because of it.*

Flourishing schools take a broad view of whom education is for, realizing that our schools do not exist just for us (however we define the "us"). Jesus's abundant vision of "life in all its fullness" is not offered just to those who think a particular thing, look a certain way, or earn a certain amount—*it is for everyone who desires it.*

Just as in Jesus's ministry, an authentic Christian vision for living well together is one that is scandalously inclusive—marked by genuine welcome, dignity, and respect. Good practices can form generations to come, helping to redefine community, replace division, foster reconciliation, and shape ways of living better together. We are called to seek the prosperity of the city in which we find ourselves (Jer. 29:7).

This is what is meant by "serving the common good."

Practically speaking, this means wherever there is division, flourishing schools should empower students (and consequently their educators) to live well together. Wherever there is social injustice, flourishing schools should open. And wherever schools are situated, they should seek to be a blessing—remembering Jesus's expansive definition, given in Luke's gospel, to the question, "Who is my neighbor?" (Luke 10:29).

This is a powerful and persuasive challenge for flourishing leaders to wrestle: holding in tension a deeply Christian approach to education with one that seeks also to serve the common good. There are no easy or quick answers, and fears related to self-preservation may present barriers. But each school that bears the name of Christ must prayerfully and thoughtfully walk through this challenge, because we are called to *shalom*.

A spiritual practice that can help shape our schools in this regard is hospitality.

Hospitality is simply about welcoming a *hospes* (the Latin word meaning "guest" or "stranger")—and Scripture instructs us that we should not neglect to show hospitality to such ones (Heb. 13:2). Schools practice hospitality when they keep their doors open (metaphorically and literally) and by embedding an invitational culture and fostering community engagement in all they do.

Flourishing schools graciously receive unexpected guests, because they seek to love, bless, and serve all, thereby living out their Christian vision in practice.

Questions for Further Reflection

1. How central is your school in the wider life of your local community? What could further develop this?

2. Who might be the *hospes* in your community and how could they be invited, welcomed, and hosted?

3. How do you respond to the language of being "scandalously inclusive" when reflecting on the life and teaching of Jesus?

4. To what extent does your school communicate that its vision for education is for all who desire it?

Setting the table

The Flourishing Schools research shows that community engagement and insular school cultures are related to flourishing in schools (positively and negatively, respectively). One way to reflect on this is to imagine that our school has set a table for a meal, at which students and families, our team members (leaders, teachers, and staff), community members, and other schools and organizations are seated at different "sides" of the table (see below). Using this image, we can discuss (as a leadership team, board of trustees, or other school group or department) three questions for each side of the table: (1) *Who is already seated (who is represented at our school)?*; (2) *Who do we need to invite (who is not represented, but should be)?*; and (3) *How can we welcome them (what do we need to do as a school to show hospitality)?*

○ ○ ○ ○ ○ ○

○
○   Students and Families
○   Community Members   Other Schools   ○
                                                            ○
            School Team   ○

○ ○ ○ ○ ○ ○

3

LEARNING

7

Learning for Flourishing

Like anything worthwhile in life, supporting adult learning and building schools as learning centers require the hidden treasure of paid attention, intention, and investment . . . Yes, this is important work. And yes, it is hard work that will take time. And yes, we can and must do it.

—Eleanor Drago-Severson,
Leading Adult Learning[1]

A Christian education can never be merely a mastery of a field of knowledge or technical skills; learning is embedded in a wider vision of who I am called to be and what God is calling the world to be.

—James K. A. Smith,
You Are What You Love[2]

The time and resource investment of societies, families, professionals, and students themselves in education across the world is incalculable. Undoubtedly, the intended outcome of these efforts is learning. But what is far less clear are the answers to questions about what is learned in schools and how that learning takes place. All schools address these questions through their structures, practices, and curricula, but often with varying degrees of alignment to their vision for learning.

A Christian vision for education views the answers to these questions as fundamental to educational flourishing, beginning with an understanding that learning is a capacity and endeavor central to the human experience. As Warren Cole Smith and John Stonestreet explain, "Throughout history, Christians not only have seen education as a common good but also could explain *why* it was a common good. To know about God's world is to know about God himself. . . . [L]earning reflects who we are in the deepest sense. We are made in the image of the One who knows all."[3]

This view of learning has compelled Christians to start schools all over the world, including in our own countries. In the United States, nearly all schools birthed some three or four centuries ago were Christian at their inception, and the Church of England's founding of free educational institutions in 1811 gave rise to the founding of thousands of other state-funded schools. A Christian vision for education and its corresponding value of learning does not just find its expression in the founding of schools, however. Such a vision for the "why" should also make a fundamental difference in the "how" and "what" of learning in schools. As John Hull of The King's University in Alberta asserts, a "Christian perspective" should lead to a "transformation of the school's educational goals, curriculum, pedagogy, student evaluation, and organizational structure."[4]

In order to explore what this transformation means for learning, we may need to engage in some *un*-learning first. This is because when it comes to learning and the structures that support it, schools are often still shaped by what Peter Senge and colleagues call the "industrial-age school system fashioned in the image of the assembly line," characterized by uniformity, efficiency, and standardization.[5] We can see this reflected in students grouped strictly by biological age versus ability or interest, in discrete "packets" of knowledge taught through partitioned subjects, in master schedules that prioritize efficient transmission of content versus open-ended time for exploration and discovery, and in high-stakes summative tests that serve as gatekeepers for progression. As noted by our coauthors in *MindShift*, "Christian schools must identify where they have been shaped by cultural forces—such as the industrial era impulse to construe schools as machines—and instead return to an education founded on God's love for humanity and creation."[6]

In two essential ways, this chapter explores how learning might be structured—and often, *re*-structured—if it is to be sufficient for the goal of helping schools, educators, and students flourish. First, learning that leads to flourishing is deeply purposeful, reflecting insights from Part 1 ("Purpose"). As Steven

Garber asserts in *The Fabric of Faithfulness*, "Meaningful education is possible only if questions of meaning are allowed in education."[7] While an industrial model of education may crowd out these important questions in favor of content acquisition, a Christian vision for education can prioritize inquiry, exploration, and reflection, which leads to the development of wisdom. Such wisdom equips and enables students to interpret, question, debate, and apply the knowledge and skills they are acquiring. And wisdom is key for character development, which empowers students to make informed ethical, cultural, moral, and spiritual choices throughout their lives.

Second, as we explored in Part 2 ("Relationships"), learning that has flourishing as its goal must be relational. Thus, instead of the individual competition that characterizes much of contemporary students' experiences—and the professional isolation that many educators experience—learning for flourishing will be marked by collaboration in the classroom and beyond. This again builds on what Étienne Wenger terms "communities of practice," where educators in schools "share a concern or passion . . . and learn how to do it better as they interact."[8] The relational dimension of learning is central to flourishing together in schools.

Most discussions of learning understandably start with students. But the premise of this book—that we are interconnected for flourishing—suggests that while student learning is the guiding star, it is situated within a larger constellation of school and educator learning. For this reason, we begin our consideration of learning for flourishing with schools themselves, which necessarily set the preconditions for both student and educator learning.

Flourishing Schools

When we think of learning, we may tend to think of a person; in the world of expanding artificial intelligence, we might even think of a computer. And yet as all sectors—from business to healthcare to education—grapple with increasingly complex economic, societal, and global realities, organizational learning has emerged as crucial for thriving. As Joseph Murphy explains in *Leading School Improvement*, "Learning climates and organizational adaptivity are being substituted for the more traditional emphasis on uncovering and applying the one best model of performance."[9] In other words, educators are finding it necessary not just to shape their schools as sites of learning but also to become learners themselves. Because organizational learning involves the collective beliefs, values, and actions of a group of people inhabiting a shared structure, such learning happens at the level of culture. Indeed, the Flourishing Schools research points to the importance of developing a *learning culture*[10] that is future-focused and marked by continual improvement. As Terrence Deal and Kent Peterson found in their explorations of school culture, "In study after study, where cultural patterns did not support and encourage reform, changes did not take place."[11]

Building a learning culture may require a number of shifts in schools, including rethinking an often-exclusive focus on teachers implementing "best practices" with fidelity. In *The Past, Present, and Future of School Improvement*, David Hopkins and David Reynolds acknowledge that while teachers should "know about 'best practice' in many fields [they must] also possess the intellectual, emotional and practical equipment to create 'better' practice . . . [by] generating knowledge themselves."[12] Knowledge generation in schools will require a foundation of collaborative inquiry around important questions— for example, What do we know about the learning of our students, ourselves, and our school? What don't we know about how we learn as a school community—and would we be willing to act differently if we knew it? Who should be at the table with us to ask these questions—and who gets to answer them?

As we ask and answer questions like these together, a few important things happen at the level of culture. First, we develop a common language for focusing on *outcomes,* which the Flourishing Schools research found was significantly linked to flourishing.[13] In other words, rather than focusing on "merely classroom and school processes,"[14] we discipline ourselves to ask the bold, no-holds barred question, "What *really* works in *our* school?" Our teams also develop a level of relational trust together, which allows us all to become more transparent about our weaknesses and to admit our humble need for others in order to support our collective growth and improvement.

In addition to asking important questions about learning, our schools need tools to be able to answer them. This may require a rethinking of our use of data, which the Flourishing Schools research also found was linked to flourishing outcomes.[15] Specifically, in schools where data is sought primarily for accountability purposes, a shift may be needed in terms of broadening the outcomes examined and in using the resulting data to inform everyday practice, growth, and development. Data sources should be qualitative as well as quantitative and may be generated by varied practices such as conducting formative and varied assessments of student learning, evaluating teacher practices, and involving students in designing their own assessments. This may require adapting the school calendar to allow time for collaboration, as well as viewing educators *and* students as co-investigators when it comes to data—and perhaps most importantly, as co-learners on the journey to educational flourishing together.

Finally, school leaders play an orchestrating and coordinating role when it comes to growing a learning culture. When leaders understand the larger ecology of the school, they are empowered to shape schoolwide approaches that lead to educational flourishing. The Flourishing Schools research found that this use of systems thinking—or the "ability to see situations from a holistic perspective"—is linked positively with school flourishing.[16] Whenever leaders consider the potential impact on students, educators, and the overall school when planning for change, they are engaging in systems thinking. This leadership function is crucial in light of research which suggests that a lack of a "coherent, big-picture approach to school improvement" is often the downfall of efforts to implement change in schools,[17] as well as in considering the cacophony of educational fads, external mandates, and constituent demands schools continually face. Systems thinking also helps leaders to better address the source of complex problems. As per the aphorism "every system is perfectly designed to get the results it gets," undesirable results are unlikely to be random, one-off, or solely attributable to a single person or program. When leaders engage in systems thinking, they can improve the likelihood that, having better understood the multilayered origins of a given issue, they can lead their teams in mapping out sufficient strategies and solutions.

Flourishing Educators

In *Schools That Learn*, Peter Senge and colleagues assert that education "can be made sustainably vital and creative, not by fiat or command or by regulation or forced rankings, but by adopting a learning orientation."[18] Having examined the importance of developing a schoolwide learning culture, we can consider how the educators who lead and teach within that culture can themselves flourish as learners. What does it mean in schools to take educator learning seriously? How can we create the conditions necessary for adult learning, especially given its centrality to flourishing not only for educators, but also for students and the school itself?

Adult learning theory and research suggests that educators often learn best by engaging authentic problems of practice in their own workplaces.[19] Thus, experimentation and reflection within the context of one's own teaching is more powerful for professional learning than addressing a hypothetical situation away from the classroom. Additionally, adults learn best when engaged in social contexts, where they can collaborate with peers rather than trying to learn on their own. Research has also shown that teachers find professional development most effective when it is active in nature, aligns with the instructional emphases and goals of the school, and has a longer-term duration (in terms of time span and total number of hours).[20]

Research on school culture suggests that improving teaching and learning "will take much more than tinkering with the types or amount of professional development teachers receive, or further scaling other aspects of our current approach."[21] Along these lines, one of the strongest linkages in the Flourishing Schools research was between flourishing outcomes and *feedback on teaching* that enables real-time adjustments in practice.[22] Although for leaders this may bring to mind the practice of formal observations as part of teacher supervision and evaluation, this is not necessarily what is meant by "feedback"; rather, research suggests that *peer* observation—with constructive feedback offered in real-time—is more powerful for teacher learning.[23] The input of teaching and learning coaches, as well as peer mentors, can likewise be an effective means of providing feedback on instruction.

In addition to teachers, we intuitively recognize that leaders need to continue to learn and grow as well. Put simply, when it comes to professional learning, schools should require of leaders no less than is required of teachers. For leaders, learning extends beyond technical "know-how" to developing the wisdom necessary for navigating competing interests and deciding among multiple "goods." This will require shifting decision making and leadership behaviors away from making the single correct decision in every situation—which is often elusive or nonexistent—toward employing the "wisdom from above" that is "pure, then peaceable, gentle, open to reason, full of mercy and good fruits, impartial and sincere."[24] Nurturing wisdom in leaders may require providing budget and opportunities for leaders' own professional development, as well as leaders' preparing annual "leadership development plans" or LDPs.[25]

In both the US and UK contexts, we have found that connecting leaders together through local, national, and international networks is one of the most effective means of fostering leaders' ongoing learning. A genuine network enables educators to ask and then answer the question, "What can I contribute?" and not just "What can I get out of this?" This reciprocity creates a commitment to mutual learning and support that leaders need to lead wisely in the complex educational environments of today. The Church of England's Peer Support Network—which was started in 2017, and since has grown to over one thousand schools—has found that successful leadership networks focus on the right things (meaning things that people are already working on) and provide leaders with a new language and new energy to enhance what they're doing (rather than expending time they may not have to just make a different version of what they're doing).[26] Such networks can reduce the isolation often experienced by school leaders, enhance collaboration between schools, and enable leaders to flourish together in new and generative ways.

More specifically, for these kinds of local and national networks to provide powerful support and development for leaders, they benefit from a focus on school category or context (such as geographical location, urban or rural school) or a common content focus (for example, a shared leadership development priority, such as curriculum design, faith formation, sustainability, and well-being). Also important is local facilitation by experienced and credible school leaders, who combine the ability to draw on their own leadership development journey along with the best national (and international) resources available. Networks that host their meetings virtually and in schools enable leaders to remain fully embedded in the life of their schools, as well as provide opportunities for leadership-focused tours, discussion and other networking activities, and touchpoints between events (for example, via videoconferencing and structured development activities). Finally, a multiyear commitment to networks helps leaders foster ongoing participation and allows time for relationships, collaboration, and collective problem-solving to occur. These factors combine to create an attractive environment in which school leaders are eager to sustain collaboration, and to generate a sense of a genuine community of practice—much like learning-focused leaders seek to develop with their own teams, in their individual schools.

Flourishing Students

It is against this backdrop of a school's larger culture—specifically shaped by organizational and educator learning—that student learning occurs. We can ask two important questions about student learning that leads to flourishing: first, *how* do students learn best, and second, *what* ought students to learn?

When it comes to the "how" of learning, Peter Senge and colleagues assert that where there is no student engagement, there is no learning.[27] The Flourishing Schools research likewise found that *engaged learning* for students is linked to flourishing.[28] As we consider what engaged learning looks like, it is helpful to mention that other researchers and practitioners employ different adjectives to modify the word "learning" (such as "deeper," "authentic," "transformational," and so forth). While there may be differences in the specific pedagogies encompassed or endorsed by each, we have found they all involve two similar goals: first, to differentiate between the "learner as passive knowledge receiver" approach and more active, collaborative, learner-centered, and student-directed approaches; and second, to broaden the scope of learning from the exclusively academic or cognitive to include social-emotional, spiritual, physical, artistic, and other dimensions. We have even been challenged to consider dropping any adjective that modifies "learning," because if student experiences are not truly engaging, deep, and authentic, can we truly say that students are learning?

In looking to other research insights, we find that when students "believe that what they are doing is important and has clear goals, they are more likely to interact with interest and absorb what is available in the classroom environment" and when given support "emotionally (e.g., via support for autonomy and intrinsic interests and feeling understood by teachers and peers) and with timely performance feedback, they adopt attitudes characterized by excitement, fun, and interest in learning."[29] This combination of deep purpose, along with relational engagement, has a transformational effect on student learning. Additionally, the Flourishing Schools research found that a strengths-based approach to learning—involving metacognition, or students' learning how they learn best—is positively linked with flourishing.[30] From a Christian perspective, this makes sense: because each student is created uniquely, the exact same approach to learning is not likely to work for two different students—let alone all students within a given classroom.

While differences in school structures and resources will allow for varying degrees of flexibility in grouping and scheduling—often owing to the industrial model of education schools have inherited which, again, favors uniform instruction, assessment, and sequencing—a number of approaches can be used in any setting to engage students in their learning. These include encouraging reflection, or helping students to think about their learning and growth and engage in self-discovery. When students are encouraged to reflect on their learning through journaling, discussion, learning portfolios, and other methods, "knowledge retention is higher, and students are able to make stronger connections across curricular areas."[31] Nurturing curiosity through unstructured (though perhaps guided) time within a class period or school day is also important, as is helping students learn how to ask good questions, which equips them with the ability to direct their own path to learning.[32] Learning also becomes more meaningful when it is placed in context; starting with real world problems and exploring them through project-based learning is one way to facilitate application of classroom learning. It not only helps students see the "why" of learning but also prepares them to be problem solvers and innovators in their careers and communities.

Interestingly, the Flourishing Schools research found that engaged learning was linked to flourishing outcomes not only for students themselves, but *also for teachers*. Where teachers reported helping students engage more deeply in their learning (to develop critical thinking and problem solving, for instance), staff turnover rates were significantly lower. This suggests that the quality of student learning improves teachers' sense of satisfaction and fulfillment in their work, further underscoring the interconnectedness of student and educator learning in flourishing together.

Finally, we turn to consider the question of *what* students ought to learn. In other words, what curricular decisions might schools make that would contribute to flourishing? As discussed earlier in Part 1 ("Purpose"), the Flourishing Schools research found holistic learning to be a key construct linked to flourishing.[33] A Christian vision of education views students as whole beings, who think, feel, act, and relate to others, which has profound implications on what students should learn in schools. As Steven Garber suggests, education should be "oriented to preparation for a calling and not just training for a career. The difference is one of substance, not semantics."[34] Again, this is often in direct contrast to external pressures to focus almost exclusively on summative testing, for which schools and teachers are often forced to backward design their curriculum and lessons to enable students to perform. The resulting education is frequently incomplete—failing to address adequately the wholeness of mind, body, emotions, and relationships necessary for people to flourish, and forgoing the character development that is essential for individuals to contribute meaningfully to flourishing communities and societies.

What might holistic learning for students—rooted in Jesus's promise of "life in all its fullness" and grounded in a Christian vision for education—look like, if realized fully in our curricula? While each school will need to ask this question of its own particular programs, we offer four general suggestions here, drawn from *"Deeply Christian, Serving the Common Good": The Church of England Vision for Education.*[35]

First, a curriculum that educates for wisdom, knowledge, and skills is one that enables discipline, confidence, and delight in seeking wisdom and knowledge, and developing talents in all areas of life. Such a curriculum should be rich and varied and allow ample room for exploration and self-direction. While this type of curriculum recognizes the value of many paths to flourishing—whether vocational or college preparatory—it does not force students to foreclose early on their future (for example, by funneling them exclusively toward one track of study). And while allowing students to dive deeply into their interests, the skills cultivated by the curriculum are sufficiently broad to prepare them for a range of career possibilities over their lifetimes.

A curriculum that prioritizes holistic learning is, secondly, one that inspires hope and aspiration in students, by encouraging them to see themselves as agents of healing, repair, and renewal. In doing so, it expands the view of education as a private good for one's personal economic benefit, to a common good that builds a foundation for living well together in communities and societies. Such a curriculum focuses on cultivating interpersonal relationships, participating meaningfully in the surrounding community, and developing the qualities of character that enable people to flourish together. This kind of learning toggles between the classroom and the larger community through peer mentoring, genuine service, and authentic leadership experiences.

Third, a holistic curriculum that is in line with a Christian vision for educational flourishing is also one that educates for dignity and respect. In recognizing the value and preciousness of each person as created in the image of God, such a curriculum treats each student—and every person that student will encounter, now and in the future—as a unique individual of inherent worth regardless of background, status, or ability. Practically speaking, this translates into textbooks and resources that share diverse stories and perspectives; ample time for students to share their own stories and listen to those of others with openness, respect, and care; regular opportunities within the school community to practice hospitality and foster belonging, especially toward those on the margins; and engagement through study and action on behalf of those who face injustice and discrimination.

And finally, a holistic curriculum geared toward flourishing also involves social and emotional learning. The Flourishing Schools research found that the predictable routines and positive reinforcement of *behaviors for learning* (sometimes referred to as classroom management, particularly in North America) are linked with flourishing outcomes.[36] It is also important to ensure that classrooms are safe for learning—which includes allowing students to make mistakes, ask questions, and express doubts without fear of punishment. Teachers also need to balance learning challenges and supports for each student, which help to keep students from becoming bored or feeling overwhelmed. Fostering student agency in the curriculum helps students to feel in control of their environment and learning, as opposed to feeling trapped or helpless in the classroom. And finally, designing curriculum which helps students to work collaboratively in groups can promote healthy peer interactions, mutual respect, and conflict resolution. All of the social and emotional skills that enable students to engage successfully in learning can translate into productive behaviors and habits for adult life and work. In this sense, promoting behaviors for learning in the school setting can prepare students to be lifelong learners. We can model this principle for students as we patiently and lovingly guide them in developing positive behaviors for learning.

As we work toward realizing a holistic curriculum that leads to flourishing, we return inevitably to the question of how we measure educational success. Unsurprisingly, research on accountability systems in the public-school sector in the United States found that often "student annual test scores serve as a proxy for the ultimate goals of education, including employability, civic involvement, and a fulfilling life."[37] This reductionist and shortsighted view of education does not reflect the breadth and depth of the holistic nature of a Christian vision for learning. While transforming a country's educational metrics may be beyond the reach of individual schools and educators, we can make a start by interrogating our everyday assessment practices—asking questions like, To what degree do these practices reflect our vision of education? What do our assessment methods communicate to students about their learning? How can we more closely align our practices with our vision? When we feel tied to practices that do not reflect our vision for student learning, how can we effect meaningful change in students' experiences—even in the smallest of ways?

The key to assessment approaches that lead to flourishing is to emphasize growth, as opposed to task completion. Believing that people can grow and change is a central tenet of Christianity, as the apostle Paul highlights in his first letter to the Corinthians: "That is what some of you were. But you were washed, you were sanctified, you were justified in the name of the Lord Jesus Christ and by the Spirit of our God."[38] Emphasizing growth and change encourages students to persevere through challenge and to celebrate learning victories. Research by Carol Dweck and others demonstrates the power of a "growth mindset," in terms of both improved academic performance and greater perseverance in task completion.[39]

While many schools seek uniformity or perfection when it comes to assessment of learning, we can instead make the choice to affirm progress and growth. Rather than pass-or-fail assessments or one-size-fits-all products, multimodal "artifacts" of the learning process, which show and celebrate multiple iterations of the creative and refinement process, can be developed by students to demonstrate and display their learning. Assessment then takes the form of engaging students in cycles of creation, peer and expert critique, and revision.[40] This approach more closely approximates how "real work" is created in the majority of professions—and certainly better prepares students for future careers than high-stakes testing. But more importantly, creating and celebrating student growth in learning reflects the process of ongoing personal and corporate restoration at the heart of the Christian journey. This kind of alignment of Christian vision and educational practice brings us closer to learning that leads to flourishing.

8

Asking Questions

Transformation comes more from pursuing profound questions than seeking practical answers.

—Peter Block, *The Answer to How Is Yes*[1]

It is telling that the first words Jesus speaks in the Gospels are in the form of a question.

—Martin Copenhaver, *Jesus Is the Question*[2]

Given the portrayals of Jesus throughout the centuries in various media, we could easily be forgiven for thinking he was exclusively an inspiring lecturer who interacted with his students primarily by passing along knowledge. It might therefore be surprising to learn that Jesus asks 307 questions in the Gospels, while he only gives direct answers to eight—making Jesus *more than forty times* more likely to ask a question than to answer one.[3] This begs a question of its own: What is Jesus's purpose in asking so many questions? And what insights can his questioning offer us regarding how we learn together in schools?

As Martin Copenhaver observes in the book *Jesus Is the Question*, "There is great value in pondering the implications of having a savior who approaches the world—and us—with questions."[4] As we consider these implications together, we will explore four key aspects of questioning—*nurturing wholeness, granting agency, permitting doubt,* and *developing wisdom.* These insights inform our understanding of how we can foster the kind of learning, for both students and educators, that enables us to flourish together in schools.

Nurturing Wholeness

When we read Jesus's words in the Bible, our first instinct may often be to look for the theological lesson that he is trying to impart to those with whom he interacted—and by extension, to us. The instinct toward interpretation is a vital one, ingrained in church practice by nearly two millennia of expository preaching and teaching. But it is helpful to pause and consider that Jesus is also talking with *real* people and asking them about their *real* lives. If we momentarily shift to consider Jesus's questions from this perspective—to take his questions at face value—we may learn something important about human flourishing.

Significantly, if we look closely at the range of questions that Jesus asked, we realize that Jesus was attuned to every dimension of human existence—mind, body, spirit, emotions, and relationships. When Jesus asks his disciples, "Do you not yet understand?"[5] he is concerned about their thinking. The question directed to the man awaiting healing by the pool of Bethesda—"Do you want to get well?"[6]—shows Jesus's care for physical needs. His repeated question "Why are you afraid?"[7] attends to his disciples' emotions. And after telling the parable of the good Samaritan, Jesus's question, "Which of these three do you think was a neighbor to the man who fell into the hands of robbers?"[8] addresses the social dimension of human existence. In addition to the spiritually rich truths we might intuit from these questions, they fundamentally reflect Jesus's desire for people to receive healing, restoration, and wholeness in all of these dimensions—in other words, for them to flourish.

In keeping with this desire, a Christian vision for education is concerned with all aspects of students' and educators' experiences and, as we have explored in the previous chapter, holistic learning is linked positively with flourishing outcomes. This convergence of theology, practice, and research in Christian schools ought to leave no doubt as to the importance of addressing the whole student through learning. But, as we have also observed, the focus of current educational policy and market forces is often exclusively on narrower academic outcomes. This persists even despite increasing calls internationally to broaden that focus, arising from modern economies in need of professionals who are able to navigate complexity, think creatively, and work collaboratively.[9] As Rex Miller and colleagues observe in *Humanizing the Education Machine*, "The current system is failing to graduate students who are prepared for the demands of the twenty-first century"[10]—ironically so, because nearly a quarter of the twenty-first century is already behind us.

Shifting pedagogy and curricula toward holistic learning will require significant intentionality and effort. But for Christian schools, there is nothing less at stake than students' and educators' ability to engage meaningfully and redemptively in a world that is increasingly in need of physical, emotional, and spiritual healing. By caring about the wholeness of human experience—just as Jesus did—our schools can attend not just to the flourishing of those within their walls, but also to the flourishing of the larger community and culture.

Granting Agency

At its most basic level, asking a question involves an exchange between the person who asks the question and the person (or people) invited to answer. Good questions—ones that are not rhetorical, and that originate from pure motives—are asked out of a desire to engage others. Taking this a step further, the very best questions are asked out of genuine care for another. We might say that such questions acknowledge that others are individuals just like ourselves, capable of thought and action, with inherent value that makes them worthy of dignity. Christians understand this concept of personhood through the lens of *imago Dei*, or the biblically based doctrine that people are created in the "image of God."[11] It should not surprise us, then, that Jesus asks people questions that not only reflect but also enable a fuller realization of this truth.

We see an example of this in Jesus's interaction with a man named Bartimaeus, who was blind.[12] As Jesus and his disciples are leaving Jericho and headed to Jerusalem, on what would be Jesus's final trip to the city, we find Bartimaeus begging by the side of the road. As he shouts for Jesus's attention, the crowd tries to stop him and deny him access to Jesus. But Jesus is the one who stops and, after telling the disciples to call him over, asks Bartimaeus a question: "What do you want me to do for you?"[13]

To us as readers, it seems the answer should be fairly obvious; indeed in the next verse Bartimaeus exclaims, "I want to see!" But Jesus's question is asked with a deeper purpose, as Copenhaver explains: "When Jesus asks,

'What do you want me to do for you?' he is showing respect for the man. He is not presuming to know what he wants. He is asking. And he is listening. It is a way of recognizing that the blind man is not defined by his disability. Jesus' question is a way of relating to the man as a human being. It is also his way of inviting him into a healing relationship."[14] Surely Jesus could have healed Bartimaeus outright without bothering to converse with him. Instead, Jesus's question models for us how the experience of being heard and of being shown respect is critical for not just physical healing but also dignity as a human being. Recognition of our personhood, of the *imago Dei*, is central to human flourishing.

The implications of this are profound for education. In the classroom, teachers must continuously invite students to speak—and really listen to their voices when they do. Likewise, school leaders need to make room for teachers' voices in ongoing decision making. In educational terms, we call this granting agency—or empowering others with the ability to represent themselves and make choices. Without this ability, students and teachers can be relegated to something less than fully human. Accordingly, experiences in our schools that serve to silence us are fundamentally dehumanizing. If we desire flourishing students, educators, and school communities, we must prioritize agency.

Arguably, the biggest challenge to this in schools (and in many organizations) is the use of power. Our rigid hierarchical structures—with students at the bottom, teachers in the middle, and school leaders at the top—have been handed down to us from the industrial age of education. As our *MindShift* coauthors note, while top-down, assembly-line models of schooling "work well for the industrial purposes for which they were invented . . . they do not, however, work well in forming human beings, who are created in the image of God."[15] Such agency-limiting structures or their remnants have a negative effect on the humans that inhabit educational ecosystems, and undoubtedly serve as contributing factors to student disengagement and teacher attrition.

Granting students and teachers the agency they need to flourish will require the sharing of power. This does not, however, mean the relinquishing of authority; in acknowledging Bartimaeus's agency, Jesus did not in any way give up his authority as the Messiah to heal him. Rather, Jesus chose to position his authority within the larger context of relationship, which had as its aim Bartimaeus's flourishing as a human being and, therefore, sought to empower him. As Copenhaver suggests, "One might expect that the savior of the world would more likely ask, 'Do you want to know what you can do for me?' After all, those in positions of power are used to being served. . . . Jesus asks the servant's question: 'What do you want me to do for you?'"[16]

As Jesus demonstrated in this question, as well as throughout his ministry, the way to employ power to benefit others' flourishing is through servant-hood. To use C. S. Lewis's words, Jesus's question is "bringing us back" to the "simple principles" [17] by which we felt called to education—in this case, the desire to serve students. While many educators entered their profession motivated by the desire to serve, some might say their daily reality is not what they had envisioned. A return to educational servanthood that leads to flourishing, as Jesus would depict it, would involve us using our authority to prioritize agency, give voice, listen carefully, and empower our students and colleagues as persons worthy of dignity and respect.

Permitting Doubt

Of all the questions that Jesus asked, the most challenging and penetrating may be the one he asked his disciples after rebuking a storm in response to their panicked cries for help. It is the same one Jesus asks Peter, who, after walking on water in response to Jesus's call, becomes afraid and begins to sink. In both circumstances, Jesus asks, "Where is your faith?"[18] It is difficult to read Jesus's question and not think the disciples have failed utterly and now their master is calling them to account. When we read these passages, we may focus on the disciples' lack of faith in the face of trouble and challenge, just as we may often focus on our own lack of faith. And just as Peter sank when he took his eyes off Jesus and focused on the wind and the waves, so too our hearts tend to sink when faced with our own doubts. If doubt is a part of human existence, what are we to make of Jesus's question to those who walked with him?

An interesting place to start is by asking what the *disciples themselves* made of Jesus's question. Significantly, none of the disciples responded as if their master had rebuked them. It is only us, as readers millennia later, who may feel only the "sting" of Jesus's question. Instead, the disciples in Luke's gospel respond with amazement, asking, "Who then is this, that he commands even winds and water, and they obey him?"[19] And in the account of this event in

Matthew's gospel, the disciples "worshiped him, saying, 'Truly you are the son of God.'"[20] In both instances, the disciples respond with marvel, adoration, and invigorated faith in light of what Jesus has done, as opposed to focusing on what they themselves had (or hadn't) believed.

As we dig deeper into these exchanges, we can uncover three principles for flourishing together. First, as stated earlier, doubt—like the storms that cause it to arise—is an inescapable part of human existence. As James K. A. Smith writes, "Even as faith endures in our secular age, believing doesn't come easy. Faith is fraught. . . . We don't believe instead of doubting; we believe *while* doubting."[21] Second, God does not punish or turn away from us in moments of doubt, but rather continues to act for our good—just as Jesus rescued his disciples in the boat, and then Peter, from drowning—because, as Christian Kettler writes in *The God Who Believes*, only "God possesses the love that dares to embrace the doubts of doubting creatures."[22] And third, by asking the question "Where is your faith?" Jesus "presses in" to our doubts in such a way that they can become springboards toward *deeper* faith. As Frank Rees writes in *Wrestling with Doubt: Theological Reflections on the Journey of Faith*, Jesus's question is in effect "God inviting us into conversation. . . . [T]here is much in the biblical witness which suggests a continuing conversation of belief and doubt, a conversation between God and the people of Israel or between God and the Christian believers."[23]

Educators can anticipate that pain, suffering, and challenges in students' lives are likely to give rise to deep questions, just as they do for ourselves. Students' doubts are often expressed in honest, nervous, and insecure questions. Indeed, the Flourishing Schools research found that *questioning*—when students have doubts about their faith—is significant for students' flourishing.[24] And just like students, we should expect that teachers and leaders will face doubts arising from pain, suffering, and challenges. How we react to students' and educators' doubts is of paramount importance. Like Jesus, we cannot turn away from or punish students or colleagues for doubting or questioning themselves and others. Flourishing together depends on the school community acting lovingly for the individual's good, which means permitting questions of doubt rather than ignoring, hiding, or trampling them.

Instead, we must come to treat doubt as natural to the human condition, and inextricably linked to our journeys toward flourishing. We can do this by permitting students' doubts and inviting them to engage in conversation with those around them, within the larger context of loving relationships. Frequently the relief of knowing that another person shares the same doubt can be deeply comforting and can enable further conversation together. Educators can do the same within our professional circles and, in doing so, build communities that thrive through mutual support. In these ways, schools can become safe and fertile ground for wrestling with doubt, for providing genuine love and care in the midst of challenges, and for sharing life together as a redemptive community.

Developing Wisdom

The central question at the heart of the gospels focuses on the identity of Jesus: Was he the promised Messiah? In John's gospel the people ask Jesus directly, "How long will you keep us in suspense? If you are the Messiah, tell us plainly," to which Jesus responds, "I did tell you, but you do not believe."[25] The people interrogating Jesus sound a bit like our own students who—wanting to know what exactly will be on the test, versus seeking real understanding— demand exasperatedly, "Just tell us the answer already!" And Jesus sounds a little like an exasperated teacher who replies, "I told you already, but you weren't paying attention!"

We see a fascinating contrast between this discourse on Jesus's identity in John's gospel and the one told in Matthew's. This time, Jesus is the one who asks his disciples about his identity: "Now when Jesus came into the district of Caesarea Philippi, he asked his disciples, 'Who do people say that the Son of Man is?' And they said, 'Some say John the Baptist, others say Elijah, and others Jeremiah or one of the prophets.' He said to them, 'But who do you say that I am?' Simon Peter replied, 'You are the Christ, the Son of the living God.'"[26] In this passage, we learn that when the tables are turned—when Jesus does the questioning—the disciples (or at least, Peter) comprehend who Jesus really is. What made the difference this time?

Whatever we might be able to say about the disciples and their differing levels of faith, one thing is clear: when Jesus asks the question, it requires careful consideration and—owing to his follow-up question, "Who do *you* say that I am?"—personalization. When Jesus asks the question and personalizes it, he is looking for far more than basic information. As Copenhaver explains, Jesus's questions "are an invitation. . . . Information is not the goal."[27]

Jesus is inviting his disciples to deeper understanding that is rich in personal meaning, born out of relationship, and imbued with commitment. We see this in Jesus's response to Peter: "Blessed are you, Simon son of Jonah, for this was not revealed to you by flesh and blood, but by my Father in heaven." Had Jesus merely been looking for the "right" answer, he might have responded with a simple "Correct!"[28]

When we think about educational flourishing in light of these passages, we are led to ask ourselves about the goals of teaching and learning. Do we want students to be able to give the right answers? Reasonably, yes—and it is certainly a good thing that Peter gave Jesus the correct response! But is that *all* we hope for them? And is teaching students how to give right answers all we can hope for as teachers? In *On Christian Teaching*, David Smith asks how often our pedagogical methods "have invited student responses that focused on successful completion of a task but bypassed deep learning."[29] And interestingly, as mentioned earlier, the Flourishing Schools research has shown that where teachers report helping students engage more deeply in their learning, staff turnover rates are significantly lower. This suggests that, like Jesus with his disciples, a Christian vision for educational flourishing requires that we desire something deeper for our students—and for ourselves.

To highlight the dichotomy between this "something deeper" and the simple acquisition of surface knowledge, we can describe a flourishing-worthy goal of learning in terms of *developing wisdom*. Many of our educational systems and schools across the world are structured around a "banking" model of education, which views teachers as absolute authorities making deposits of static knowledge into passive students, with the goal of students successfully regurgitating correct answers upon request.[30] Returning to the account of Jesus's questions to his disciples, we might view the banking model as the educational equivalent of "flesh and blood"[31] that Jesus describes—superficial, impermanent, and unable to impart life-changing meaning. Regrettably, our models of professional development for teachers and leaders may fall into the same trap, if they focus solely on educators acquiring static knowledge or skills rather than developing a community of practice with a shared vision, focus, and language.[32]

By way of contrast, wisdom is much more than a drudging repetition of knowledge bearing no importance or meaning for the person reciting it. Wisdom is something deep that develops within a person, as the mind and heart engage together in apprehending truth. When Jesus tells Peter, "This was not revealed to you by flesh and blood, but by my Father in heaven,"[33] he is describing something incarnational and transformational that has happened to Peter, rather than Peter's simply memorizing facts that he successfully recalls on a test when asked.

We are encouraged by the prayer of the apostle Paul in his letter to the Ephesians, "that the God of our Lord Jesus Christ, the Father of glory, may give you a spirit of wisdom and of revelation in the knowledge of him."[34] Allowing room for the spirit of wisdom and revelation—versus crowding students' and educators' minds with shallow information acquisition—is essential to a Christian vision for flourishing schools. As James K. A. Smith writes, "A Christian education can never be merely a mastery of a field of knowledge or technical skills; learning is embedded in a wider vision of who I am called to be and what God is calling the world to be. How does *my* learning fit in this Story? And what practices will cultivate this *ultimate* orientation in me?"[35]

Questions in Action

As we come to the end of this chapter, we can reflect on the richness of Jesus's questions for nurturing wholeness, imparting agency, permitting doubt, and developing wisdom in our schools. We can also consider the value of Jesus's pedagogy—of questioning as a way of teaching and learning—in our professional practice. At Little Rock Christian Academy (LRCA) in Arkansas, president Gary Arnold has worked for the past fourteen years to craft a learning environment for students that is collaborative and discussion-based and that is also mirrored by a professional culture of shared inquiry among leaders and faculty. Regarding the school's vision for learning, Arnold explains, "Faith and intellect are equal partners for our well-being, our *shalom*. Both grow when curiosity is set free. In order for Christian schooling to flourish, faith and intellect must grow in tandem as equal partners. The best way—perhaps the only way—for that to happen is to be comfortable with questions."[36]

At LRCA, this vision is operationalized at all levels—in elementary, middle, and secondary grades—where essential questions frame learning standards and guide curriculum development. Questioning also deeply informs outcomes: the school's 1,400 students are trained to become "good questioners" who test out their ideas with peers, listen to and incorporate feedback, and refine their thinking. And, compellingly, questions also provide a framework for "student-driven" pedagogy in the classroom. From middle school on up, this includes a "workshop" model consisting of a ten-minute didactic "mini-lesson," followed by nearly an hour of collaborative discussion around key readings, and then capped by a ten-minute wrap-up by the teacher. In the high school, this model follows the Harkness method, a dialogic approach to instruction developed at Phillips Exeter Academy in New Hampshire. Justin Smith, LRCA's head of upper school and vice president, explains that in this method,

> Students sit facing one another in some version of a circle and then discuss the text, looking for meaning and connections. The teacher acts as facilitator, guide, and coach and discussions typically ebb and flow: a question, a response, a pause, a connection outside the classroom, more questions and so on. Unlike teacher-centered instruction, this method of student-centered teaching [is] designed to capture the imaginations of students, challenge them to grapple with complexity, and create a space where they can refine their thoughts on things ranging from literature, Scripture, historical documents and theology to scientific discoveries.[37]

Members of the teaching staff report that, through involvement in Harkness, students have grown in their abilities to connect new and previous learning and retain information learned in class. They also learn to disagree with others thoughtfully and respectfully, which is a skill in short supply in today's world. As the students and staff "work together through challenging problems, and enhance understanding by way of a shared learning experience," they have "witnessed the systemic change [in] how our teachers approach student learning and how our students perceive the learning experience."[38] Importantly, Harkness proves an immensely valuable pedagogical tool when it comes to the intersection of faith and learning. As Smith explains of the pedagogy: "You are allowed to doubt. And we do say, Christianity is a worldview that you can walk into and ask the big questions."[39]

The importance of questioning at LRCA is not just limited to students, but also extends to faculty and leaders—reflecting Arnold's belief that "school cultures are strengthened by an open inquiry environment." To this end, teachers engage in a number of practices, such as critiquing each other's essential questions and providing suggestions for ways to improve on lesson plans, as well as conducting peer observations and providing regular feedback to colleagues. Professional development is conducted primarily on-site by teachers, often based on readings related to Harkness learning, discussion-based instruction, inquiry, and other active learning models. And when teachers do attend external events, it is frequently for training to support the pedagogical methods at the school. For example, LRCA staff members have been among a small group of educators selected to attend annual Harkness leadership conferences at Phillips Exeter. And yet even in these instances, the staff work to bring their learning back to campus (notably with regard to Harkness, LRCA also hosts a two-day summer workshop conference for their own teachers, plus teachers from other Christian schools across the country). Finally, LRCA teachers also must create an annual professional learning plan (PLP) which incorporates instructional risk and reflection. When looking across each of these components of faculty culture, the school has found that,

> Taken together, stronger bonds have grown across campus due to quality time observing and conversing about teaching and learning. Through the process as a whole, teachers are encouraged to take risks—to get outside of their comfort zones, and try something new that has the promise to improve student learning. Crucial to this is an atmosphere where risk is corporately encouraged, collaborative support is provided, and fear of failure is mitigated . . . [which] has created a culture where instructional challenges and limitations are viewed as hurdles to be jumped together, rather than insurmountable walls facing each individual teacher.[40]

To support this dynamic instructional environment, leadership teams engage in collaborative inquiry as well. For example, instead of appointing single chairs of academic departments, LRCA has co-chairs (often a seasoned faculty member who is paired with a more junior colleague). This structure not only increases the likelihood that different perspectives within a given department will be engaged, but also expands the table for a larger group of instructional leaders to meet regularly around questions of teaching and learning.

Across all levels of the school, LRCA students, teachers, and leaders interact as learners who ask good questions together. This requires a degree of vulnerability, humility, and loosened control, and at the same time encourages the building of life-giving trust and interdependence. This alignment of vision and practice throughout the school reflects a core value at LRCA: "We learn in community. We grow through fellowship."[41] As the story of LRCA demonstrates, when we entertain questions from—and pose questions to—our students and ourselves, we make space for learning that can lead to greater flourishing. Conversely, failure to make room in our classrooms and schools for questions will serve to stifle flourishing. This is because a vision for flourishing together requires that we grow more in touch with (versus ignoring or deprioritizing) our human experience, in both its mountaintops of joy and its valleys of pain. As Jesus demonstrated with his disciples, questions help us flourish together in the face of inevitable challenges by inviting us to find faith, pursue meaning, and act redemptively in our own lives and in the lives of others.

9

Reimagining Learning

To remain open to understandings—perhaps even to principles—
as yet not determined is the least that learning requires, its barest
threshold. With every friend I've known, in every situation I've encountered, I have found something to learn.

—Sonia Sotomayor, *My Beloved World*[1]

Intellect, emotion, and spirit depend on one another for wholeness.
They are interwoven in the human self and in education at its best,
and we need to interweave them in our pedagogical discourse as well.

—Parker J. Palmer, "The Heart of a Teacher"[2]

I f visitors walked around a school or into a classroom, how might they be able
to tell whether students and educators are flourishing? Some outward signs
of flourishing might be visible, whereas others might lie deeper beneath the
surface, hidden from view like the roots of a tree. In this series of short reflections, questions, and activities, we consider the kinds of signs we might look
for visibly, as well as the kinds of orientations that might underpin a flourishing approach to learning. Ultimately, the pursuit of flourishing together
should be reflected in the most central activity of the school—learning.

In this chapter, we explore six reflection pieces on what flourishing in learning might look like for students, educators, and schools, as shown below:

You are still a learner too—you ask and answer great questions.

You release the creativity of your students—your imagination shapes your teaching.

schools flourishing educators flourishing students flourishing

We align our pedagogy with our vision—our curriculum reveals our shared values.

We invest in our teams—we pursue our learning journeys together.

I back myself to take risks—I take the first step.

I make mistakes every day— I don't mean to disappoint you.

We start this chapter with two reflections that help us to again imagine ourselves in the place of a student, to explore risk-taking, courage, vulnerability, creativity, and imagination in learning. As you read these reflections on flourishing students, it may be helpful to picture a particular classroom in your school, or even a particular group of students (past or present). As adults, it may be challenging to think about students of this current generation without bringing our own experiences as students to bear. How often do we ask our students to describe their experiences of learning—and really listen? To this end, it may be helpful to read part or all of these student-focused reflections *with* students, as well as spend time engaging the questions after each.

The interconnectedness of flourishing together takes us next to consider flourishing educators. As we have emphasized throughout the book, it is quite right to prioritize the flourishing of students—but this requires flourishing educators who are leaders of learning. For where there are few flourishing educators, there will be few flourishing students. First, we consider teachers as learners themselves—not to put more pressure on educators to complete professional development programs or advanced degrees, but rather to ask whether we orient ourselves as learners first. When we do, teaching is enriched—and by extension, so too is the learning of our students. For the second reflection for educators, we explore the key role that creativity has to play in enabling flourishing together.

Finally, we offer some thinking about the way that teaching and learning must stand at the heart of flourishing schools. In these reflections we offer the chance to think about a simple but important question: we may say we have a certain vision for learning, but *how would anyone actually know?* The extent to which our vision is revealed in our pedagogy is the extent to which it *actually is* our vision, expressed through the normalized behavior of "the way we do things around here." This question of the alignment between what we believe about teaching and learning, and what actually happens in our schools, is all important. Finally, we consider the learning journey that we take together in schools, including the ways we invest in our teams as we build cultures of learning.

As in previous "Reimagining Our Practice" chapters, we encourage you to read slowly and reflectively. We also invite you to connect with colleagues to engage the leadership development and schoolwide discussion activities offered throughout the chapter. As you do, may you find a fresh vision for flourishing together in the learning you are leading.

"I back myself to take risks—I take the first step."

Students quickly learn what happens when they attempt something difficult, try something new, or take a risk. They acquire feedback and judgment from their peers (sometime tacitly, sometime audibly). This can become something that is feared, but the mirror that it holds up can also be valuable and motivating—so long as the conditions for flourishing together have been established.

Risk-taking in learning is underpinned by teaching that imparts dignity—in fact, such dignity is a precursor to learning, and thus foundational to flourishing.

Real learning is quite different from merely repeating what we can already do. Stepping out beyond our current place of security, particularly publicly, requires imagination and a vision of what is yet unseen. Flourishing students allow themselves to take risks, when they learn that educators and their peers notice and nurture the small green shoots of growth.

At times the teacher's insistence on progress can lead to a diminished desire for risk-taking, particularly around the pressure points of assessment—sometimes leading students to do enough to pass but perhaps not enough to excel. Even when grading rubrics call for creativity and innovation, teachers need to create the conditions for risk if students are to flourish in these ways.

This means normalizing and praising failure as a precursor to success— demonstrating the love that knows students have to fall off the bike before they fully know how to ride it.

Through this, the student's self-concept is strengthened, which in turn enables them to ride out a few mistakes—forming their character through this positive cycle of grace. Flourishing students demonstrate that the development of character is intrinsic to the pursuit of academic success, and the likelihood of taking a risk under pressure is often far more a test of character than of cognitive recall.

And when working with students who have already experienced deep pain, trauma, separation, isolation, and loss, teachers need to exhibit patience, understanding, and grace if students are to develop the confidence to take the first step.

Flourishing in the classroom is often not so much about completion and final product; rather, it is evidenced by students making the first move or taking the first step. The student who makes the first paintbrush stroke, writes the first sentence, sings the first note, or attempts the first math problem shows vital, if early, signs of flourishing. Even if that step differs from the teacher's expectations, the very fact that the student took a first step is something on which the teacher can now build.

Taking the first step is sometimes taking the wrong step (otherwise it wouldn't be a risk), and flourishing students need to experience the safety of a growth mindset that is centered on their potential, not their past. Like adults, students have a limited capacity for getting things wrong in front of their peers before they give up, avoid, pretend, or distract. They need to see teachers taking risks themselves and leading risk-taking in the classroom. Teachers need to model what is required for progress. This means building close relationships that understand the detail and the story of each student well enough to recognize what it will require to enable each student to take the first step.

If we imagine a garden bed with the right soil, water and light for its planted seeds to grow—the initial green shoots of growth cannot be seen from a distance. *Even though the shoots have sprouted, one needs to get close to see them.*

In the same way, a leader or teacher needs to get closer to notice the early signs of life. Leaders and teachers who choose to get to know students, and not just their data, will recognize and understand much more quickly what may be developing. The flourishing of students starts with the experience of wonder and celebration of the first green shoots, grown in the conditions that have enabled students to take the first step.

Questions for Further Reflection

1. What conditions help your students take risks? What hinders risk-taking? How could you create conditions that are better suited for risk-taking?

2. What does risk-taking feel like? How can you model risk-taking for students?

3. How might you cope wisely when things go wrong in learning?

4. To what extent do you need to get closer to see the "green shoots" in students? How might children be best placed to see (and celebrate) these in each other?

"I make mistakes every day—I don't mean to disappoint you."

"Flourishing" is not a synonym for "success."

While no doubt a sense of forward momentum and positive change is part of flourishing, there is no guarantee that everything will always be improving in *every* area for *every* student at *all* times. In fact, this is highly unlikely to ever be the case. The acceptance of things going wrong is fundamental to flourishing. Vulnerability is the first step to learning and development, and flourishing students understand the importance of making mistakes. They learn this importance by observing it daily in themselves, their peers, and their teachers.

The best teachers create and sustain environments and relationships where mistakes are expected, applauded, cheered on as the necessary precursor to progress. Students are treated with the utmost dignity as they fall, *and are then lifted back up to begin again stronger*.

Even though students would (much like adults) prefer to repeat what they can already do (often to reinforce their own security and self-image), the love that flourishing students can experience in the classroom takes them into spaces where they may be far more likely to make mistakes. Yet when things go wrong, flourishing students know that there is always a way back. They know this not by what is written on a wall, or in a school brochure, but by the grace that characterizes their teachers, rooted in the love of a God whose desire to give fresh starts knows no limits.

Students all flourish at different times and speeds (regardless of examination systems that are predicated on one-shot test performances at particular times of the year), and so students' flourishing needs the patience, perspective, and wisdom of educators. In fact, this flourishing may be more contingent on the relationships in the room than any pedagogical technique or experience.

Flourishing students love to experience learning as a communal journey, not just as an individual striving for success. They know "we" is more important than "I." Equally, they thrive on the personal validation—academically, emotionally, socially, and relationally—from educators.

Students in schools are, in the main, experiencing new content for the first time every day, taught by educators who, again in the main, are not encountering that material for the first time each day. Flourishing students feel the excitement of approaching new learning, and yet they need their teachers to remember what the trepidation of the new feels like, in turn shaping their teaching with empathy, curiosity, and wonder.

Some students may fear judgment or disappointment as they take risks, and as a result their flourishing is fueled by accurate and timely feedback. They are buoyed by the courage their teacher instinctively instills in students.

Sometimes the patience from educators that the flourishing student needs will demand far more than a day, month, or year and will require a very different long-term perspective from the team to hold out for a positive outcome. *Fledgling green shoots do not grow as a result of the disappointment of the gardener but rather from the patient, expectant, tender wisdom of long-term care.*

Students live in a world that is constantly telling them they are not good enough, with every swipe left or right, and with every like or follow. Therefore, even though their students get things wrong and make mistakes, great teachers never choose to put them down personally.

Flourishing students do not get everything right all the time, but in knowing that they are loved for who they already are, they come to appreciate the bumps in the road as important and necessary parts of the journey.

Questions for Further Reflection

1. What might grace actually look like in the classroom?

2. How do we find the balance between encouragement and correction in our feedback?

3. When was the last time you tried to learn something new? How did it feel? How might reflecting on this experience affect your teaching?

4. To what extent do you resonate with the idea of a world that daily tells children they are not good enough—and how might that affect your approach to teaching and learning?

ACTIVITY: COMING ALONGSIDE STUDENTS

Looking closely, looking expectantly

Green shoots are often hard to spot when they first emerge, especially if observed from a distance. A careless or hurried gardener—despite being well-meaning and fully desirous of growth—might accidentally crush a shoot underfoot, while trying to complete a routine task quickly.

The solution for gardeners, as well as for educators, is to slow down and look closely—and with expectation—for those first steps and signs of growth. This takes intentionality, practice, and above all patience, especially given the harried pace of both education and life in many settings.

To practice looking closely and looking expectantly, choose a student in your care. Using the prompts below, spend some time thinking about how you might spot shoots of growth that you may have missed or that might be coaxed to emerge with just a bit more encouragement (instructional sunlight and water).

Student's Name: _____

1. Something that is uniquely wonderful about this student is . . .

2. When it comes to learning, something I have noticed about this student is . . .

3. When it comes to this student's learning, I wonder . . .

4. If I have missed something in understanding this student, I think it might be . . .

5. What this student most seems to need from me in order to learn is . . .

6. When I think about whether or how I provide that, I . . .

7. If I could invest more time with this student, the first thing I would do is . . .

8. If I could ask a talented and trusted colleague about this student's learning, I think what I would ask is . . .

9. Reflecting on my answers to these questions, I think this student might blossom in learning if I . . .

"You are still a learner too—you ask and answer great questions."

For students, there is something magical, attractive, and deeply compelling about teachers who do not simply appear interested in their subjects from a professional point of view but who actually practice those subjects outside of the classroom—the English teacher who writes and publishes short stories online, the art teacher who exhibits at the local gallery, the music teacher who plays in a local band, or the history teacher who volunteers as a guide at a historical site on the weekends.

The joy of the subject is revealed through the life of the teacher, which is highly motivating to students, who love to learn from a fellow learner. *Flourishing educators are still learners too—and they love to learn.*

They establish habits, disciplines, and practices which help to release this. They read widely and often and retain the wonder and intrigue of discovery—the joy of learning, the glint in the eye at an unanswered question, or the line of inquiry without obvious conclusions.

Flourishing educators also love learning about pedagogy. They delight in refining their craft, they take pride in marginal gains, and they establish relationships with peers to support their development. They recognize that teaching on one's own can create an echo chamber of practice, so they seek the opportunity to watch and learn from others whenever possible.

Flourishing educators realize that different ways of teaching are possible, and they are stimulated by personal reflection, peer coaching, and networking among schools, which takes teachers out of their own spaces and structures to see how others approach their subjects and students. Flourishing educators are hungry for these new perspectives, and they think wisely about how to refine their practice as a result of encountering them.

Creativity and risk-taking begin simply with asking great questions, without agendas or expectations of simple answers. They catalyze the new and make space for the fertilization and germination of fresh thinking and practice.

Great questions always lead to further great questions.

Questioning is of course a very important pedagogical technique, which centers learning on the releasing of questions, rather than the transmission of answers. Finality and resolution are rare, and learning through questions can be chaotic, confusing, and disorientating. Yet flourishing educators give (and are given) time and space for questions to be explored. Questioning is fundamental to flourishing because it nurtures wholeness, grants agency, permits doubt, and develops wisdom.

There is something wonderful about the moment when you realize another person is asking a question similar to yours—it feels reassuring when our questions are normalized. But something deeply destructive happens when our questions are shut down. Somehow the silencing of a question extinguishes hope and immediately reduces the likelihood of further useful questions emerging. In fact, it is almost worse than having our opinions dismissed, as silencing questions removes possibility.

Great questions are fundamental to flourishing—they are water in the desert, light in the dark. Educators who show they have the courage and safety to ask questions will grow in this fertile soil and empower others to do the same.

Questions for Further Reflection

1. What do you still love to learn, or love about learning? How would anyone know?

2. Whose teaching (or leading) do you look up to and how are you working with your peers to further improve each other's practice?

3. How central is questioning to your pedagogy (or leadership)?

4. What makes for a great question? How do we construct questions that lead to further questions?

"You release the creativity of students—your imagination shapes your teaching."

B ill Lucas, who has written extensively on the notion of creativity in education, offers five helpful dimensions to describe creative students—those who are *imaginative* (playing with possibilities, making connections, using intuition); *inquisitive* (wondering and questioning, exploring and investigating, challenging assumptions); *persistent* (tolerating uncertainty, sticking with difficulty, daring to be different); *collaborative* (sharing the product, giving and receiving feedback, cooperating appropriately); and *disciplined* (reflecting critically, developing techniques, crafting and improving).[3] These dimensions provide much-needed balance to the notion of adult-designed learning, whereby students are merely the recipients or users of a product that may be already out of date.

Flourishing educators understand that knowledge is crucial and that without acquiring it and using it, very little new thinking can occur. However, they also understand the limitations of memorization of facts as a principal method of learning (as they know that this generation of students is able to access technology in such a way that the need for recall or memorization will never be the same).

Flourishing educators foster a greater sense of practical wisdom because they can design and create from the starting point of a question. This is the built-in curiosity and exploration that most students bring with them when they first arrive in the educational system as young children.

The opportunity to design learning is intensely attractive to flourishing students, and it is a clear indicator of learning that contributes to flourishing together. It is the way we build learning from meaningful starting points and ground our teaching in the individual stories and imaginations of the students in front of us. While it is easily squeezed out of the pedagogical craft when lost to the narrow pursuit of productivity, the imagination of a student has immense potential for good or ill. It is a raw force present in students, there for the teacher to encourage, refine, and cheer on.

Walter Brueggemann writes, "The imagination must come before the implementation. Our culture is competent to implement almost anything and imagine almost nothing. It is our vocation to keep alive the ministry of imagination."[4] Visionary teachers equip their students to ask great questions (even when at times these are subversive). *Imagination, inquisitiveness, and curiosity are like the water, light, and heat needed for the plant to grow.*

A first step on this journey is simply giving airtime that permits questioning, and recognizing the reality that the questions flourishing students ask may be quite different from those the teacher wishes to pose. Prioritizing the voice of the student like this means thinking carefully about the structure, assessment, and feedback of learning, and finding a healthy or symbiotic tension between performing on required testing and exploring the broader subject area from a place of genuine curiosity.

To build learning from questions (or at the very least to validate and give space to students' questions, in midst of a more fixed approach to instruction) can enable the flourishing of students, who are empowered to think and design for themselves.

Imaginative and inquisitive questions are fairly easy to conceive: What if I . . . ? Why does it have to be like . . . ? Could I try . . . ? What difference could it make if . . . ? How does this work . . . ? Where could I find . . . ? Who could I connect with to learn . . . ? What is wrong with . . . ? I wonder . . . ?

Persistent and disciplined questions need space: Why do I still not get . . . ? How can I keep going when . . . ? Why are we learning this . . . ? How does this fit with . . . ? What routines would help me to . . . ? Why is the structure like . . . ? Can you help me understand why I keep . . . ?

Collaborative questions move us from "I" to "we." They reveal our desires, hopes, fears, and pains.

In addition to helping our students learn to ask these kinds of questions, we need to ask the same of ourselves as educators, collaboratively with our colleagues. Imaginative teaching that results from good questioning has the potential to spark flourishing learning for students and educators alike.

1. How and to what degree are our students able to design learning for themselves?

2. If creativity was a desired outcome of a particular class's lesson, subject's curriculum, or school's portrait of a graduate, how would you know (beyond reading it in a curriculum map or mission statement)?

3. How can you use questioning to spark your own learning as an educator?

4. In what ways might you open up avenues for greater creativity in your teaching or leading, and why might that be important?

Encouraging creativity

This activity helps us as leaders to reflect on the five domains of creativity as outlined by Bill Lucas and Ellen Spencer in their inspirational book *Teaching Creative Thinking*.[5]

Imagine a group of people in your school (students or educators) and evaluate the extent to which you observe the creative behaviors shown in the model below.

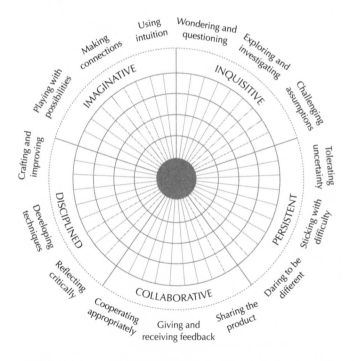

The Centre for Real-World Learning's Five-Dimensional Model of Creative Thinking. From Bill Lucas and Ellen Spencer, *Teaching Creative Thinking*, 22. Reprinted by permission.

Color in this creativity wheel to show the relative strengths and areas for development. This can be a helpful individual or group activity (in which individuals' wheels can be compared with one another to generate discussion). It can be done in a single class period or over a more extended timeframe.

Next, consider how flourishing schools can encourage, equip, and celebrate creativity across every subject, and how the attributes in the creativity wheel allow flourishing among students across all disciplines and deepen flourishing for educators in all roles. Explore ways you could use this exercise with students, staff, families, and others as a framework to evaluate and expand approaches to creativity.

"We align our pedagogy with our vision—our curriculum reveals our shared values."

I n discussing the way that a school's vision or values are lived out, Max Coates describes "an often uncertain journey from print to practice."[6] This is the leader's quest to ensure that vision is lived and not just laminated. While the journey is not always straightforward, if our approach to teaching, learning, and curriculum does not reflect our vision, it may not actually be our vision at all.

Flourishing schools are known for and run by inquisitive, creative, reflective, thinking leaders and teachers. They weather the challenges of external assessment methodologies (and their often too frequent changes), and yet they find ways to grant agency in the classroom. They naturally question and evaluate externally imposed models, asking "why" questions about teaching and learning. Such schools pursue the highest standards, creating similarly inquisitive, creative, reflective, thinking students.

Asking the "why" before the "what" questions reveals much about our vision and intent for curriculum. Some external accreditation or inspection groups, in both the United States and the United Kingdom, explore this area in depth as part of their school visits. This recognizes the importance for flourishing schools of developing curriculum pathways that reflect their vision.

Such curricular thinking is not simply about choosing standards, assessments, textbooks, or supporting websites. Rather, it challenges us to have deeper and more engaging conversations (particularly around complex issues); dismantle false hierarchies (for example, "academic" over "vocational" programs, or "university" over "career" paths); challenge hurtful prejudice (for example where cultural assumptions, omissions, or stereotypes exist in the curriculum); and debate "known unknowns" (for example, equipping students to think wisely about environmental sustainability, despite the significant consequences their thinking may have for changes in policy and action).

The Church of England Vision for Education offers four areas for leaders to think about in relation to their leadership; each has potential implications for curricular thinking focused on the flourishing of students and educators:

- *Educating for wisdom, knowledge, and skills*—Fostering discipline, confidence, and delight in seeking wisdom and knowledge (including a healthy and life-giving tension between knowledge-rich and biblical-wisdom curriculum approaches), and fully developing talents in all areas of life.
- *Educating for hope and aspiration*—Seeking healing, repair, and renewal, coping wisely with things and people taking wrong turns, and opening horizons and guiding people into ways of fulfilling their goals.
- *Educating for community and living well together*—Ensuring a core focus on relationships, participation in communities, and the qualities of character that enable people to flourish together.
- *Educating for dignity and respect*—Ensuring the basic principle of respect for the value and preciousness of each person, and treating each person as a unique individual of inherent worth.[7]

The *Vision for Education* is not intended as a blueprint to be imposed on schools (or superimposed over their own specific curriculum models, policies, and practices) but rather offers an opportunity for school leaders to gather around a shared language, and interdependent conversation, to develop a clearer sense of purpose and how it shapes what we teach.

Flourishing together means making the "journey from print to practice" together. Flourishing schools choose this journey, and as a result, their curriculum comes to more closely reflect their intended values.

Questions for Further Reflection

1. Does our organizational vision have implications for the kind of learning that happens in our school? What are the implications?

2. How intentionally do we align our vision with our practice of teaching and learning throughout our school?

3. What specific examples of alignment between vision, curriculum, and pedagogy can we identify?

4. How could we increase the number and strengthen the quality of examples of this alignment between our vision and our practice?

"We invest in our teams—we pursue our learning journeys together."

When we go on a journey, our destination is very important—it is our intended outcome, our hoped-for result. Our destination determines the direction, and often the speed and method, of the travel we choose.

However, in so many cases, *the journey itself turns out to be much more important than the destination.*

Journeys rarely progress exactly as we expect them—there are hold-ups, diversions, disruptions, delays. There are phases that go much better than we think, views we stop to admire, and changes in perspective we may not anticipate until we experience them. Sometimes our destination even changes as a result of the journey itself—new possibilities open up, original thinking changes, fuel runs out, vehicles break down, and sometimes we even have to turn around and head back.

Commitment to learning together in schools is similar. Our development is as much about inviting colleagues to experience a journey together as arriving at a final, fixed destination.

Leaders know that if teachers are actively learning and developing, they are far more likely to unleash learning in their students. Flourishing schools therefore place learning (of students *and* educators) at the heart of all they do. But while we often reduce this learning in educators to individual appraisal processes and professional development plans, the journey can be so much more vibrant if undertaken together, not alone.

Our choice to journey together affects everyone. My development affects yours, and yours affects mine. Per the writer of Proverbs, "As iron sharpens iron, so one person sharpens another."[8] Committing to a colleague's professional development is a statement of investment in and encouragement of that individual. It is life-giving, relationship-binding, loyalty-securing, and commitment-building. It says you matter, both to me and to our organization, and not just in the present and in your current state, but in the future and in all that could unfold for us as a result of your development.

The momentum and energy of the journey can help us bring out the best in one another, thereby creating new possibilities and connections. They can counter our tendency to reduce colleagues to lists of skills or competencies, and they can encourage us to think in more holistic ways about one another's flourishing.

Flourishing schools are full of educators who are energized toward a future that they cannot yet see. This energy is directed into the pursuit of excellence in today's tasks, but it also extends into a medium- and long-term commitment to learning and development. If I am committed to us journeying together, I may not need to fully know the destination. The journey is enough.

In *On the Road with Saint Augustine*, James K. A. Smith provides a rich and compelling view of spiritual formation not as an intellectual answer to be found, or a fixed position to be reached, but a lifelong journey of discovery. Smith explains that, for Augustine, "the Christian gospel . . . was more like a shelter in the storm, a port for the wayward soul, nourishment for a prodigal who was famished." He points to a beautiful image of God from Augustine's *Confessions*: "Look, you're here, freeing us from our unhappy wandering, setting us firmly on your track, comforting us and saying, 'Run the race! I'll carry you! I'll carry you clear to the end, and even at the end, I'll carry you.'"[9]

There are countless examples of how individuals can journey further, longer, and deeper if they go together rather than alone. Anyone who has climbed a mountain, run, biked, or kayaked in a race with others knows the deep encouragement that comes with going together versus continuing alone.

If there is no journey together, there is no conversation. Without conversation, any individual learning remains bottled up and unshared. When we go together, we hear different voices, give time to others' views, and escape our own echo chambers. At all ages and stages of our careers, the intergenerational dialogue that schools can offer—through mentoring, coaching, and supervision—can be key to our individual flourishing.

The extent to which we and our colleagues can articulate our developmental journeys (looking both backward and forward) is an indicator of how much we are flourishing together, as is our willingness to accept the invitation to the journey—even when the destination does not seem clear. At many stages of our careers, we may not need to fix the destination, but rather simply trust the journey.

Questions for Further Reflection

1. What is the most exciting journey you have been on? What did you learn? What did you regret? Who did you journey with?

2. For whose professional growth are you essential (perhaps without realizing it)?

3. How challenging is it to "simply trust the journey"?

4. Which colleague might you need or want to have a conversation with about teaching and learning? What questions would you just love to ask them?

SCHOOL DISCUSSION **ACTIVITY**

Mapping our learning journey

In this chapter, we have underscored the importance of aligning instructional vision with practice, as well as recognizing how student learning and educator learning are intertwined. When it comes to assessing how well we accomplish this in schools, we have repeatedly asked the question, "How would you know?" This activity is designed to help answer that question.

Using the prompts in the chart below, engage each group in mapping out the learning journey it is taking *as a group*. This activity can be done with one or two representatives from each group to get a "snapshot," or it can be done with greater numbers (either all together or in focus groups) for a panoramic view of learning at the school.

Then, as a team, map out points of convergence and divergence between groups. Finally, rate each group's journey in terms of its alignment with the school's vision for learning. Once completed, this activity can provide important insight and discussion points for reflection around the learning journey of the entire school.

Group	Small Group Discussion Prompt	Points of Convergence and Divergence with Other Groups	Degree of Alignment to Our Vision from 1 to 4 (1 = not aligned; 4 = fully aligned)
Students	As students, our learning journey at this school . . .		
Faculty	As teachers, our learning journey at this school . . .		
Support Staff	As support staff, our learning journey at this school . . .		
Leaders	As leaders, our learning journey at this school . . .		

4

RESOURCES

10

Educational Abundance

Nothing that you have not given away will ever be really yours.

—C. S. Lewis[1]

No one ever becomes poor from giving.

—Anne Frank[2]

W hen we consider our own schools in the United Kingdom and the United States, perhaps nowhere do they diverge more than in their resourcing models. Church of England schools are publicly funded by the national government, while Christian schools in the United States are privately funded, meaning they are primarily resourced through a combination of family-paid tuition and fundraising (though publicly funded school choice programs are available in some locales). And while resourcing may be the point of greatest difference for our schools, it is simultaneously a point of greatest convergence. When we have asked school leaders on both sides of the Atlantic what keeps them up at night, they almost always respond with a variant of the same question: "Will we have enough to meet the needs of our students?"

A Christian vision for educational flourishing addresses the issue of resources by taking our thinking about the scarcity we may experience and reorienting it within the biblical narrative. As discussed in Part 1 ("Purpose"), we know from the Old Testament account of creation that God's original intent was for humanity to serve as caretakers and cultivators of the "good" world he created. The lack of resources we experience in the world results from the willful abandonment of this purpose by humanity. In the foreword to this book, the Rt. Revd. Rose Hudson-Wilkin, Bishop of Dover, eloquently describes this arc:

> We're told that God made us one human race in his image, that he provided for us with a beautiful environment—the sea and everything in it, the different animals, the land with its trees and fruits and flowers, the natural resources all spread across the world. God wanted us all to flourish together.
>
> God wanted us just to take what we needed. Remember the words of the Lord's Prayer? "Give us this day our daily bread." God wants us just to take what we need for each day so that we can flourish together.
>
> Sadly, as humans, we have been selfish. We have taken much more than we needed, and in order to do this we have enslaved other human beings, and animals. We have told some people that they are not good enough, because of the color of their skin or because they are disabled. We created weapons of warfare, and we have destroyed our environment.
>
> This is one of the reasons why millions of people are on the move, leaving the countries they were born in to try and get to another place where they can prosper and flourish with their families.

This Christian vision helps us to understand the scarcity of resources we face not only in education but also across much of human experience. While we must certainly advocate for just distribution of resources and address disparity where we find it (which we will discuss later), the problem of scarcity originates in something much deeper than misallocation. Scarcity originates all the way inside the human heart; by extension it becomes visible in how well—or how unwell—we live together.

Jesus's promise of "life in all its fullness" offers a new frame through which to view ourselves and the resources entrusted to us. First, when we engage in *stewardship*—by wisely recognizing and investing the resources we already have—new horizons and possibilities for flourishing open up for our schools, for us as educators, and for our students. Second, Scripture makes it clear that this abundance is not meant to end with our own private benefit, but rather should overflow in *generosity* toward others. We can see these two principles and their connection in the apostle Paul's second letter to the church at Corinth, when he writes that "God is able to bless you abundantly, so that in all things at all times, having all that you need, you will abound in every good work," followed just two verses later by, "You will be enriched in every way so that you can be generous on every occasion."[3] Thus, a Christian vision for education radically reframes our thinking about resources through the twin biblical lenses of stewardship and generosity.

Flourishing Schools

In *The Steward Leader: Transforming People, Organizations and Communities*, Scott Rodin calls out "the cacophony of voices screaming to us the gospel of wealth, consumerism and consumption" in society, as well as "authoritarian voices from our own ranks" in our organizations that are focused on the trappings of "a world that is passing away instead of a creation" that we are called to help liberate and restore.[4] These pressures will not only be familiar to most school leaders, but also are likely a source of constant concern when it comes to our school cultures.

A vision for flourishing together helps us to refocus, though not in an effort at wishful thinking or reflective of a "name it and claim it" prosperity gospel. Rather, as our coauthors outline in *MindShift*, a Christian vision enables us to move from a mindset of scarcity to a mindset of abundance. By "mindset" they are referring to the way in which our beliefs about resources inevitably turn into patterns of thinking and behaving. Schools and educators operating from a scarcity mindset "believe that the challenges they face serve to limit who they are and what they do . . . [while an] abundance mindset looks at the same restraints and challenges, but [reframes] them as opportunities for greater impact."[5] Our mindset in turn limits the kinds of questions we may ask and therefore the possibilities we can see. For example, leaders functioning with a scarcity mindset might singularly focus on how to increase enrollment, while an abundance mindset might lead to questions like, "What new opportunities exist that we haven't yet considered, that would allow us to expand our reach as a school? What new partnerships—with other schools, churches, ministries, businesses, or community groups—could we forge to do kingdom work together?"[6]

We might think of this as a school-level equivalent of Carol Dweck's "fixed" versus "growth" mindset.[7] Research suggests that our mindsets matter, as they ultimately can create a kind of "self-fulfilling prophecy" for students and educators. Similarly, the Flourishing Schools research shows that leaders' beliefs about resources can play an inhibiting role when it comes to school flourishing. Specifically, the research identified as significant the construct of *resource constraints*—a belief held by leadership that the school could be more effective if not for fiscal restraints, and that the school lacks the resources to make changes.[8] Critically, this belief focuses the attention of leaders on what their schools *do not* have. Again, it is indisputable that lack of resources is a problem for schools everywhere. The issue here is leaders' *focus* on what is lacking, which in turn contributes to a belief that school effectiveness is hampered and needed change is stalled.

A Christian vision suggests that leaders can shift their focus—or effectively, their mindset—by reframing their relationship to resources from one of *ownership* to one of *stewardship*. Ownership is as it sounds: leaders see resources as belonging to them and to be used for the purpose of furthering their own agendas, whether good, bad, or mixed. By way of contrast, the entire arc of Scripture calls us to live as stewards. As Rodin explains, "Whether it is the understanding of the grace of God for us in Christ, our place and vocation as the creatures of God in this world, our fellowship and communion with our neighbors, or our standing and relationship with God's created world in which we live, our call to be stewards is based on our *acceptance of each as a gracious gift and a rejection of the lure to play the owner*."[9] This essentially "flips" the leader's focus from what one can *add* to one's possessions (ownership), to wise cultivation of what one *already has* in one's possession (stewardship). For this reason, as Rodin explains, stewardship "does not derive from or depend on . . . external increase."[10]

A key practice which can help schools move toward a stewardship orientation is the reshaping of strategic planning, particularly in the areas of finance and facilities. The Flourishing Schools research found strategic planning to be positively linked with flourishing, particularly when *financial planning* was a strength of trustees.[11] When this planning is viewed through the lens of stewardship, it can become a powerful tool for school flourishing, as Rodin explains: "By its very nature, strategic planning seeks to match the best resources of an organization to the most important issues that will determine its long-term vitality and growth. . . . Marshaling the right people to do the right jobs with the right resources to achieve the right goals at the right time is one of the highest callings of the steward leader. And for that reason, effective strategic planning is one of the highest forms of organizational stewardship."[12]

Strategic planning conducted from the perspective of stewardship can open up new possibilities for flourishing which hitherto were invisible from the vantage point of ownership. For example, space may be repurposed in unconventional ways to meet new needs; programs that have enjoyed historic success may be sunsetted to make way for innovative offerings that better advance the school's mission into the future; and staff may be reassigned based on strengths and opportunities for growth versus seniority or rank.

When operating from a stewardship perspective, leaders may experience a new willingness—even an eagerness—to pool or exchange resources with other schools, because they know that sharing can lead to better stewardship of our collective resources as an educational community. And as we begin to see these new possibilities, we move away from focusing on what we lack, to beholding afresh the resources with which we have already been gifted and which we are free to share. As Paul writes in 2 Corinthians regarding giving generously, "But since you excel in everything—in faith, in speech, in knowledge, in complete earnestness and in the love we have kindled in you—see that you also excel in this grace of giving."[13]

Flourishing Educators

Rather than new buildings, ample annual funds, spacious athletic facilities, and the latest and greatest in technology, a vision for flourishing together considers people to be the most valuable resource within our schools. Certainly, financial and physical resources are essential for schools to thrive. But absent social capital, our schools would quickly become bankrupt. The Flourishing Schools research confirmed that having *qualified staff* at a school—defined as those who are credentialed and have sufficient professional experience—is linked with flourishing outcomes.[14] This finding highlights the importance of developing robust hiring practices that help leaders recruit, select, and welcome staff who are a good missional "fit" and who also have the background and experience necessary to execute the mission. Trustees also play a critical role in this process, by prioritizing planning for, and allocation of, the financial resources that make it possible for school leaders to build flourishing teams. However, it is not enough to "get the right people" for the job; people must be nurtured once hired. And as we shared in Part 3 ("Learning"), one of the best ways to nurture people professionally is to develop a "community of practice"[15] where supportive relationships, ongoing feedback, shared inquiry, and mutual commitment help professionals to grow.

If we are seeking to engage well with people in the context of community building, we will need to steward another of the most valuable and scarce resources in our schools—time. The development of relationships, collaborative engagement on tasks, and cultivation of others' talents are all life-giving activities that are time-intensive. Certainly managing one's time well is important, and an entire industry exists to support our ability to work efficiently (with everything from books and seminars to web- and app-based time management programs). However, we do not need to manage our time efficiently so we can accomplish more; rather, we need to steward our time in such a way as to create the margin necessary for human activities like cultivating relationships. This is because much like the students in our schools, educators need unstructured, "free" time to "play"—individually and together—as a precondition for effectiveness. In commenting on our world's state of constant acceleration, Pulitzer Prize–winning journalist Thomas Friedman asserts, "In such a time, opting to pause and reflect, rather than panic or withdraw, is a necessity. It is not a luxury or a distraction—it is a way to increase the odds that you'll better understand, and engage productively, with the world around you."[16]

A Christian vision for flourishing together does not allow us to stop with stewarding our time well, however; such a vision calls us onward to invest our time generously with and in others. Being generous with our time leads us to listen deeply, pay rich attention, welcome others, and practice hospitality. This can involve leadership approaches that may already be familiar to us, such as keeping an open door policy, "leading by walking around," and greeting staff and students at the school doors each morning. A view toward flourishing in schools holds "people work" as the most important investment that can be made by educators. This is because education, at its heart, is about people—nothing more, nothing less. Flourishing schools not only recognize but also celebrate this reality by aligning personal and corporate practices with a posture and culture of generosity. Though it will surely not be easy, it is transformative work at the deepest level of school culture; as leaders consistently prioritize people through these investments of time, they set expectations and free others to do the same.

Flourishing Students

We began this chapter by asserting that scarcity of resources is a lived experience of educators everywhere, and that an abundance mindset will help to open up new possibilities for flourishing that may have been hidden previously. At the school level, and for leaders and teachers, we fully stand by this principle. When we move to examine and discuss education as a sector or a national system, however, our perspective and our responses necessarily shift. This is because resource scarcity is one thing, but educational *disparity* is quite another. Not surprisingly, the Flourishing Schools research shows that *sufficient resources*—including classroom materials, technology, and school buildings in good condition—are all positively linked to flourishing.[17] But the reality in both the United States and the United Kingdom—and indeed around much of the world—is that gaping disparities in resources exist between schools in different communities and settings.

These worldwide gaps can be caused by educational funding systems and schemes that produce inequity, by lack of economic opportunity and mobility within a community, by violence and exploitation, by cycles of poverty fueled by institutionalized racism and gender bias, and by the tragedies of genocide, war, and displacement. Where these issues and resulting disparities exist in our communities, they often manifest in our schools through dropout rates, mental health issues, bullying and violence, and student and family disengagement. Ultimately, this is a question of how our societies steward the potential of our children and young people, who are our most valuable resource.

As educators, we create the possibility for remedying action when we ask whose potential is maximized through access to resources like excellent school choices, enrichment opportunities, safe housing, quality medical care, and technology. We can then ask whose potential is inhibited by lack of access to the same—to the detriment not just of individual children and young people but also of families, neighborhoods, communities, and entire countries. And when we have answered these questions, we need to ask what our schools, educators, and students can do—together—to work toward removing disadvantage in our institutions, our communities, and our societies.

Of all manner of schools, those founded on a Christian vision should lead the way in asking these questions. This is because a clear mandate exists in the Bible to seek justice and correct oppression, to defend the rights of those who are destitute or exploited, to do no wrong to refugees, and to show kindness and mercy to anyone in need.[18] Not only are these actions mandated in Scripture, but the apostle James actually labels them "religion that is pure."[19] Donovan Graham, in *Teaching Redemptively*, sets the stage for applying this in our schools: "Those who are redeemed will act in that creation and toward others in ways that bring healing and restoration—a tangible demonstration of God's character. . . . God did not sit back and say 'how awful, but that is just the way it is.' Neither can those who seek to reflect who He is. . . . God Himself identified with His people and came to them to live in their presence. The incarnation is a marvelous lesson in how we are meant to live out the image of God in the current age."[20]

Although we may feel powerless when faced with the deep roots of educational disparity, there are still tangible ways we can "live out" the image of God in addressing disadvantage. We have already mentioned some of them in Part 2 ("Relationships"), including coming into proximity with those on the margins, meeting together and breaking bread, and pursuing *shalom*-filled relationships in and with our communities. We can also examine our admissions processes and requirements with a view toward remedying disparity, as well as considering and bolstering the ways we support our students who come from disadvantaged backgrounds. And to the degree we have influence with local and national governments, we can advocate strongly for greater educational access, equitable allocation of resources, and increased family and student choice regarding schooling.

Finally, in stewarding our students' potential, we would be remiss—ironically so—if we did not involve students centrally in all of these efforts. This will require far more than a one-off field trip to visit a politician or attend a rally. Instead, the biblical command to learn how to pursue justice, relieve oppression, defend the rights of the exploited, and care for the displaced must be included in the curricula and programs of schools. This can be done, for example, through service-learning, student-led outreach, and partnerships with churches and community groups. As we engage in these efforts together, our students can learn how to advocate for themselves and others, address disparity of resources wherever they find it in their lives and communities, and develop perseverance in the face of what may seem to be insurmountable challenges at the core of society. Undoubtedly, these are all skills the next generation will need in abundance if they are to lead the way toward flourishing together.

11

Breaking Bread

Another of his disciples, Andrew spoke up, "Here is a boy with five small barley loaves and two small fish, but how far will they go among so many?" Jesus said, 'Have the people sit down."

—John 6:8–10 (NIV)

And he took bread, and when he had given thanks, he broke it and gave it to them, saying, "This is my body given for you: do this in remembrance of me."

—Luke 22:19

"Give us this day our daily bread."

—Matthew 6:11

W hatever we write down in our mission statements, present in our promotional films, or discuss in our policy meetings, our use of resources is frequently a clearer indicator of our vision for flourishing together. This is because how we invest our time and money is often an accurate reflection of what we actually believe as individuals and organizations. Certainly, most schools and educators have neither limitless resources nor complete agency over their use, and the pressures surrounding resources are significant—from disparity in classroom resources in different communities; to a lack of preparation time for teachers; to demands on leaders to do more with less. Even so, we have room individually as well as corporately for variance in how we think about, acquire, manage, and share resources.

To explore the domain of resources further, we reflect theologically in this chapter on one of the most commonly discussed resources in the biblical narrative—bread. This resource is referenced hundreds of times throughout the Bible in both metaphorical and literal ways. We might think of the hurried baking of unleavened bread by the fleeing Israelites, the miraculous provision of bread (*manna*) in the Sinai desert, or the symbolic use of twelve loaves of bread on the Old Testament altar. There is even a wide diversity of types of bread described in Scripture: *sappihit* (a flat cake or wafer, in Exodus 16:31); *niqqudim* (a hard biscuit or cake, in 1 Kings 14:3); *kikkar* (a disc-shaped thin loaf, in 1 Samuel 2:36); *halla* (a ring-shaped bread, in 2 Samuel 6:19); *lebiba* (a heart-shaped cake, in 2 Samuel 13:6); *massa* (an unleavened cake, in Leviticus 2:4); and many more. We even find a recipe for bread recommended in the book of Ezekiel—"Take wheat and barley, beans and lentils, millet and spelt; put them in a storage jar and use them to make bread for yourself."[1]

Breaking bread together appears to be foundational to an understanding of Christian community in the New Testament, perhaps starting with the birth of Jesus in Bethlehem, which means "House of Bread." The breaking of bread is frequently the setting for moments of deep encounter with Jesus, such as the lawyer Nicodemus or Zacchaeus the tax collector.[2] The radical changes in their lives did not come about as a result of a rousing speech, sermon, or miracle—but rather through breaking bread with Jesus. This becomes a core feature of community for the early church as it establishes itself in Acts: "They devoted themselves to the apostles' teaching and to fellowship, to the breaking of bread and to prayer."[3]

Bread is accessible, simple, and a staple—adaptable to all climates, budgets, and tastes. It meets our needs in extreme poverty, and can also reflect great opulence and extravagance. Bread is presented in the biblical narrative as a means of provision, a divine gift, and a medium for generosity and sharing. To consider the implications of this physical resource and its metaphorical meaning for flourishing in schools, we turn to three moments in the gospels: the miraculous feeding of five thousand; the Last Supper that Jesus eats with his disciples; and the "daily bread" in the Lord's Prayer that Jesus teaches his disciples. We begin with the first, as an episode featuring a hungry crowd, some bewildered mass caterers, and the emergence of a generous though surprisingly humble protagonist—an unknown child, who offers up his meager lunchbox to get things started.

Feeding the Five Thousand

Although the story of the feeding of the five thousand appears in all four gospels, we are left very much with a highlight reel—a story told with high energy and using only key details emphasized for the reader. The style leaves us with many tantalizing questions in between the lines of the familiar text— for instance: Why did such a crowd gather so quickly and so far away from food provision? Were the people rich enough to have afforded food and were merely unprepared, or were they poor and therefore hungry well before dinnertime approached? Who was the boy who offered up his own provisions, and did Andrew, the disciple, know him? Why was there so much food left over, and what became of it?

Although we may not be able to answer all of these questions, the details we do find in the story can suggest insights for how we might think about resources in schools—beginning with Jesus's question to the disciples, "Where shall we buy bread for these people to eat?"[4] The response Jesus receives signals the scarcity mentality of the disciple Philip, who exclaims, "It would take more than half a year's wages to buy enough bread for each one to have a bite!"[5] Philip's reply signals panic and disbelief—so much so that he does not even offer a real suggestion of how to proceed. Similarly Andrew, having found a young boy's resources with which to begin the task, expresses doubt that they will suffice: "Here is a boy with five small barley loaves and two small fish, but how far will they go among so many?"[6] While the connotations of a barley loaf may not be immediately obvious to us as contemporary readers, at the time it was seen as a bread for the poor (also used as fodder for horses); thus by drawing attention to the type of bread—as well as the "small" size of the bread and the fish—Andrew was likely underscoring even further the paltry nature of the limited resources on hand.

Both disciples' responses may resonate with many school leadership teams facing uncertain resource decisions, such as where to build a new building or how to repair an existing one, how to support students with disabilities, where to invest technology in ways that will truly benefit learning, and how to develop talent management programs to improve staff diversity. While we may in principle say that we seek to educate for "life in all its fullness" in these and other decisions, the flourishing we seek in our schools is often reduced to considerations around scarcity of resources. Certainly, flourishing does not result from unrealistic, irresponsible, or poorly designed planning. However, a scarcity mentality—which says, "We don't have enough" or "It'll never work," or simply "We can't"—will cut off our ability to find the path to flourishing together every time. Just like the disciples, we will quickly arrive at a dead end when we focus on our own limitations instead of the possibilities that may be available to us, if we refuse to let those limitations foreclose our thinking.

All readers can marvel at the way in which the story moves forward toward resolution, but the solution to the disciples' problem is made all the more beautiful for educators. This is because it is not generated by the disciples as leaders, but rather offered up by a child. We find no suggestion that the child was pushed forward by his aspirational parents or was sent forward as a representative of a wider family group; he is portrayed alone—humbly offering an idea to a leadership team that had no way forward. Even despite Andrew's unenthusiastic response, the child's offering is precisely what opens up the possibilities for miraculous provision. This is a wonderful moment for educators to consider how often we are missing out on similar provision, when we fail to include students in our decision making. We can so easily create educational systems and environments that ironically disempower the very students we are seeking to serve, thereby limiting not only the flourishing of students through the boundaries we impose on them, but also our flourishing together in schools.

This moment in the story is also important for a Christian understanding of children and young people, as influencers of the present who are worthy of full inclusion. Frequently students' perspectives, creativity, energy, and vision are far more inspiring than that of all the well-meaning adults. Jesus reinforces this idea in Matthew's gospel when, in response to his disciples' question about who is the "greatest," he calls a child to himself and replies, "Whoever humbles himself like this child is the greatest in the kingdom of heaven."[7] Some of the miracles that our schools are seeking for the communities they serve are too important not to involve students. Genuine agency of students—achieved by placing them front and center of our thinking and planning—releases tremendous opportunity in the present and can also set students on a trajectory of influence and leadership for the rest of their lives.

We can point to one final lesson in the "setup" for the miraculous feeding of the crowd. Once the resources to be used have been identified, Jesus tells his disciples to have the crowd sit down in groups of about fifty.[8] It is easy to skip over this detail and register it simply as an organizational step, something that only serves to make the larger task (the distribution of provision) easier.

In doing so, we miss an important principle that the text may be suggesting—that the imminent miracle will be enacted through smaller groups of people eating together, versus separately as individuals or family units. This is not an "everyone for themselves" miracle. Rather, in the face of a seemingly endless need, smaller communities are formed in which the resources on offer are passed around, from person to person, until all have enough. Further, there appears to be no criteria or check boxes for who is to benefit—all who are present are equally eligible, regardless of their background, status, or even their faith position in regard to the teacher whom they have come to hear.

This account provides tremendous hope to those of us in schools who are faced with limited resources—and who as such are not only doubting our ability to care for those in our immediate charge but also questioning how we can ever reach and engage those who have been historically distanced or excluded from our schools. The feeding of the five thousand suggests that it is in and through community, as we generously distribute and share what we have with each other, that the opportunity for miraculous multiplication will present itself—whether through the divine transformation of physical materials, or a stunning unlocking of human generosity that runs completely counter to human nature. And as Jesus's giving thanks before the distribution reminds us, all of our resources have their origin in divine provision, whether or not it is obvious to the human eye. It is in the generous sharing out of those resources not only that our collective needs are met but also that we have overflowing surplus—seen in the twelve baskets of leftovers in the story—with which to provide for others whom we have not yet engaged.

This mindset of abundance gives us the confidence we need to obey Jesus's command to his disciples—"They need not go away; you give them something to eat"[9]—whereas a scarcity mindset will lead us, like the disciples, to immediately conclude that our only option is to send them away. In education, this might mean starting a building campaign, accepting students with greater learning needs than that to which we are accustomed, developing a technology acquisition plan that seems unrealistic given our resources at the moment, or setting ambitious goals to increase diversity among our staff and student body. A Christian vision for education views each challenge from an orientation of possibility. Hope-filled learning, teaching, and leading involves school communities choosing to see an abundant future that does not yet exist, and then walking together toward it.

The Last Supper

As we follow the disciples through the gospels, we might imagine the team holding "planning meetings" to think through endless logistics—where to travel, what and whom to visit once they arrived, and how to accomplish each day's work efficiently and effectively. But for this intense community, and as was common in the culture of the day, it was likely mealtimes that brought them together to laugh, share, discuss, argue, repent, dream, imagine, and enjoy one another's company. They must have eaten together countless times—on the road, in people's homes, in the open air, on beaches, in boats, on hillsides, on mountains, and in towns, villages, and cities. Likewise, their master Jesus must have blessed and broken bread, as was the religious tradition in that context, innumerable times as well.

Within this larger framework of eating and breaking bread together, we can feel even more deeply the gravity of Jesus's final meal with his disciples. This meal has of course given arise to one of the central practices of billions of Christians across the globe over the past two thousand years, through the sacrament of the Eucharist. Communion is enacted in countless different ways, liturgies, settings, and languages, thereby drawing together in unity a local group of believers as well as all those worldwide. However it is practiced, the breaking of bread in observance of the Last Supper calls us to remember Jesus's death on the cross, as the text says, "And he took bread, and when he had given thanks, he broke it and gave it to them, saying, 'This is my body, which is given for you. Do this in remembrance of me.'"[10]

We also know from an earlier passage in John's gospel that Jesus had already identified *himself* with bread—in fact, just a day after the feeding of the five thousand, when he says, "I am the bread of life [*zoē*]. Whoever comes to me will never go hungry."[11] Beautifully, John uses the word *artos* for bread here, which conveys a much more flavorsome, extravagant (and expensive) artisan bread than the barley loaves brought by the young boy the day before. This signals the costly and precious nature of the sacrifice which Jesus was about to make. The purpose of bread then was as it is now—to provide sustenance, nourishment, and support for life; and in a very tangible sense, the disciples understood bread as something to be broken, and distributed, and shared, much like we do today. But the bread Jesus is offering is his own life, and the breaking which the bread undergoes is the expending of that life, in order to give life to others.

As educators, we can take encouragement from this in two ways. First, this has implications for the availability of resources to us, whether readily visible or not; as Paul reflects in his letter to the Romans, "He who did not spare his own Son but gave him up for us all, how will he not also with him graciously give us all things?"[12] A Christian vision for education thus does not perceive limits on what is possible when it comes to resourcing, because Christian schools are founded in the name of a savior whose life, death, and resurrection signal the possibility of all things. As Jesus himself says, "Humanly speaking, it is impossible. But with God everything is possible."[13] This reminds us of the challenge issued in *MindShift*: "As Christian educators, we need to think critically about whether a scarcity mindset or an abundance mindset is more in line with the gospel."[14]

And second, in the life of Jesus, educators can find inspiration and affirmation for their own roles. Rather than physical riches, a conquering army, or a physical homeland (all of which would have been reasonable to expect from the Messiah), Jesus gave the greatest resource he had to give—his own life. Similarly, the best thing we have to offer our students and our colleagues is not a beautiful building, a cutting-edge STEM lab, or expansive athletic fields. These are wonderful resources to be sure, but regardless of what we think we have or lack in terms of resources, the best resource we have in schools is ourselves. We have often heard phrases like "the greatest textbook a student will ever have is a good teacher." This is because education is inherently an incarnational practice. Unlike the production of goods or the provision of services, education happens relationally, life-on-life, in and through people. Because of the example we have in Jesus, we can be encouraged as we live and serve incarnationally in our schools, no matter the pressures for "bigger and better" that we often face.

Finally, as we reflect further on the "bread of life" in the gospels, we realize quickly that giving oneself requires sacrifice. Again, Jesus is our model and inspiration as educators. School leaders and teachers everywhere will affirm that education, as a helping profession, makes intense demands upon those who serve within it. We will discuss these demands and their impacts in detail in Part 5 ("Well-Being"), but for now we acknowledge that educators often significantly sacrifice their own time and resources as they expend themselves on behalf of students and colleagues. In this too, we can be inspired by Jesus's giving of himself freely, fully, and completely; as Jesus told his disciples, "Whoever would be great among you must be your servant . . . even as the Son of Man came not to be served but to serve, and to give his life as a ransom for many."[15]

Even though we call it the "Last Supper," the meal in which Jesus institutes the Eucharist is not the final time he breaks bread with his disciples. In one such account after the resurrection and at the close of Luke's gospel, we meet two unnamed disciples traveling on a country road to a village called Emmaus. They are perplexed, confused, and in doubt about all they have heard and experienced in the previous days in Jerusalem. As they walk, the resurrected Jesus joins them—but they completely fail to recognize him. They talk, question, and debate with Jesus, but they still do not see him for who he is. As they pause their walk together to share a meal, it is only at the moment of breaking bread together that they realize it is Jesus: "When he was at table with them, he took the bread and blessed and broke it and gave it to them. And their eyes were opened, and they recognized him."[16] This account encourages us as educators that even on our most difficult days—when we feel spent beyond what we can bear or overwhelmed by our insufficiency amid the need we see around us—Jesus is recognized in the breaking of the bread. This speaks to the reality that the true source of provision for our need is *already present*. The challenge lies in our ability to see it. And as we turn to our final passage of Scripture, we explore how the spiritual practice of prayer can open our eyes to perceive abundance.

The Lord's Prayer

Our last passage to examine is found in both Matthew's and Luke's gospels, when Jesus teaches his disciples how to pray.[17] In Jesus's explanation of the kinds of things to pray about, some of them appear more cosmic and spiritual—such as God's kingdom coming on earth, his divine will being done, the forgiveness of sin, and rescue from evil. Yet in the midst of this we find a simple line: "give us this day our daily bread."[18] Depending on how we experience the world, this line can either feel like a casual nonprayer of the rich (that is, we pray as we are commanded, but daily bread has never been in doubt in our lives), or the despairing cry of the needy, for whom the provision of bread, however simple and plain, is a daily matter of life and death. This continuum might be reimagined in a school leadership context when thinking about resources; some leaders are praying for things that, while enriching for their school communities, would be luxuries for other leaders who are praying for the barest of educational essentials, often owing to the local, national, and global disparities with which we live.

Given this continuum of possibility, it is striking that Jesus's prayer is a *plural* one, which appears to be designed for community and groups rather than individuals. Christians may have overemphasized notions of personal prayer and individualized spirituality in recent years, yet this model of prayer appears to be primarily corporate—it would read quite differently to pray "give *me* today *my* daily bread," yet this might be often how we actually think. Jesus's model suggests that while praying involves an individual's choice to engage in prayer, it becomes a plural, corporate, collective, and relational "we-us" activity in the main, versus an "I-me" transaction. This fundamentally reflects an understanding of flourishing as not solely an individual pursuit, but as a journey that must be made together. Considering the provision of bread within this framework helps us to see that our resources are not just for thirty or so individuals in a classroom, or three hundred individuals in a school, but rather for a collective class or school of interconnected and interdependent people. The kind of learning that leads to flourishing is not an individual pursuit for students; nor is it solo teaching or hero leadership. Our prayer for resources is one to be said together in community—not separately, in isolation, or in competition.

We also need to recognize that while our prayers are very real requests for provision, the process at work when we pray is deeper than a transactional one (that is, our supposing that if we just say the right words, we will receive the things requested). Jesus even discourages this thinking when he instructs his disciples not to "heap up empty phrases" or think they "will be heard for their many words," because "your Father knows what you need before you ask him."[19] If God already knows what we need, then perhaps as Richard Rohr eloquently explains, "[Prayer is] a transformation of the consciousness of the one who was doing the praying, the awakening of an inner dialogue that, from God's side, had never stopped. . . . In simple words, prayer is not changing God's mind about us or anything else, but allowing God to change our minds about the reality right in front of us."[20] In this way, praying for our daily bread—the resources we need—is a spiritual discipline that can invite God to shift our mindsets from scarcity to abundance.

One way in which prayer accomplishes this is by enabling us to reject the pervasive narrative of always needing "more" that surrounds us. The prayer for daily bread recalibrates our thinking by challenging us to be thankful for the resources we do have, and ultimately frees us from the pressures and fears of our not being or having "enough." Cultivating a posture of gratitude for what we have can then lead us to become more generous with our time, money, resources, and expertise—because we are starting from the recognition and appreciation of what we have, rather than striving for what we think is not yet there.

We can see from these insights that "give us this day our daily bread" is not a throwaway line in the middle of the more "spiritual" prayers surrounding it. Rather, the request for daily bread *is* a spiritual prayer. This is because the daily breaking of bread together, though a simple act, is in reality how our mindsets are transformed, generosity is birthed, and our communities come to flourish together. Praying for our daily bread challenges us to reject a dichotomy that says some elements of life and resource sharing are more or less spiritual, or more or less valuable. In the gospels, as we have seen, flourishing is found together in the unknown child's lunch donation that gets a community miracle going. It is found together in the daily prayer of collective gratitude and sharing practiced together by billions of Christians in need and in plenty. It is found together in the remembrance of Jesus at the simple moment of breaking bread together.

An "Upward Spiral of Abundance"

We can witness this vision for resources in the story of Sneinton Church of England Primary School, which is a large elementary school serving a highly diverse community in inner-city Nottingham. It educates students from ages three to eleven and draws young people in its local community from a significant range of socioeconomic, ethnic, and faith backgrounds. In serving their community, school leaders have sought to avoid thinking they are there to solve the community's problems. Rather, they view the richness of the community itself as integral to their flourishing together. Headteacher Kelly Lee explains,

> It all begins with loving each part of our community without exception, prioritizing inclusion and ensuring that everyone gets to play their part. So often the answers we're looking for are already present in the community—for example our "Inspire Parents" group who come together regularly in the school to share their cultural experiences, food, festivals, and learning. In hosting such groups, we are able to celebrate learning together, and we all benefit from what each person brings. We don't have all the solutions as educators, but we see the community as foundational to our flourishing together.[21]

Central to this vibrant understanding of community is the welcoming of all, with the school motto "Together We Achieve" lived out in the opening of doors, the laying of tables, the writing of invitations, and the embracing of guests from all backgrounds—a sharing of the "daily bread," received and enjoyed together.

This creates a deep sense of generosity, an outward-looking vision, and an orientation of service to the community. The school has also sought to rethink its own conceptions of disadvantage and has removed many of the labels often used to categorize students. They have focused in particular on dismantling the sometimes-misleading economic proxy measures of flourishing; as Lee explains, "clean clothes and a good breakfast do not necessarily equal love." Frequently they have seen that the deeper relational flourishing of students is far less linked to their socioeconomic background than stereotypes may suggest.

While the school places the student at the center of all it does, it does not limit its mission to the students. Much like the centrality of the boy in the gospel story who offers his lunch (leading to the wider flourishing of the crowds through the miracle that is then released), the school's vision is for the families they serve. Lee explains, "We're not just teaching children; we're seeking the flourishing of the whole family." As they do this, their generous vision brings into center stage the transformative impact on the whole community.

In this sense, much like the feeding of the five thousand, the resource for the miracle originates *from* the community, and is then multiplied and released *in* the community. At the heart of this approach is a deeply grounded Christian vision of "life in all its fullness" for all. Lee outlines further:

> Because we say there are no limits, there are no ceilings, this leads to no excuses. It all comes back to releasing the richness of the community itself— the school is not the savior, it is the catalyst for the community to change itself. This creates an upward spiral of abundance, where each person's use of resources inspires the next. We want all of our people to feel this is a place they can grow and will be invested in, even though this hasn't always been a part of the city for which this has been true.

This abundance mentality releases growth and permits possibility. It asks "what if" questions and fuels imagination of what could be.

The school still faces challenges like any other, but through this vibrant vision for flourishing together—and an approach to resources that backs this up in action—it aims to become a beacon of hope to which the whole community is drawn. In seeking to love the community first, the school has recognized that its greater resource is already present in the community itself—in the children of course, but also in the mothers, fathers, uncles, aunts, grandparents, cousins, friends, and neighbors. It is not a miracle that is forced or contrived; rather, the miraculous abundance of flourishing together is already present, drawn out and enacted each day.

In schools, we are called to flourish together in the provision of the simplest of resources and not just in the grandest of outcomes and accomplishments we seek. It may be that through this process of "dailyness" we will find our Christian vision in action in unexpected places: in the cleaning of classrooms; the allocation of budgets; the maintenance of IT equipment; the cooking of meals; the provision of security systems; the sharing of expertise with other schools; and the giving of time by parents and families. We may find flourishing provision in the most commonplace experiences: in the transportation of students across town; the opening or renovation of buildings; the assessments of health and safety risks; the project management and accountancy; the meeting of legal, governance, and legislative requirements; the accreditations and inspections; the human resources and professional development; and the acquisition of chairs, books, tables, projectors, calculators, test tubes, 3D printers, sports equipment, and musical instruments.

Flourishing together is thus released through—and not in spite of—our normal day-to-day decision making around resources. This is as important an expression of our Christian vision for education as any other, and is deeply integral to the flourishing together of students, educators, and institutions. This is our daily bread in education—normal, necessary, life-giving, empowering, humbling, and enabling—to be broken and shared together.

12

Reimagining Resources

[Leaders] use their core beliefs about the deep purpose of education and the capacity of all students to motivate their staffs and sustain their own courage and stamina in the face of obstacles.

—Karin Chenoweth and Christina Theokas,
Getting It Done[1]

Nothing is wasted—not even our mistakes. . . . The ego demands successes to survive; the soul needs only meaning to thrive.

— Richard Rohr, *Just This*[2]

We live in a world that seems to be forever wanting more. No matter whatever we have, we still need just a bit more. However far we have come, we still need to go just a little bit further. Cumulatively, it can feel as if we are living in a culture of enforced dissatisfaction. Whatever "it" is, it is never enough. This cultural narrative can echo down the corridors and through the classrooms of our schools, where the larger educational paradigm often communicates that, whoever we are and whatever we have achieved, there is always more.

To some extent this is true—there are unending waves of improvement to be accessed. Yet, when we consider our approach to resources in seeking flourishing together, it may be that our conception of what is "enough" is in need of balance and perspective. This does not mean losing ambition or pace, but rather grounding our approach in gratitude. This perspective enables us to play our part in releasing the miracle, like the child in the gospels whose lunch offering became a meal for thousands, with twelve baskets of leftovers. It also helps us ground our practice in the simple request (and consequent thanks) for our daily bread, for which we are commanded to pray together.

As we turn now to reflect more deeply on what this could look like for students, educators, and schools, we invite you to read the corresponding six reflections and questions (see below) slowly and to invite colleagues to engage in the team and school activities offered in this chapter.

flourishing **schools** *flourishing* **educators** *flourishing* **students** *flourishing*

You are good enough—you already have all you need within.

You are a reservoir of hope—your door is always open.

We pursue the broadest of outcomes—we love each student as we would our own.

We ask what we can give—in doing so, we reflect the divine.

I aspire not to have more, but to be more.

I have what I need to flourish— I am treated justly.

In our reflection on flourishing students, we seek to open up what might really matter the most in the classroom, by offering a picture of students whose flourishing is dependent as much on their character development as on their attainment. The call to character over possessions—to *be* more, instead of just *having* more—is completely countercultural, flying in the face of every advertising campaign or social media influencer to which students have been subjected. The second reflection opens up questions of disparity our education systems can sometimes create and reinforce, which necessitates redemptive action on local, regional, and global levels, as accessing such resources is essential for belonging, learning, and thriving together.

The resources that educators have at their disposal is not unlimited; there are few that are not stretched (usually up to and beyond their limits). However, when we delve deep within, how do we as flourishing educators really see ourselves? Are we good enough? Do we have what it takes? The answer is usually factually yes, but frequently our self-concept allows doubt and perfectionism to take the place of self-compassion and confidence. Our flourishing relies on our collective ability to fill our reservoirs with hope, such that we are then equipped to give away.

Finally, as we consider what this might look like in flourishing schools, we think about what it means to love students wholeheartedly. This includes pursuing the broadest outcomes, not simply those that are valued externally, which in turn has implications for how we think about resources in our schools. The pursuit of flourishing together also necessitates the wise sharing of resources and the cultivation of a deep sense of generosity. In so doing, we reflect something of the divine—there could be no higher call. And as we remember the simplicity of the prayer to "give us this day our daily bread," we continue to be reminded that this is a "we" prayer, not an "I" one. A flourishing approach to resources can only ever be collective.

Ultimately, the choices we make about resources communicate our vision and values far more than the words written on our walls or websites. As we take time with these reflections, reading slowly and planning to collaborate with colleagues, we can reframe our vision of resources and how we steward them, share them, and give them away.

"I aspire not to have more, but to be more."

Flourishing together can be easily reduced to fairly narrow academic metrics and transactional outcomes for students—we go to school to learn things, to pass tests, to receive numbers or letters, and all this enables us to take the next steps toward economic security and success.

In many countries, school measurement systems force leaders and teachers to direct most of their energies toward these numeric outcomes, which are of course extremely important. However, the danger is that such systems implicitly and explicitly communicate that the purpose of education is ultimately to acquire more—as in, "learning more leads to getting more."

A Christian vision for flourishing together calls for something more expansive for our students, showing that to "be more" is just as important, and foundational to the vision for *zoē* "life in all its fullness."

Education is also about developing young people's character. As defined in the Church of England's report *Leadership of Character Education*, "Effective character education will have a legacy far beyond the school gates, impacting young people as friends, neighbours, parents, team members and employees, benefitting both the individuals themselves, their wider communities and broader society."[3]

Rather than serving a forced dichotomy or counterpoint, *character development is fundamental to the pursuit of academic excellence*, and it stands at the heart of all aspirational teaching, learning, and pastoral care. The balance between economic success and character development will have a significant impact on the kind of education we provide, the learning we value, and ultimately the life trajectories to which we contribute as educators.

Flourishing together involves a vision for decoupling education from its simplified societal function as a means to an end, and taking a much broader view of developing young people's perspectives on resources. It fans prophetic flames in the minds and hearts of young people eager to make their mark and have their voice heard. Establishing the conditions for flourishing means understanding that these orientations and postures toward the world are valuable, and they are to be encouraged in young people—who can come to see their life as the greatest resource they have been given, and which they can generously reinvest in others.

Flourishing for the long term can be energized by the development of "why" moments as students develop their sense of vocation and calling. Approaches to careers and futures can typically take quite transactional approaches, imposing false hierarchies of vocation (such as university over career). *This is to misunderstand the beautiful ecology and diversity of callings for a society in which all can flourish.*

Much of this ultimately centers on our vision for the student. Whether we approach as a parent, relative, teacher, administrator, leader, or trustee, our foundational question must be, "What is it that I want education to release in this student?" This might have implications for curricula. It might call for broader vocational experiences in schools—for example, service learning, internships, and leadership activities.

A vision for flourishing together will require hard work to manage the tension between the pressures of reductionist metrics experienced in most countries and the promise of this richer, broader vision. Courageous leaders and teachers choose this path together—because young people's vision for their future is forming now.

Questions for Further Reflection

1.   What kinds of experiences and relationships have shaped your character?

2.   What kind of pressure does an economic model of education put on students to succeed in particularly measured ways?

3.   What possible activities or structures could help broaden students' experiences of education, such that their character is developed?

4. How could students be helped to think more expansively in terms of the resources they themselves are called to steward and with which they are called to be generous—so they could aspire to "be more" and not just to "have more"?

"I have what I need to flourish — I am treated justly."

Flourishing together expands our vision for the resources which students need to learn well. This requires thinking deeply about equity and the potential disadvantages that may be implicitly normalized or permitted. Few schools would deliberately seek to widen these gaps; however, there are many examples in our practice where our assumptions can reinforce rather than remove disadvantage.

One might think of the experiences of schools during the COVID-19 pandemic beginning in early 2020, as they sought to provide learning experiences either remotely or in a way that blended remote and face-to-face opportunities. The education sector had never faced a challenge like this before, and thus each institution found itself suddenly improvising, adapting, and responding to a rapidly changing situation. However, the personal experience of most leaders and teachers inadvertently created blind spots and assumptions in our solutions. Specifically, the notion that education could be delivered effectively online assumed that all students could access this learning via adequate IT provision and internet access. We know that this assumption was true for some students, in some communities—but not for all students, and not in all communities.

In more normal times we might also consider the significant disparity in educational resources between institutions, of different sizes and scopes, or in different regions of the same country—not to mention the global disparity that is readily evident. Flourishing together involves being comfortable opening up uncomfortable conversations on these matters and truly thinking deeply about what equity and justice might look like across a region, a nation, or the globe.

This is not confined to physical resources (such as technology, books, desks, libraries, and sports facilities), although these are some of the outward signs of provision or inequity for young people. It extends to wider social considerations and requires us to think deeply and engage in reimagination to ensure that all students can access the same resources and opportunities to enable their flourishing. This will also include fighting for appropriate resource levels for students from more vulnerable groups, for whom additional resources are clearly essential to foster flourishing.

Alongside the physical provision of such resources, it also involves ambitious evaluation of the most precious of resources for students' development—the quality of teaching, learning, and pastoral care. Sometimes leaders need courage to open difficult conversations with colleagues about improvements required, but these are a necessary and important part of releasing the correct resources for each student to flourish. Students need leaders to be ambitious for their learning, and keen to redress any sense of mediocrity in pedagogical practice. This can then lead to the equality of opportunity that each young person deserves.

There may also be particular implications and opportunities for those tasked with considering where schools should *open, close, merge, and divide*, such that we do not inadvertently create systems and structures that steward resources unwisely, thereby reinforcing disadvantage and closing off opportunities to flourish for individuals and communities.

Access and resource issues are at the heart of such concerns, which we address by placing the student at the center and working to open up resources that give professionals and families a better chance of accessing, developing, and thriving together.

Questions for Further Reflection

1. What kinds of disadvantage may be "implicitly normalized or permitted" in our classrooms and schools?

2. To what extent might our own personal experiences create blind spots and assumptions?

3. To what extent is there equity in my school for the most marginalized and those most in need?

4. What might a vision for equity in education look like across our community, region, nation, or globe? How do we seek to effect change on behalf of our students, schools, and communities?

ACTIVITY: COMING ALONGSIDE STUDENTS

Having more/being more

One of the greatest opportunities in education is to invite students not only to see their gifts and talents as some of the greatest resources they have received, but also to recognize the unique ways in which they can use those resources generously in the service of a greater cause than simply "acquiring more." In this activity, consider how this tension between "having more" and "being more" is experienced by students in your school. You might use the main prompt at the top of each box as the basis for an activity with students, and the reflection questions offered at the bottom of each box to spark discussion with your colleagues.

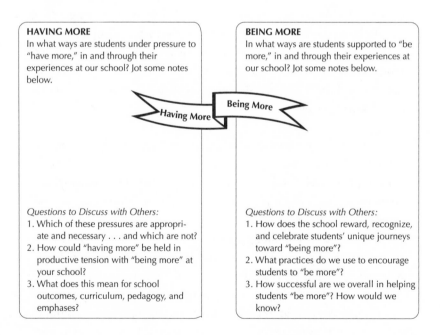

HAVING MORE
In what ways are students under pressure to "have more," in and through their experiences at our school? Jot some notes below.

BEING MORE
In what ways are students supported to "be more," in and through their experiences at our school? Jot some notes below.

Questions to Discuss with Others:
1. Which of these pressures are appropriate and necessary . . . and which are not?
2. How could "having more" be held in productive tension with "being more" at your school?
3. What does this mean for school outcomes, curriculum, pedagogy, and emphases?

Questions to Discuss with Others:
1. How does the school reward, recognize, and celebrate students' unique journeys toward "being more"?
2. What practices do we use to encourage students to "be more"?
3. How successful are we overall in helping students "be more"? How would we know?

"You are good enough — you already have all you need within."

The global advertising industry revolves around some fairly simple messaging, offering people something they can purchase to improve their lives—a new car, outfit, house, or image—all based on a notion that whatever we have, and whoever we are, we are not good enough.

Every social media swipe, like, comment, or follow has the potential to do the same to the upcoming generation of value seekers: Am I attractive enough? Talented enough? Fast enough? Liked enough? Connected enough?

Flourishing together is not yet another thing to work on, or to add to a growing list of things at which we are not yet "good enough." It is not something more to do, nor does it imply that we are not enough as we are.

There is a moment in the creation narrative that is easily passed over, but which demands our fullest attention. It is a repeated motif that occurs most days in the story—"And God saw that it was good."[4] It's the hook, the chorus, the earworm that should get stuck in our head as we read the first chapter of Genesis.

You are good enough.

It is worth repeating—even taking a moment to repeat it in front of a mirror (either a literal piece of glass or a conversation partner who can speak truth in love). You are good enough. It's a moment of recalling creation, where God looks at you—yes, you—and says, "You're great! You're everything I intended."

Of course there is nothing wrong with wanting to improve things—to train, develop, and extend ourselves and our teams—but we should embark from a starting point of confidence and assurance that who we are reflects the very nature of God and he has designed us for flourishing.

Flourishing is already there to be drawn out, as opposed to something to aim for or measure progress toward because it is not yet there. For those of us blessed and bold enough to be in conversation with others about their personal flourishing, we need to start with a posture of, "You are enough."

This strengths-based approach does not mean that we excuse things that are going wrong or accept poor performance—these still need to be addressed with dignity and love. However, drawing out that which is already within others is completely foundational to our approach to flourishing—just as it is a fundamental orientation of pedagogy. It is at the heart of great coaching and what leaders do instinctively—cheering on the growth that they can see, even when it is just a small green shoot.

Contrary to the dominant educational narrative—which can tell students, educators, and schools that whatever they've achieved, they are not yet good enough—our flourishing rests on an understanding of a God who looks at each one of us as precious and loved.

In fact, sometimes the Christian narrative can be presented in an overwhelmingly demanding light—painting God as a rather dissatisfied supervisor or line manager consistently appraising us and finding we do not quite yet measure up. Not only does this contradict God's resounding assessment of his creation as "good," it also contradicts the New Testament promise that his "divine power has given us everything we need for a godly life [*zoē*] through our knowledge of him who called us by his own glory and goodness" (2 Peter 1:3 NIV).

Saying that we are "not good enough" not only denies the truth of God's creation but also rejects his provision of "everything we need" for a *zoē* life. God calls us to abundant flourishing, and then extravagantly equips us to answer the call. In both creation and through the *zoē* he provides, God truly makes us "good enough."

This means the dominant, unforgettable, foot-tapping, dance-inducing, turn-the-volume-up-to-eleven central riff of creation is that God sees you and thinks you are good—*you are good enough*.

Questions for Further Reflection

1. What processes and experiences in education can lead to us feeling that we are not "good enough"? How might we navigate or reshape these together?

2. What kind of vision does God have of you as an individual and as a team? How might this affect your thinking and actions?

3. If flourishing is "already there to be drawn out," how might this affect how we view our colleagues? Our students?

4. Amid all the challenges of the education systems in which we serve, what habits and practices could help us remind ourselves that we are "good enough"?

"You are a reservoir of hope—your door is always open."

Alan Flintham provides a wonderfully rich metaphor of a school leader—as a *reservoir of hope.*[5]

He paints the picture of a staff team consistently going to the reservoir (the leader) to draw water (resources), and he describes this as being an expected daily occurrence—so much so, that it is the nature of leadership, by definition. Staff members approach the leader with questions, problems, and issues, all of which draw from the leader's resources, and all requiring hope. *One of the greatest resources we have to offer one another is the gift of ourselves.*

Flintham also shows that it is incumbent on the school leader to ensure that the reservoir is well topped up and refilled regularly, through a range of sustaining activities, rest, and relationships both within and (frequently) outside of the school. This releases the personal flourishing of the leader, but also by implication, the flourishing of the other educators in the institution. Students need to be taught, coached, and cared for by hope-filled educators.

Flourishing educators prioritize the resources needed to refill their own reservoirs and ensure that their colleagues do the same as well. We will explore this dynamic as it relates to well-being in Part 5, but we foreshadow it here, because giving of ourselves as a resource requires that we have something to give.

Despite the relentless busyness of the school day, it is crucial to engender in colleagues and students a sense that the door is open and that there is time (even if there is not!). Equally, as we relate to one another as educators in school, there is constant pressure for greater efficiency and productivity. Yet we each need to feel listened to, loved, and valued— which is only really possible if we feel that others' doors are open.

This raises challenges of resourcing and access, and very practical issues of offices, doors, communication, phones, and email, but we each need to know there is a place to go, a person to talk to, and a relationship through which we can process and grow.

Most of all, this raises questions around how we use one of our most precious resources: *time*.

Many of us certainly desire to use our time better or more efficiently, or we may simply wish we had more time in each day (a physical impossibility of course). But these are not solutions that will get at the root of the problem for most of us (though better time management is certainly not a bad goal, and trying various approaches and systems to find ones that work is a worthwhile activity).

The reason these efforts will ultimately fall short is because they are aimed at increasing our productivity and getting more and more done—when in reality, the key is doing less of the same, *so we can make room for doing better things.*

This may require honest conversations with ourselves, our teams, and our supervisors or line managers, as we seek to restructure our days to do more of what matters in schools. Spending quality time with the people in our care should be at the top of our job descriptions, not somewhere near the bottom. And if they are at the top of our job descriptions on paper only, and not in our daily lives, then we need to renegotiate our workloads—and perhaps most importantly, empower others to do the same.

This will be key if we are to keep our door open to others, instead of brushing past them as we run off to our next meeting, strategy, or goal. "People work" is not something that we can squeeze in among our other tasks or treat as an add-on to our schedules, for the simple reason that *"people work" is what education is all about.*

Questions for Further Reflection

1.   How does it feel when your colleagues demonstrate genuine interest in how you are doing?

2.   How might we slow down and question the hurry that our organizations tend to be in?

3.   What practical steps could you take as a team to prioritize "people work" better?

4.   What would it mean if your school or team were to be truly characterized by "open doors," where hope is freely dispensed?

LEADERSHIP DEVELOPMENT **ACTIVITY**

The examen: "You are good enough"

The "examen" prayer is a venerable practice of Ignatian spirituality. It encourages us to reflect deeply on our journey of faith, typically through the consideration of and reflection upon a day. It is a prayer of contemplation, courage, and reshaping. Work through the example steps carefully, permitting yourself to move slowly, as you consider the implications of having and being "enough" for your life and work.

Part One: GRATITUDE (5 mins)
- What things have given me life today?
- What moments revealed something of God in me?
- How could seeing today through God's eyes help me reshape it?
- What relationships are helping me to see I am "good enough"?
- What has fed my soul today?
- Where have I seen hope rise over fear?
- What is moving forward in my life, even though it might not yet be finished?

Part Two: ASKING FOR HELP (5 mins)
- What do I long to see more of?
- What do I long to see come to a conclusion?
- Who might I need a conversation with?
- What do I need God's eyes to reframe?
- Where do I need to be kind to myself?
- What do I want? What does God want? How might I know? Is there a difference?

Part Three: DESOLATION/CONSOLATION (5 mins)
- What things did not help me flourish?
- In what ways might I have held back other people's flourishing?
- Where did my choices need reshaping?
- To whom do I need to say I'm sorry?
- As I "play back" the film of the day, what do I observe—what went well, what could have gone better?
- What do I need to ask forgiveness for?

Part Four: RESOLUTION (5 mins)
- What might I resolve to do tomorrow?
- Who might I need to ask to give me courage to make this resolution?
- What do I now need to let go of?
- How can I take the next steps, knowing my inherent worth is not dependent on whether things go well?
- What habits and practices can I commit to in order to remind myself I am "good enough"?

"We pursue the broadest outcomes—we love each student as we would our own."

Teachers spend *a lot of time* at school.

Teachers spend a lot of time with students, and in the complexity of an institution, relationships with particular educators are of course key to the flourishing of individual students. Therefore it is not surprising that as academic years progress, and even roll into one another, our attachment to and love for the students we serve grow.

Such love underpins the growth and flourishing of the student, like water in the soil taken up by the plant's roots below or sunlight being photosynthesized in the leaves above. Flourishing schools can create the conditions therefore for each student to be loved wholeheartedly, to be welcomed in, and to enjoy a secure and empowering sense of belonging and attachment. This journey underpins great pedagogy and pastoral care, and flourishing schools thus create a more expansive vision for the kind of outcomes they seek.

This makes a difference, then, to the kinds of resources that are allocated, and the priorities that are chosen, as the school broadens its vision for the student beyond academic performance to wider personal, character, social, moral, cultural, and spiritual development. *Flourishing in all of these areas is what we want for our students.*

This leads to very practical considerations of timetables, classroom experiences, extracurricular opportunities—all of which need to be supplied within a finite budget. However, a school that is set on cultivating the broader flourishing of its students will find the leadership resources to make courageous decisions to open broader opportunities.

We are often challenged, or even incentivized through performance measures, to take up more utilitarian approaches, whereby schools feel forced to narrow the experience of the student to suit a particular assessment approach. One might consider a simple example of the tension between teaching detailed grammatical constructions to students and the desire to engender a love of reading. The two are not mutually exclusive, but it requires courage and vision for a school to pursue the broader outcome of the latter, when it may only be the former that is assessed (and therefore valued externally). Equally, the narrower our curriculum becomes (or is forced to become), the fewer opportunities there will be for every student to flourish.

When considering a deeply Christian vision for education in this regard, a further question opens up: *What does it mean for us as a school to see each student through God's eyes?*

How might this affect our vision for the students we serve, include, teach, inspire, and cheer on? What kinds of outcomes might we really want to aim for if we have this view, for surely such outcomes would broaden and deepen?

There are no simple answers for schools with finite resources and mounting pressures to perform in particular metrics. However, the vision of flourishing together will seek to open up ambitious opportunities across a broader range of subjects and experiences, through which a greater proportion of students are likely to flourish. If we are parents, a good question to ask is what we might desire for our own children—and then we can think through whether we desire (and deliver) the same for our students.

- We want to resource our students to learn to *sing, run, dance, act, create, and design*, even if there is no test on that.
- We want to resource them to *listen, celebrate, forgive, grieve, reflect, and empathize* even if none of these are on an examination paper or a gateway exam for university.
- We want to resource them to develop love, compassion, empathy, commitment, creativity, patience, resilience, and kindness, even if these will never be written on their résumés.
- We want to resource them to create opportunity, challenge inequity, give generously, serve willingly, question thoughtfully, lead wisely, and rest easily, even though these will never show up on their report cards.

We do not just want to allocate resources to help them pass—we want to release the resources to help them become fully alive.

Questions for Further Reflection

1. What might it mean to love the students in our care as our own? How might it affect the way we see them, teach them, and desire certain outcomes for them?

2. What difference could it make to see each child "through God's eyes"?

3. If you had to list the outcomes your school is seeking for its students—not what is written on your website, but what is evidenced by the time spent in the classroom related to those outcomes, what is assessed, and what is celebrated—what would be on your list? And in what order?

4. What kind of resources might you need to help students (and staff for that matter) "become fully alive"?

"We ask what we can give—in doing so, we reflect the divine."

The education sector is heavily influenced by external forces that shape the definition of a successful school. This can lead to a marketplace approach to learning, where we overly associate flourishing of the institution with financial growth or test scores. In many countries our systems incentivize this, by shaping education into a transactional experience for customers who expect particular experiences and value.

For schools needing numbers of students to survive, this narrow notion of flourishing can become central. Similarly, when the majority of examination systems are set up such that performance becomes relativized, schools become comparative in league tables—and not everyone can win. The consequences of this are often the most pronounced for the most vulnerable, who may have the least ability to play a competitive educational game.

Very few schools would report having an abundance of resources—in fact, our current climate is one of the most challenging in recent decades for both public and private funding. This can lead to a pragmatic tendency to look inward. However, the flourishing of our schools is not simply to serve their own purposes—we do not simply exist for the benefit of ourselves.

Genuinely flourishing schools choose to look outward, seeking to serve others, sharing resources generously, and leading as if the success of other schools matters just as much as our own.

The economy that Jesus appears to advocate in his teaching is generous and extravagant, where the marginalized are brought to center stage and prioritized. Functioning from an abundance versus a scarcity mindset, genuinely flourishing schools ask not what we can gain—*but what can we give?*

Christina Rossetti's famous Christmas poem, "In the Bleak Midwinter," offers us a range of examples of giving:

> What can I give Him,
> Poor as I am?
> If I were a shepherd
> I would bring a lamb;
> If I were a Wise Man
> I would do my part,
> Yet what I can I give Him,
> Give my heart.[6]

Most often we focus on the climax of the stanza, whereby the primary thing we need to give is our hearts. While this is of course central, the example of the shepherd and the lamb is also very important—it is tangible. It is literally giving that which we have to give.

A flourishing school might reconceive this poem and consider giving a science technician, a set of textbooks, a sports field, or a supervision and evaluation system.

A flourishing educational system could be primarily built on the ability to give—rather than simply the ability to compete.

Schools and educational systems built on competition may be disincentivized to work with the most vulnerable (arguably the communities and families most in need of schools which reflect the divine). But as Jesus announces his ministry in Luke's gospel, he chooses a highly practical text to quote from Isaiah in announcing his ministry: "The spirit of the Lord is upon me, because he has anointed me to proclaim good news to the poor. He has sent me to proclaim freedom for the prisoners and recovery of sight for the blind, to set the oppressed free" (Luke 4:18–19 NIV).

It's a striking launch quotation, one that gives us some insight into the nature of Jesus's mission and purpose. It raises questions about how our schools are serving those who are poor, in need, and disadvantaged in our communities. It also suggests that flourishing is not "winning," but giving. And it suggests that the flourishing of a school may be defined less by its financial security or academic success and more by the wider flourishing it effects within and beyond its own walls.

Questions for Further Reflection

1. To what extent does the success of other schools matter to you? How would anyone know?

2. When you think of the relationships within and between schools, what difference could having an abundance mindset make?

3. What does your school have to give? What could release the giving?

4. How might your school's use of resources reflect something of the divine?

SCHOOL DISCUSSION **ACTIVITY**

"Problem-tunities"

Mindset matters. Often the difference maker for whether we can find resources to accomplish our mission is having an abundance mindset—rather than one of scarcity. This means it is critical to reframe our resource problems in light of our opportunities, so that we are better able to see the possibilities for flourishing that we might have otherwise missed.

The word "problem-tunity" is a combination of the words "problem" and "opportunity," and it reminds us that every problem can be reframed as an opportunity. In this exercise, have your team list their top resource problems in the first box. Then, list your top resource opportunities in the second box. Next, use the third box to consider how you could reframe your resource problems in light of these resource opportunities, to create new "problem-tunities."

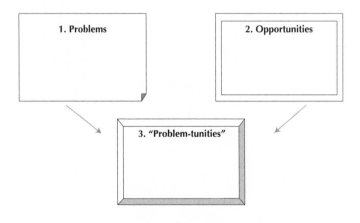

5

WELL-BEING

13

Well-Being in Schools

Too often busyness is not a means to accomplishment but an obstacle to it. . . . A life that focuses on what matters most, makes time for rest, and declines unnecessary distractions may look simple on the outside, but from the inside it is rich and fulfilling.

—Alex Soojung-Kim Pang, *Rest*[1]

Self-care is never a selfish act—it is only good stewardship of the only gift I have, the gift I was put on earth to offer others.

—Parker Palmer, *Let Your Life Speak*[2]

Although placed at the end of this book, the fifth domain identified by the Flourishing Schools research—"Well-Being"—is as essential for educational flourishing as the domains that preceded it. The Children's Society in the United Kingdom defines well-being in its annual *The Good Childhood Report* as "'how we are doing' as individuals, communities and as a nation, and how sustainable this is for the future."[3] And renowned psychologist Corey Keyes of Emory University asserts that well-being is not simply the absence of illness; rather, well-being can be assessed along a continuum of *flourishing* to *languishing*.[4] Our vision for Christian education focuses on how well students, educators, and the school community are as they move toward flourishing together.

The question of well-being in schools has become a particularly challenging one in recent years. Most educators would readily identify a decline in student well-being and its impact on learning, the classroom environment, and the school overall. This would appear to be supported by statistics; for example, the US Centers for Disease Control and Prevention notes that rates of depression and anxiety among children are on the rise, with one in six young children having been diagnosed with a mental, behavioral, or developmental disorder (that number increases to more than one in five for children living in poverty).[5] The Children's Society found that in 2020, 18 percent of children in the United Kingdom were deemed to have low well-being, which was the highest percentage in the last five annual household surveys and reflects declines in children's happiness with life overall, as well as with their appearance, schools, and friends.[6] A supplemental report on the impacts of the COVID-19 pandemic in the same year showed increases in feelings of isolation and adverse effects on cognitive well-being for children.[7] Further, the UK children's mental health charity Place2B notes that one in eight children have diagnosable mental health problems, many of which continue into adulthood.[8]

The importance of well-being in schools is not limited to students, however. In their article "School Mental Health Is Not Just for Students: Why Teacher and School Staff Wellness Matter," University of Maryland psychologist Nancy Lever and colleagues cite data showing that 46 percent of teachers report the highest levels of professional stress—at the same rate as nurses and higher than physicians—and that 78 percent of teachers report feeling both physically and emotionally exhausted every day. Perhaps most importantly for the question of how we flourish together in schools, Lever and colleagues identify a *symbiotic relationship* between the well-being of educators and students in school. As they explain, "teacher burnout is predictive of student academic outcomes, including being correlated with lower levels of student effective learning and lower motivation. . . . [Moreover] teacher burnout appears to affect the stress levels of the students they teach."[9]

The reality in many of our schools is that budget strain, market pressures, and external accountability demands can work against our attempts to prioritize the well-being of staff and students alike, often favoring more "concrete" measures of success like college acceptance rates, standardized testing scores, and league tables. But if educators and students are not well, we by definition are not flourishing together—and if we do not address well-being in schools, much of what we do when it comes to teaching and learning simply will not matter. In their book *WHOLE: What Teachers Need to Help Students Thrive,*

Rex Miller and colleagues assert: "Schools should be natural environments for peace, embracing and encouraging social and emotional literacy. Yet educational institutions seem to have their own fight-or-flight trigger that prevents administrators from stepping back, reflecting, and then reestablishing what we know is necessary for learning—healthy and resilient teachers who care for their students as individuals and then communicate hope and possibility."[10]

We have been encouraged over the past few years by the growing attention to social and emotional learning, which signals a greater attention to the well-being needs of students. But we often fail to address the concurrent and related needs of teachers and leaders in our schools. A Christian vision for educational flourishing together elevates the conversation around well-being to one that must be had schoolwide—not as something we must address so we can "get on" with the more important business of schools, but rather as a central foundation for flourishing together.

Flourishing Schools

A starting point for well-being in our schools is the school environment itself. Rex Miller and colleagues make a profound statement in their book on educational well-being: in schools, "the building is an additional teacher."[11] In other words, our school buildings and grounds themselves are communicating things about well-being every day to our students and educators. When they are well-designed for human beings who need ample natural light, movement, nutrition, interaction, and rest—providing places where students and educators alike can explore, create, collaborate, and play—they set the stage for well-being. Alternatively, our buildings and grounds can present obstacles to flourishing when they are designed for something other than human flourishing—such as when they resemble educational "factories," designed for efficiencies like large-batch instruction, uniform movement of students, and "assembly lines" of subject matter and content.

Although most new school buildings are based on healthy design principles, many schools do not have the luxury of constructing new buildings and face limited funds when it comes to refurbishing existing ones. Miller and colleagues emphasize that in such cases, targeted and sometimes small changes— enhancing natural lighting, opening spaces where possible, reducing noise, and improving indoor air quality—can have a positive impact on well-being.

One particularly powerful approach to improving well-being in schools is to connect educators and students to the outdoors. As psychologist Sue Stuart-Smith notes in *The Well-Gardened Mind: The Restorative Power of Nature*, involving adults and children in gardening, or "therapeutic horticulture," can encourage not just environmental sustainability, but also "psychological sustainability" marked by improved mood and self-esteem as well as reduction in depression and anxiety.[12] This also makes good sense from a spiritual perspective, as reconnecting with God's creation—where the cycles of planting, growth, harvesting, and rest are on full display—can help us reflect in healthy ways on the different seasons of our own lives. Thankfully, schools do not always have to "go it alone" in making these changes. For example, grants may be available for eco-friendly lighting upgrades, community groups will often happily volunteer to assist schools with planting gardens, and task forces involving students can design and implement creative concepts that also can serve to meet science learning goals. Urban schools with limited access to outdoor spaces can bring the outside in through aquaculture and pop-up greenhouses to accomplish many of the same benefits.

When it comes to physical well-being, another area to consider is how our scheduling practices support or inhibit students and educators. For example, research suggests that schools can significantly improve well-being by better prioritizing rest. In *Rest: Why You Get More Done When You Work Less*, Alex Soojung-Kim Pang of Stanford University examines the neuroscience around rest and concludes, "We shouldn't regard rest as a mere physical necessity to be satisfied grudgingly; we should see it as an opportunity. When we stop and rest properly, we're not paying a tax on creativity. We're investing in it."[13] A Christian vision for education prioritizes rest based on the biblical principle of Sabbath; in Scripture, God's design and provision for us to pause from our work and recharge is viewed as a "holy" command.[14] In this way, rest may very well be one of the most spiritual practices in which we can engage. When we think of ways we can promote rest in schools, Pang's insight that rest may not look the same for everyone—or even look very restful at all—is instructive: for some, rest may involve physical, creative, or even social engagement, rather than a pause of all activities. Thus instead of just scheduling times for young children to lie down or teachers to have a coffee break (though both are of course important), we should integrate various kinds of breaks in our daily schedules that allow for diverse expressions of rest.

Along these lines, educators have long been aware of the physical and psychological benefits of movement for students, especially when experienced through frequent, small spurts of activity sprinkled throughout the daily schedule. But not only are opportunities for movement crowded out of students' days in many schools, they also are not extended to the educators in the building. Often open periods in teachers' schedules are given for classroom preparation only, but adding in short breaks for activity—whether structured or unstructured—could create time and space for movement. Even taking a brief walk around the grounds or off campus can help teachers and leaders to recharge and refocus.

Taken together, these approaches can contribute to *healthy living* in schools, which the Flourishing Schools research found to be positively linked with flourishing outcomes.[15] There are many other considerations in school life that contribute to well-being, such as nutrition standards that promote healthy eating for students and staff alike. But importantly, a program "here and there" does not always add up to an overall school environment that promotes well-being—rather, an integrated and intentional approach is needed. This might start with a "well-being audit," in which a cross-constituent team convenes to discuss issues of concern in the school environment and daily schedule, as well as target and prioritize areas for improvement. Such a team should include students, who in addition to providing valuable insight, can also gain practical problem-solving experience and meet various learning objectives related to health, science, psychology, and other subjects. The guiding question for such efforts should move us from viewing well-being in schools as something we would address "if only we had the time" to something that is a primary emphasis because it creates the preconditions for our learning, growth, and overall flourishing together.

Flourishing Educators

C. S. Lewis asserts in *God in the Dock*, "None can give to another what he does not possess himself. No generation can bequeath to its successor what it has not got. . . . Nothing which was not in the teachers can flow from them into the pupils."[16] No matter how good their teaching skills are, if teachers are not well, they will have little energy to engage, instruct, and care for students. Where there are few flourishing educators, there will be few flourishing students. The very same is true for school leaders, whose ability to set priorities, cultivate people, and accomplish tasks is at risk when leaders are unwell. As Miller and colleagues assert, our necessary "first step is to make sure that the educators in the building are being genuinely cared for. We must prioritize the collective well-being of those charged with teaching children. They cannot do that if they are stressed, sick, broke, or hopeless."[17]

Not surprisingly, the Flourishing Schools research found that *stress* for both teachers and leaders—defined as experiencing constant feelings of being overwhelmed, accompanied by a lack of time to prepare or to focus on health—is negatively correlated with flourishing in schools.[18] We have already mentioned that educators experience stress levels on par with frontline healthcare workers with whom they share "the caregiver's dilemma," when they "care so much that it leads to fatigue, burnout, and demoralization."[19] Research shows that stress can lead to physical and psychological issues for teachers, including increased illness and fatigue, lack of energy, emotional numbness and loss of interest, and difficulty with decision making.[20] And thanks in no small part to increasing demands made of school leaders, around 75 percent of principals experience a wide range of stress-related symptoms that hamper their self-efficacy, impair executive control functions, and contribute to significant turnover in school leadership.[21]

In their review of the research, Lever and colleagues found that the most common sources of stress for teachers are what we might expect: high-stakes testing; large class sizes; student behavioral challenges; poor physical space; bureaucracy; workloads; and paperwork. But some of the more "hidden" causes include gaps between preservice training expectations and teachers' actual experiences in schools, a perceived lack of adequate recognition or autonomy over their classroom, and a lack of collective influence over school policies. The educational field is not doing nearly enough to address these concerns; for example, only a quarter of schools in the United States offer formal stress management education.[22]

Failure to address stress in systematic ways not only represents a missed opportunity to nurture teachers' well-being but also reinforces enduring stigma around mental health and unhelpfully relegates stress-related challenges to questions of performance and supervision. When it comes to addressing stress, opening up communication will be key; schools may need to utilize community resources, such as the assistance of qualified mental health professionals, to initiate and sustain conversations around teacher stress. In terms of reducing leaders' stress, strategies can include sharing responsibilities through collective leadership, careful examination of workloads, increasing leaders' agency and decision-making power, and making mental health a priority.[23]

It is important to note that educator stress may go beyond a situational concern to a clinical one in need of referral for professional attention and treatment. In addition to workplace concerns, a wide range of stressors can affect educators' well-being; these can include relational difficulties, financial insecurity, physical illness, and mental health challenges, to name but a few. Because stigma surrounding mental health persists in our societies, educators who are struggling may not be transparent about their concerns with others or be willing to seek help when they need it. Miller and colleagues assert that we can mitigate this by creating school cultures marked by care and mutual accountability:

> True communities are comprised of people who care . . . [and] keep an eye out for the "signs" in and from each other. You know the signs—when a friend, family member or colleague seems increasingly tired, negative, cynical, erratic, or disappears. . . . It takes another human to notice the signs, such as when the physical clues of health and well-being suffer. When the worldview and sense of self wobble. When the medical and psychological indicators of burnout are too obvious to ignore. That's the time to speak.[24]

We can empower educators to speak by deliberately creating safe spaces and ample time within our schools for conversations around well-being, and we can offer support by being aware of community mental health resources to which we can connect others. By watching out for one another and taking action when others are struggling, we can flourish together in and through the challenges we face as professionals and as human beings. These challenges may manifest at different levels and intensity in the various seasons of our lives, but a Christian vision for education anticipates, accepts, and addresses them as part of a flourishing journey together.

Flourishing Students

As we have explored, the well-being of students is inextricably linked to that of educators; this means that prioritizing educator well-being can yield a salutary effect for many students. At the same time, of course, students face significant challenges to their well-being both in and out of school. For example, according to the Pew Research Center, "When it comes to pressures teens face, academics tops the list: 61% of teens say they feel a lot of pressure to get good grades," while 29 percent feel the greatest pressure when it comes to physical appearance, 28 percent to fitting in socially, and 21 percent to being involved in extracurricular activities or being good at sports.[25] While these pressures are certainly not new for adolescents, they are compounded for this generation through the influence of social media; according to the Prince's Trust in the United Kingdom, more than half of youth (57 percent) believe social media exerts an "overwhelming pressure" to succeed.[26]

In the face of these pressures, the Flourishing Schools research identified *resilience* as an important construct linked specifically to student well-being.[27] As Nan Henderson and Mike Milstein note in *Resiliency in Schools*, resilience refers to the ability to persevere through difficult circumstances of life by drawing on one's "capacity to spring back, rebound, successfully adapt in the face of adversity and develop social, academic, and vocational competence despite exposure to severe stress or simply to the stress inherent in today's world."[28] Resilience can also be described as "the existence of assets and protective factors in the social context, the ability to adapt to combat adversity, or the developmental outcomes that result from coping positively with adversity."[29] A high level of resilience is associated not only with better academic performance in school, but also with higher levels of critical thinking and a range of non-cognitive outcomes, including greater opportunities in life.[30]

Thankfully, resilience has been receiving increased attention in schools in recent years. Across educational sectors, schools are incorporating social and emotional learning goals as well as training faculty and staff in ways to nurture resilience through research-informed practices.[31] Of particular interest for Christian schools is a report from the Harvard Graduate School of Education, which indicates that students are more likely to have positive outcomes in the face of adversity when they have at least one stable, caring, and supportive relationship with an adult, as well as an affirming faith or cultural tradition that contributes a supporting context.[32] Schools founded on a Christian vision for education are uniquely poised to provide both, through flourishing relationships with caring educators and the affirming faith at the very heart of Christian schools.

This is particularly important for students who are recovering from adverse childhood experiences, such as poverty, neglect, abuse, or bullying. As mentioned earlier in our discussion of flourishing relationships, Louise Bombèr's work on trauma-informed education—with a basis in attachment theory—is helpful for considering ways to care appropriately for these students. Bombèr suggests a four-step process for teachers to use pastorally, before diving into teaching, to support students who have experienced adverse childhood experiences: *regulate*, which means helping students learn to self-soothe; *relate*, which involves connecting meaningfully with each student; *reason*, which entails equipping students through reflection; and *repair*, which facilitates reconnection through ongoing relationship.[33] These insights are also helpful for students who may not have a diagnosis or documented trauma, as all students will face some form of trouble and pain in their lives, though of course to varying degrees. We are reminded again of Jesus's words to his disciples, as recorded in the Gospel of John: "In the world you will have trouble. But take heart! I have overcome the world."[34] Resilience involves being able to "take heart"—literally to "take courage," from the Greek *tharseite*—and keep going. As Steven Garber describes in *The Fabric of Faithfulness*, rather than "being shipwrecked by the brokenness of the world," students can "learn to navigate their way through"[35] with teachers as loving guides, and an education rooted in the hope-filled promise of Scripture.

On a final note, the Flourishing Schools research found a positive connection between flourishing outcomes and students being *other-oriented*[36]—meaning they not only enjoy helping others, but also are known for showing love and care. Similarly, research from Swinburne University in Melbourne, conducted on the relationship between resilience and spirituality, suggests that "sense of purpose" is tied to the development of resilience among students.[37] And so, in this last domain of flourishing, we have come full circle—returning to the importance of *purpose* for our Christian vision for flourishing together. When students are oriented toward serving, loving, and caring for others, it grounds them in purpose-filled, authentic, real-world work. This stands in direct contrast to the perfection-driven and curated lives that students often feel pressure to sustain on social media.

Educators can support and reinforce this positive desire of students to love and care for others in genuine ways, first by modeling this for students inside their schools and classrooms. Schools can also undertake explicit efforts to develop students' capacities for caring for others through curricula related to character development and through authentic service-learning.[38] Involving students in significant decision making and leadership roles within the school can also help them develop listening and communication skills, as well as cultivate empathy and humility in working with and leading others.

We began this chapter by defining well-being as something greater than just the absence of illness. Likewise, flourishing is something greater than an absence of difficulty and pain. Miller and colleagues suggest that, instead of a highly stress-inducing experience where the focus is exclusively on academic performance, schools can become places where we help students to see beauty *in the midst* of brokenness:

> Kintsugi, a Japanese art form, reassembles broken pieces of pottery. The pieces are glued together by golden beads. That's how the artistry of Kintsugi highlights each vessel's unique pattern of brokenness. The beauty is the pattern and its signature. To accomplish this, a teacher must be free to teach, not driven by tests or bureaucratic efficiencies. Allowing a teacher to be human and touch the life of a student can be a life-changing experience for both. And that life is returned back to the teacher in the fulfillment of their calling. Teachers are naturally gifted to restore the broken pieces in children's lives. Learning is healing.[39]

A Christian vision for flourishing together calls for schools to be characterized by mutual care for and service to one another, among educators and students alike. In the process, our schools can become communities of healing that contribute to our collective flourishing.

14

Jars of Clay

But we have this treasure in jars of clay to show that this all-surpassing power is from God and not from us. We are hard pressed on every side, but not crushed; perplexed, but not in despair; persecuted, but not abandoned; struck down, but not destroyed.

—2 Corinthians 4:7–9 (NIV)

The collective well-being of the students and educators in our schools is central to the pursuit of flourishing together. As we have seen, well-being is deeply personal and relational for students, grounded in secure attachments with adults that confirm and build personal value. These relationships set the stage for learning and impart confidence with which to approach the future. For educators, well-being can frequently determine many of our day-to-day actions, words, and decisions, by coloring our view of the past, altering our experience of the present, and underpinning our expectations of what is possible in the future.

While health-related awareness days, provision of services like counseling, and collection of data on our school culture from satisfaction surveys can contribute to well-being, in and of themselves, these tactics will likely miss the mark on their own. This is because caring for one another's well-being—deeply, meaningfully, and holistically—goes beyond a program, event, or strategy. Rather, collective care for our community's well-being encourages us to choose kindness, patience, and courage as we face the next hour, day, semester, or year. It supports students unconditionally, helps us to see colleagues as whole beings versus job titles, and engages every member of the school in healthy rhythms of work, play, and rest. Caring for our collective well-being is a nonnegotiable for a community to live well together.

Well-being is also foundational to the Christian narrative, which does not promise the absence of challenge or suffering but rather offers a grounded, holistic vision for our lives—social, moral, cultural, physical, spiritual—in essence, "life in all its fullness." The prophet Jeremiah shows us that the fruits of flourishing are dependent upon roots of well-being: "But blessed is the man who trusts in the LORD, whose confidence is in him. He will be like a tree planted by the water that sends out its roots by the stream. It does not fear when heat comes; its leaves are always green. It has no worries in a year of drought and never fails to bear fruit."[1]

While well-being is personal, Scripture is clear it is also social; the central teaching of love of God and love of neighbor positions our caring about well-being as a mark of love for one another. Throughout Paul's epistles, we find the importance of caring communities that live well together in seasons of doubt and confusion, creation and growth, suffering and despair, and hope and innovation. As a path to exploring well-being, we focus on what is perhaps Paul's most personal letter—his second to the church at Corinth—in which the apostle is at his most prone, clearly expressing great passion regarding those to whom he was writing and revealing significant amounts of suffering and challenge in his own life. It is an anthem to vulnerability, a celebration of realism, and a call to a more honest understanding of the challenges of leadership. Paul's letter is richly instructive for educators, whom Parker Palmer describes as engaging in "a daily exercise in vulnerability. . . . Unlike many professions, teaching is always done at the dangerous intersection of personal and public life. . . . [W]e make ourselves, as well as our subjects, vulnerable to indifference, judgement, ridicule."[2]

The fourth chapter of Paul's letter offers a stunning metaphor of strength emerging from frailty and strength: "But we have this treasure in jars of clay to show that this all-surpassing power is from God and not from us. We are hard pressed on every side, but not crushed; perplexed, but not in despair; persecuted, but not abandoned; struck down, but not destroyed."[3] As we unpack this passage, we will consider the implications of this metaphor of "treasure" contained in "jars of clay" for our well-being, and then consider the conditions in which we may find ourselves in schools and the hope offered in the two simple words "but not" as we pursue collective well-being that is foundational to our flourishing together.

"Jars of Clay"

We may imagine the churches planted by the apostles as large, successful, flourishing communities of thousands of people. While the rapid geographical spread of Christianity is remarkable given the travel challenges of the first century, it is thought that the Corinthian church to which Paul was writing was still in its early days—perhaps around five years old and of modest size, with around fifty to seventy people at the most. It was in the early phase of its life, with plenty of green shoots to be encouraged, but still having a long way to go to establish itself and grow to maturity. The city itself was commercially significant—strategically located for trade, recently rebuilt, and flourishing economically. Corinth had a rich heritage and reputation for exquisite pottery which would have been well known at the time, thereby making Paul's choice of metaphor—a simple and fragile clay jar—all the more meaningful to the first readers of the letter.

To understand the context of Paul's metaphor, we need to venture back into the previous chapter to understand what kind of "treasure" Paul is talking about storing in the jars. At first glance, it may seem to refer to actual treasure—to a way of storing up money and riches, that which is precious and reflects success and security. But the purpose of the word used here is not in fact to imply actual riches (cash in the bank, security of resources, and so on) but rather to offer a different kind of treasure to be kept in the jars of clay, namely the ability of each human to reflect something of the divine. The word used for treasure here, *thesauron*, is the same word used in the gospels by Jesus when he speaks of storing up "treasures in heaven," which he directly contrasts with actual financial resources.[4] Those listening to Jesus in his discourses are asked to release themselves from the pursuit of material resources, sell their possessions, give things away—and thus position themselves to be on the receiving end of such "treasures in heaven."

In schools, we are far from immune to the pressure to be defined and affirmed by outward success, visible achievement, and resource-based security. In many ways our educational systems are based on these ideals, with comparison defining classroom practice, attainment grouping, inter-school rivalries, and market force competition. This can have significant effects on our well-being, whether we are students choosing not to answer a question for fear of failure in front of peers, or school leaders plunged into self-doubt and anxiety as reenrollment numbers come in or examination results are published. (If only we could all be "above average"!) Our understanding of security defined by outward markers of success may have a profound impact on us, to the point that we may conflate well-being with externally visible signs that things are going well.

However, the metaphor of "jars of clay" redefines the treasure we are to seek. Although our societies may encourage us to acquire more, this metaphor suggests that the truest of treasures is not something that is immediately visible or that we accrue on our own. Scripture makes clear this treasure is not something material in nature that can be chipped away, stolen, or destroyed.[5] Rather, it is divinely deposited, of worth that far exceeds anything physical that could be obtained and of lasting value—as the second half of the verse indicates: "to show that the surpassing power belongs to God and not to us." This is the treasure stored in jars of clay—which, as simply made vessels, would have been suitable for daily service rather than display or decoration. This juxtaposition points to an overflowing source that, rather than being hoarded, is meant to be shared generously with others. This provides a compelling vision of the generous nature of God, as well as a helpful picture of how the flourishing of a school, educator, or student is not just for that institution or individual's benefit. Rather, it is also intended for the benefit of others. As we have mentioned earlier, this is how community builds—through the asking of "what can we give?" and not just "what can we gain?" The daily choice to give away enables the flourishing of our communities and the individuals that inhabit them.

Despite this picture of a priceless treasure within, the reality of clay vessels was such that they were easily cracked or broken, especially when used in regular service as they were intended. Paul goes on in this passage to offer four very rich metaphors depicting this dynamic: "We are hard pressed on every side, but not crushed; perplexed, but not in despair; persecuted, but not abandoned; struck down, but not destroyed." The two very important connectives that hold the four metaphors together—"but not"—serve as a motif for the dynamic that Paul is foregrounding: our flourishing is revealed in and through our lived experience of challenge, and even crisis. It would be such a different passage if it just listed the challenges—"We are hard pressed on every side . . . perplexed . . . persecuted . . . struck down"—which echoes the tempting downward spiral of hope being extinguished that can grip a student, educator, class, or team. Likewise, if the passage simply offered the positive—"We are . . . not crushed . . . not in despair . . . not abandoned . . . not destroyed"—it would suggest an overly positive caricature of Christian education, wishfully claiming all is well, when clearly it is not. Each of Paul's "but not" dyads offer insight for living well within this tension, which all of us—educators and students—experience in our schools. Put simply, our well-being can be found by dwelling together in the "but not" of our circumstances.

"Hard Pressed, but Not Crushed"

In the first metaphor, Paul describes the sense of pressure that he is feeling—"we are hard pressed on every side, but not crushed." The language used here takes us to the first-century vineyard and the process of grape crushing as the starting point for the production of wine. The word used here means literal, physical pressure—a force acting upon us and squeezing us into a space too small to bear. The idea of being hard pressed is a daily experience for most leaders, teachers, and students in education, as they frequently cope with the prospect of having to do more with less as they work through a seemingly unending to-do list. This leads to the stretching out of the day, well beyond any sense of "normal" working hours, and to a general atmosphere of constant busyness and hurry. There is nothing wrong with a pace amplified by purpose, and in many seasons that is exactly what our organizations need; we see this particularly in seasons of growth and turnaround, where we become rightly impatient on behalf of our students who only get one shot at learning. However, too much pressure undoubtedly leads to significant consequences for our individual well-being and the sustainability of our teams.

But as Paul signals with his choice of the pronoun "we" instead of "I," flourishing together involves bearing that weight together. We are reminded of Paul's instructions in his letter to the Galatian churches: "Bear one another's burdens, and so fulfill the law of Christ."[6] While such pressure might be enough to crush us on our own, we have greater capacity to endure challenge and trials when we help to bear each other's burdens. This metaphor is highly relevant to a class of students seeking to learn and flourish together rather than compete with one another, supported by teachers who create a "we, not I" atmosphere in the classroom—wherein students encourage and spur each other on, enable the asking of questions, and support one another particularly at pressure points like examination times. We can also apply the metaphor for our teaching teams and leadership structures, whereby we help carry the weight for others to enable their flourishing—not ignoring or underestimating the pressure, but ensuring that the sharing of weight distributes and relieves the strain.

There is significant responsibility for leaders here in choosing what to transfer onto their teams and teachers, and by extension onto students. For example, because we operate in systems that are frequently defined by financial and market pressures that often appear insurmountable, or by the dominance of external performance measures and accountability, there is a possibility of transference of fear within an organization. In a negative spiral, this macropressure can become an internal pressure, which can translate into fear that drives our actions. Certainly, no school leader sets out to deliberately transfer this fear to their teams, and equally no teacher would set out to do the same with students. And yet, it is a daily possibility for our schools and classrooms. Being "hard pressed but not crushed" leads us to consider not just how we can collectively absorb pressure, but also how we can transfer hope and perspective to others in our care, whether teams, teachers, or students—something for which Paul's next dyad offers insight.

"Perplexed, but Not in Despair"

For leaders, there will be few days that go by without complex decisions to be made, without obvious or comfortable answers. For teachers, no matter how many times they may teach the same ages or lessons, every school year presents a new group of students who are unique in their learning and in some way completely unlike those that have come before. And unless there is appropriate challenge in pedagogy, students will probably just find themselves repeating what they can already do, as opposed to attempting new things and pursuing questions to which they do not yet have the answers. In each of these examples, we see that being "perplexed"— "at a loss" or "uncertain," from the

Greek *aporoumenoi*—reflects some of the daily reality of working in schools. Yet for Paul, this is not the end of the story—"we are perplexed, but not in despair." In other words, even though we face uncertainty, we do not give up.

The temptation to "give up" in education—for students, teachers, and leaders—is very real. We have already mentioned high turnover rates for educators, and student dropout rates are likewise concerning (not to mention those who disengage in other ways, even though they physically remain in school). The reality is that leading, teaching, and learning are complex human activities for which there are seldom very easy or clear-cut formulas. Paul's dyad here leads us to ask the question, How do we hold in tension the "but not" of being perplexed—of not having all the answers we think we need— but not giving up in the midst?

The idea of "wisdom," so central to the biblical narrative, is again helpful here. The Bible's wisdom literature is substantial and diverse—the book of Job, many Psalms, Proverbs, Ecclesiastes, the Song of Solomon, and much else. As part of that tradition, Jesus "grew in wisdom" when he was a child.[7] Reframing perplexity not as a conundrum to be resolved, but rather as an opportunity to pursue wisdom, enables us to more resiliently face the ongoing complexities of our professions (for educators) and of the educational journey (for students). Well-being in the face of uncertainty involves being prepared to be "perplexed" for a good deal of the time. It also entails our being proactive, for instance by scheduling time for our teams to consult before arriving at decisions or using well-structured group work that enables students to benefit from collective insights as they tackle problems together. This can become part of the way we set up our teams and classrooms, as well as undergird the rhythms and relationships we establish to address ongoing uncertainty. Perplexities are thus transformed from irresolvable problems that push us to give up, to navigable realities in which we are growing in wisdom together.

"Persecuted, but Not Abandoned"

Paul's third metaphor is frequently translated "persecuted," but the Greek word used, *diokomenoi*, has the literal meaning of being pursued or chased down. In first-century Corinth some of this pursuit would not just be mental or psychological but also physical. Paul goes on in the letter to explain the lengths to which he and his companions have had to go—facing beatings, hunger, imprisonment, and loneliness, which suggests that literally being pursued must have played a part in their lived experience. Certainly for some of our students, and even some of our colleagues, physical harm, neglect, or abandonment is a reality. For even more, feelings of isolation and emotional threat are a struggle. And for all of us, our well-being can often feel determined by the extent to which we "measure up" to the expectations of those around us: the heightened social media pressure under which all teenagers now find themselves creates fear of judgment; school leaders can feel chased down by the seemingly relentless concerns of financial viability or external performance measurements. Regardless of the sources, very real challenges can gather around us and elicit that sense of being pursued or chased down. And yet, as Paul continues, we are not "abandoned" (or left behind) as we are being pursued.

Paul's words call to mind the Old Testament account of the encouragement given to a new leader, Joshua, right at the point where he is about to succeed Moses, his long-serving mentor. After Moses's death, God assures Joshua, "Just as I was with Moses, so I will be with you. I will not leave you or forsake you."[8] It is on the basis of this assurance, and in light of imminent war and battles, that Joshua is instructed to "be strong and courageous" three times over the next four verses. God's promise to not abandon this new leader, even in a season of intense challenge, is extended to all of us through Jesus—whom the Bible calls "Emmanuel," meaning "God with us."[9] The knowledge that God does not give up on or abandon us requires that we likewise do not give up or abandon others. This sense of togetherness provides a buffer against, and a hopeful pathway through, the inevitable challenges that arise. In order for us to not give up we need to be surrounded by others who refuse to give up on us.

As discussed in earlier parts of this book, a Christian vision for flourishing together suggests that authentic, caring, life-giving relationships are key to moving from merely "surviving" to thriving in education. When these relationships are enduring and stable, they transform "I" into "we," reflecting Paul's language. As a result, our hope rises exponentially—because we are not alone when we are pursued. For example, few school leaders or teachers have not felt the relief and release of sharing a difficult problem with a colleague from a different school and finding that colleague has encountered a similar challenge (even if that challenge has not been fully "solved"). Similarly, teachers can impart encouragement to students when they highlight how the class as a whole is struggling with a concept, not just individual students who "don't get it"—and by allowing students as a group to work through a common problem, which is far more effective for learning than students hiding their confusion out of embarrassment or shame. The hope that a school community, team, or class can tackle any issue that comes its way—provided we "stick together"—contributes greatly to the individual and organizational resilience that is essential for our collective well-being.

"Struck Down, but Not Destroyed"

Paul's final metaphor will resonate with any teacher who has had the joy of teaching Roman history as a topic to their students. The language may evoke a military picture of the Roman army's "tortoise" formation, in which a group of soldiers provided each other with a defensive structure through the careful interlocking of their shields above and around the group, thereby making their joined shields impenetrable to arrows and other weapons. It was a highly effective approach that relied not on any individual soldier's skills or bravery but rather on teamwork and the corporate maintenance of structure. While the structure was intact, the defenses remained, but as soon as the structure was knocked out of shape, every individual soldier was put at risk of attack. The word usually translated "struck down" here has that same military implication—that the formation has been broken, the shields are knocked over, and the group's defense is compromised.

Structures, rhythms, relationships, and practices do not guarantee the absence of challenges, but nonetheless their careful construction and maintenance provides the opportunity for a more consistent and collective approach to well-being. For students, especially those who have experienced trauma or loss, such structures are vital for their secure attachment and positive orientation to learning (in fact, learning is highly unlikely to take place without such structures and relationships in place). Equally, healthy systems and patterns for educators make a positive difference in well-being—ranging from formal processes such as team meetings and coaching, to the embedding of healthy habits and practices like rest, prayer, counseling, physical activity, creativity, and many other life-giving engagements that are easily squeezed out by pressures to work harder and longer.

This military metaphor points again to the collective nature of our flourishing—it is "we" and not "I," "us" and not "me." When the tortoise shape was intact in Roman defenses, every single solider was safe, regardless of their individual confidence, skill, aptitude, or military prowess. When the structure was compromised, individuals were exposed and their vulnerabilities could be easily exploited by the enemy. This has clear implications for collective leadership, as well as for those responsible for governance. Trustees are often able to see the bigger picture, and their perspectives may provide insight that the formation is breaking up before it actually does.

Organizations and individuals will face crises—it is a certainty for your school. There will be moments for students, educators, and institutions as a whole where major challenges will knock us out of shape. The response to such situations will rarely just come down to individual inspiration or brilliance, though often of course a leader plays a significant role in drawing the structure back together. It is rather the ability of the class, team, or school to move forward as one—in discipline and purpose—which can create and sustain the conditions for everyone to flourish.

Living Well in the Tension

Throughout these verses, we see Paul and those he is leading in constant tension between two realities. The jars of clay are used to store invaluable treasure, but at the same time are fragile and prone to damage while fulfilling their intended service to others. Paul makes clear the first-century Christians were under duress of nearly every conceivable kind, yet without succumbing to the challenges that encircled them.

These verses will likely resonate deeply with those who work in schools. Leaders may find themselves in the most challenging times they have ever known, seeing little encouragement, confused by current events, or fearing they have made wrong choices, all while working with teams who are hemmed in and losing hope. Teachers may be instructing students who are at their wits' end, whose self-esteem is battered by self-criticism, and who may believe they are unlovable and unreachable. We may find ourselves in a school that is straining, creaking, and knocked out of formation—with teams that have lost their way, no longer trust, and feel no desire to forgive.

These are all real situations, and yet we can take great encouragement and have great hope because of the repeated "but not" that Paul writes with confidence, knowing he is part of a bigger story, which in turn enables him to live well in the constant tension. As he writes in a different epistle, this time to the church at Philippi, "I have learned in whatever situation I am to be content. I know how to be brought low, and I know how to abound. In any and every circumstance, I have learned the secret of facing plenty and hunger, abundance and need. I can do all things through him who strengthens me."[10] As Paul's words suggest, our well-being is frequently revealed and consolidated in a crisis—and is then sustained over a long period of time by choosing the appropriate lens through which to see our situation. Our collective well-being is dwelling in the "but not" together.

The leadership story of Alan Hardie, chief executive of the Northumberland Church of England Academy Trust (NCEA), shows these principles in action. Throughout his leadership journey, Hardie has, like so many leaders, learned that putting vision into practice is about flourishing together in challenges. Hardie's original journey to become a school leader came about in abrupt, shocking, and painful circumstances. It began when he took over his first school the day after the sudden and unexpected death of a much-loved, inspirational leader—who had led the school to significant success and established herself as a key figure in the community—literally one day before the new school year began.

Hardie's first meeting with senior staff some ten years ago was of course deeply humbling and enormously challenging, and required him to trust in God continually despite the incredible challenge and strain. He recognized that unless he led the community to put its trust in the faith that underpinned its vision, it could not survive. As he recalls,

> Sharing that news with the whole staff on the first day of the year was the hardest thing, and quite a first day in my role. Then when we held a memorial service, we gathered the entire community, turning our large gymnasium into what I can only describe as a cathedral. We could never have gotten through that season without a sense of faith and calling, and in so many ways that was made so real in having to face such difficulties. I never faced any of them alone—we faced all of them together.[11]

So, step by step, day by day, Hardie developed "but not" lenses for himself and his team—enabling them to name the challenge, but at the same time begin to build a narrative of renewal from this point of crisis. The realism of this leadership approach meant the school could gradually take its next steps together toward recovery. Over the coming years the school received the World Class Schools designation (similar to Blue Ribbon status in the United States), such was the extent of its academic and character development success with the students it served.

Having been shaped in the crucible of this challenge, Hardie later changed roles to lead the Northumberland Church of England Academy Trust (NCEA), which is a family of eight schools in northeast England comprising one high school, six elementary schools, and one school serving children with significant and multiple learning difficulties. Like many leaders who transition into a new role, he found it a place needing many changes, but with an ethos statement that gave everything a chance: "Enabling everyone in our community to let their light shine." NCEA serves an area marked by socioeconomic disadvantage, much like the community in which Hardie himself grew up, facing challenges in academic standards, budgets, and staffing. Yet Hardie has found that the key is to ensure that the vision defines every structure, development plan, and relationship. In reflecting on Paul's notion of "but not," he shares:

> When you have a lofty ambition for your schools, everyone in the community needs to actually believe it, and then adjust their expectations accordingly. It is very easy to dwell in those things that can lead us to discouragement, but while we recognize we face major challenges, we are comfortable in that space. Our collective well-being does not get determined by everything going well. If we're serious about enabling everyone to let their light shine, that means the students, but also the adults too—as a result, our community's well-being is so much more secure and we are equipped to face other unknowns, as we have been shaped together by the storm.

Having faced storms together in the past, this group of schools, which now serves nearly three thousand students, jumped into action during the summer of 2020 amid the COVID-19 pandemic lockdown in the United Kingdom. The schools sought to continue to serve the community in extremely practical ways, such as delivering and serving weekly food parcels to nearly a thousand families in need across the eight school campuses. Shining their light as a school community is a commitment not just for when the world is all "as it should be," but rather the sustaining of vision is revealed in the challenges.

Very few school leaders, upon reflecting back, will not be able to name moments of significant challenge that proved highly formative in their journeys. As leaders reflect on their own journeys, we can understand better how Paul was able to write elsewhere in the second letter to the Corinthian church, "Therefore, since through God's mercy we have this ministry, we do not lose heart."[12] Losing heart may be a helpful lens through which to consider the idea of well-being in the ministry of education, with its many pressures, uncertainties, and challenges. As we notice the "loss of heart"—or the diminishing of students' or educators' flourishing—and take generous and other-minded action in response, we acknowledge that the idea of flourishing together stands at the heart of sustaining community well-being. This view of well-being is not simply about being happy or sad, or unencumbered or challenged, but rather is about living well through the changing seasons together and building up treasure that lasts.

15

Reimagining Well-Being

There is something at the very center of our faith which reminds us that Good Friday may occupy the throne for a day, but ultimately it must give way to the triumphant beat of the drums of Easter.

—Martin Luther King Jr.[1]

If we are brave enough often enough, we will fall. Daring is not saying "I'm willing to risk failure." Daring is saying "I know I will eventually fail, and I'm still all in."

—Brené Brown, *Dare to Lead*[2]

As we think about reimagining our practice in schools toward well-being, there are a few misconceptions we need to continue to clear from our thinking. First, our well-being is not the same as happiness. Well-being should not rise nor fall with the successes and failures of each hour, day, year, or decade. Flourishing together is not necessarily correlated with winning or losing, but as we have seen from the apostle Paul's writing, it is forged in challenges and shaped by storms. Our collective well-being is found in the ability to dwell in the "but not" of 2 Corinthians 4:8–9, which names the challenges, but is not defined or limited by them.

Second, we can easily think of our well-being in physical or psychological terms only. While certainly bodily health and mental health are both crucial parts of well-being, they are not the sum total. Rather, they are joined by our sense of purpose, the quality of our relationships, and our spiritual formation. We are in need of a holistic view to consider well-being in schools and in ourselves.

It is also easy to think of well-being in individual terms (particularly when we are tempted to conflate well-being with happiness). But the reality in schools is that how well we are doing as individuals impacts the well-being of many others around us, whether students or colleagues. As we have highlighted earlier, Paul makes clear that we are all part of the same "body," so that "if one part hurts, every other part is involved in the hurt, and in the healing. If one part flourishes, every other part enters into the exuberance."[3] Imagine how vibrant a picture of well-being would emerge if we, as an entire body, flourished together.

As we reflect on what this might look like for students, educators, and schools, it is important not to oversimplify or caricature. Every person is uniquely created, and every person's situation is entirely unique. With this in mind, we aim to draw out some larger themes that can be helpful for re-imagining our practice together, through the reflections (mapped below) and activities in this chapter.

You guard and treasure your time—you rest wisely and often.

You are not your job title—your life outside of work matters to us all.

We share each other's wounds—we grow in the crucible of challenge.

We know when and what to stop—we know we are not without limits.

schools flourishing · *flourishing educators* · *students flourishing*

I am loveable—I long for relationships and value.

I have a secure base from which to explore the world—I can face the future with confidence.

The ecology of flourishing says that students need to have a secure sense of being valued in order to learn. The simple question, "Am I loved?" stands at the heart of the classroom. This may be particularly important for students with adverse childhood experiences, such as trauma, neglect, bullying, or marginalization. Where there is love—not just felt, but also consistently extended in and through our school structures and routines—there is the possibility of flourishing together. Flourishing does not mean everything goes well for students at all times, but investing in students' well-being positions them better for exploring and engaging the world that is coming into view. Flourishing students do not face a known future with certainty, but an unknown future with confidence.

The well-being of educators is one of the most fundamental conditions of the school's soil in which flourishing students can in turn grow. Our reflections unpack how the collective well-being of flourishing educators is dependent upon our developing patience and rhythms of rest. None of us can keep going indefinitely, yet we work in educational sectors and systems that continually demand more. Our well-being as professionals is deeply related to our well-being in other parts of our lives—meaning outside of school—because we are not just our job titles. From this understanding, we can work toward shaping professional cultures that are more supportive of our colleagues and ourselves.

Finally, we explore how flourishing schools are places where we share our wounds, and not just our triumphs. Through relationships and shared experiences, we strengthen one another to grow in the crucible of challenge. And as we support one another in our journeys together, we prioritize healthy school cultures where we understand when and what to stop. This understanding is frequently lacking in schools, and the pressure to "keep up" transfers directly to students and educators without questioning this pressure's impact on well-being.

Although this is our final chapter on "Reimagining Our Practice," it is by no means the least important. In fact, flourishing together in schools is built upon practices that support and enhance our collective well-being. The reflections and related activities offered in this chapter ask us to consider how we can proactively and collaboratively develop these practices.

FLOURISHING **STUDENTS**: REFLECTION 1

"I am lovable—I long for relationships and value."

There are all kinds of ways that schools like to categorize, compare, rank, and distribute students—reading age, running speed, musical ability, height, birth month, test performance, or socioeconomic status. Some of these are useful, while others can prove discouraging or even damaging.

However, when we really dig deep into the nature of a flourishing student, perhaps one thing sits at the very heart—"love-ability." Imagine ranking your class or school on the extent to which each student was lovable! Love is a fundamental human experience, a central necessity for life itself, and arguably the pivotal point from which all education flows.

In a family context there will of course be many times when children and young people don't meet expectations, respond in unexpected ways, and display disagreeable behaviors, yet do we as a result love our children any more or less? Students are growing up in a society that can communicate that love is conditional—on success, beauty, wealth, intelligence, and "follows" or "likes." Our students experience pressures that are hard for educators to imagine. However, being loved is a timeless concern, regardless of generation or background, from infancy all the way through young adulthood (and beyond).

The flourishing of students is related to their self-concept as lovable and their regular and expected experience of love, grace, forgiveness, and restoration. This is a challenge for a system that enjoys categorization and comparison. It will require teachers to focus on who the student is, not simply on what they do or do not achieve.

Consistently experiencing this love enables students to let go of other scripts or narratives in whose shadow they dwell—those of fear, of comparison, of the sense they are not good enough, or of the belief they do not truly belong. And as a result of experiencing this love, flourishing students can show love themselves in their relationships with one another and the wider community.

When the student trusts the educator in the room, learning will accelerate. When the student feels attachment needs being met by peers in the room, learning will improve. Strong peer relationships between students help to validate an emerging sense of well-being, while it is still fragile and growing. But a deficiency in or the absence of the above can dismantle everything we hope for in schools.

Relationships are integral to the well-being of students. They are not secondary, or something we can attend to "if we have time."

The flourishing classroom is interdependent, made up of very different interacting parts. Here we all recognize (and demonstrate in words and actions) that education is not an individual endeavor, but rather that students' well-being is secured much more readily when students and educators think in terms of "we" and "us," and not "I" and "me." Love, relationships, and value form the bedrock of well-being for flourishing students.

Questions for Further Reflection

1. How might the categorization or ranking of students affect their well-being?

2. How might we make the experience of love, grace, forgiveness, and restoration "regular and expected" in our classrooms?

3. To what extent do our students have the ability or confidence to let go of "the scripts or narratives in whose shadow they dwell"?

4. How can switching from "I" and "me" to "we" and "us" affect the well-being of students?

"I have a secure base from which to explore the world—I can face the future with confidence."

E ducation is in a hurry.

There is a hurry to teach quickly, to make greater progress, to cover more content, to transmit more knowledge, and to demonstrate greater understanding through a greater number of assessments.

Time for exploration, play, and learning from failure can be sidelined. Space for relationships, conversation, trust, and social engagement can be difficult to create. Yet in this hurry, we may actually (if unintentionally) skip over deeply important precursors to the learning and progress we wish to see. In failing to establish security in relationships, safety, and attachments, *we inadvertently destroy the roots from which everything can grow.*

The pioneering work of John Bowlby's theory of attachment in the late 1960s centered on the need to provide safety and security to students, thereby enabling them to regulate their emotions by comforting, creating joy, and facilitating calm. This in turn offers a secure base from which to explore the world. Bowlby's theory then informed the development of Gillian Schofield and Mary Beek's "Secure Base Model,"[4] which highlights the importance of *availability* (enabling the child to trust), *sensitivity* (helping students to manage their feelings), *acceptance* (building the child's self-esteem), *cooperation* (helping the child feel more effective), and *family membership* (helping the child to belong). These five elements offer a helpful framework to assess students' flourishing and help us consider how students' well-being is fundamental to any hope of academic learning and progress.

From a neurological perspective, we can understand flourishing as mediated through brain development and functionality, involving a journey from the brain stem (where safety and the fight or flight response are dealt with as a priority), to the limbic brain (where relationships, trust, and attachment can be secured), before arriving at the cortical brain (where learning can take place). Because our educational system is in such a hurry, we can frequently create the conditions in schools whereby we jump over the first two stages entirely—hoping to get to the third without doing the necessary work that precedes it. Flourishing together demands we take the time to secure the first two elements, in order to enable learning to occur. This journey is applicable for each and every student's well-being, though of course it is particularly challenging for students who have experienced developmental trauma, including adverse childhood experiences.

Developing well-being does not require us to dwell in the past forever. It also does not mean we need to protect students from difficult experiences. Not all stress is harmful, and set within the context of positive relationships, challenging experiences can shape and form us. Learning to cope with manageable threats to our well-being is in fact critical to the development of resilience. But such resilience needs relationships, time, trust, and dependability. These build students' confidence to take the next step, even when they cannot yet see where to place their feet. Focusing therefore on well-being and attachment is central to pedagogy, because it creates the structures and security that enable new learning to take place.

Building this secure base together creates the social conditions and relational climate for each individual student's confidence to be built, and for appropriate and healthy risks to be taken (without which real learning cannot take place).

Each day, we ask our students to step into a future they cannot yet see. There will be few students who flourish where they do not first feel trust and security in the present, which endows them with the confidence they need to step into their future.

Questions for Further Reflection

1. What factors do you think make for a secure learning environment in which students' well-being can grow?

2. To what extent are we under pressure to rush past confidence-building in order to "deliver" the curriculum? How could we slow down?

3. What difference might attachment theory make for our approach to students' well-being?

4. What relationship do you see between well-being and resilience for your students? Is there a difference? If so, what is it?

ACTIVITY: COMING ALONGSIDE STUDENTS

"Love is . . ."

Paul's description of "love is" in his first letter to the Corinthians is no doubt very familiar to us, not only through personal reading of the Bible, but also because of the passage's prevalence in wedding ceremonies, church sermons, devotional art, and religious education curricula.

What if we used Paul's descriptions to stimulate imaginative thinking around what love—which grounds our collective well-being—could look like in schools? Using the chart below, record (in three or four words) an action that students, teachers, and leaders might take if they embodied each dimension of "love is" in their respective roles. Ask students or colleagues to join you in making their own lists, then reflect and discuss together.

"Love is" . . .	Students	Teachers	Leaders
Patient			
Kind			
Does not envy			
Does not boast			
Not proud			
Not rude			
Not self-seeking			
Not easily angered			
Does not record wrongs			
Does not delight in evil			
Rejoices with the truth			
Always protects			
Always trusts			
Always hopes			
Always perseveres, never fails (does not give up)			

"You guard and treasure time—you rest wisely and often."

There are few employment sectors that would not regard time as a vitally important part of working practice. Most employment contracts outline a clear quantity of expected hours, often aligning remuneration with the completion of such time. A career in education may typically find many of us working well beyond these expectations—and normalizing extremely high tariffs of working hours per week. This is as true for teachers in their first year as it is for seasoned leaders nearing retirement.

Whatever vision we have for our lives (and within the limitations of the agency we actually have to decide, both for ourselves and others), flourishing together means recognizing and honoring the preciousness of time. Time can become our treasure.

Time is something to be organized, understood, hidden, valued, protected, and shared. Time well spent can result in feelings of amazement, wonder, beauty, and desire. However, we must resist where possible the tendency to allow work to permeate every moment of our schedule and thus every part of our being.

Productivity and effectiveness are important, but flourishing is not just about getting more done. *It also involves cultivating joy, fun, sensible pace, sustainability, and living well together with a wise perspective.*

Flourishing together calls us to value one another's time by planning carefully, sticking to deadlines, making space in our calendars, and finding the courage to stop (even when we may perceive that the rest of the organization just wants us to work harder). Much of our well-being is contingent on our ability to rest effectively.

Of course, this has implications for actual rest (sleep), but rest is not measured simply by REM cycles. For many of us, rest will come in other forms—for some, time spent in solitude; for others, in intense physical exercise; for some, in crafts or music; for others, in replenishing company and fellowship.

Our flourishing will be proportionate not to how hard we work, but to how well we rest. Flourishing educators therefore develop habits and practices that ensure rest as an essential part of life in all its fullness.

Many of us need to understand time better, largely because we are jammed into a system that requires everything immediately. There is little patience or perspective—we want answers and change now, not wisdom that waits. There are many wonderful instant miracles in the biblical narrative, but yet the major narrative arc of Scripture is a very slow process, often filled by long periods of waiting and doubt.

This is perhaps epitomized best in the Psalms, written in a variety of seasons, which Walter Brueggemann helpfully categorizes into a three-stage cycle of "orientation," "dis-orientation," and "re-orientation."[5] These seasons each present their own challenges to our individual and collective well-being. However, they can be energizing and life-giving as well.

We can be certain that we will experience all three seasons at different points in our lives (sometimes even simultaneously, for example, if our vocational season looks very different from our season at home). While our seasons will change, we can learn much from the current season in which we find ourselves. We may even be in the midst of a change in season right now, which in and of itself has lessons to teach us.

The key is to understand which kind of season we are in, and then patiently choose to rest wisely, as appropriate to the current season.

Members of flourishing teams are interested in the rest their colleagues are getting. Students will learn better if they are taught by well-rested teachers, and teachers will be supported better by well-rested leaders. In the spirit of honoring the Sabbath, why not develop a "rest policy" for your institution?

There are people on our teams right now who need rest more than professional development, and who need to prioritize holistic well-being more than increased productivity through to-do lists and meetings. For leaders, it is essential to lead by example—putting into place structures and relationships that help guard this most precious treasure of time.

1.   How do you view time in your organization? Have you ever discussed this resource and how its use affects your collective well-being?

2.   How do you rest? How do your team members rest? And if you do not know, how might you go about finding out? Why might that be important to know?

3.   What might a "rest policy" look like in your organization?

4.   What is the particular responsibility of leaders in relation to rest and role modeling?

"You are not your job title—your life outside of work matters to us all."

What is your job title? Whatever your response, it's sure to be a compression of an expansively holistic, multifaceted human being into a few words that can fit on a business card.

Most of us have been drilled in this way of thinking through our own education, and yet rarely do we open up the space in conversation about our jobs for discussion around desire, character, passion, joy, relationships—all things that, in the long run, turn out to matter so much to most people in society.

This can lead to a view that places our work above everything else in our lives. As a result, we tend to build structures that are not particularly interested in what happens outside of the workplace. This results in workplaces and sectors that are rarely sympathetic to consideration of more flexible working practices that could in fact unlock greater flourishing not just for each individual, but for the organization as a whole.

Over the past few years, our professions have generally become more effective in talking about something called "work-life balance." Frequently, however, this conversation comes with an undertone of functionality—that is, our organization or team is interested in how you are doing outside of the workplace, so that when you're in the workplace you can do a job better or last longer in it.

Flourishing together is based on the opposite approach. Love for each person—manifested in genuine interest in our colleagues beyond their status as employees—places collective well-being at the heart of our relationships.

For those of us leading schools, we might simply ask, "Would I like flourishing educators to be teaching the students in my care?" If the answer is yes, we need human beings who are flourishing physically, emotionally, spiritually, relationally—not just professionally.

Flourishing together means talking in detail about our expectations of one another when we are off the school premises, establishing clear rhythms and patterns, aligning our mutual understanding, and ensuring that we each contribute to one another's flourishing.

We can cherish one another's time through our collective practices: we can listen wisely to one another's stories, empathize with each other's context, and recognize that while the vocation to teach or lead can become all-pervasive, we are more than our job titles. Our lifestyle and our interactions with one another should reflect mutual support, and we can create cultures of trust that release flourishing, rather than cultures of suspicion and surveillance that choke our growth.

Those in healthy cultures take time to fill each other's reservoirs (rather than simply drawing from the source again and again), and thus build one another up in such a holistic way that our hope rises over fear. Such cultures also moderate speed wisely—we do not always need to rush. Frequently, the call to complete more tasks needs to be quieted, because there appears to be little evidence that great communities can be built in a rush.

Finally, the onus is not simply on the institution or the team—each of us as educators must maturely and wisely understand that which gives us life and rest, and then choose to use our time wisely. Without this, our personal reservoirs will gradually drain beyond a safe point, and we will begin to make poor decisions and judgments due to lack of resources.

In reflecting on the John 10:10 call to "life in all its fullness," we see that so much of this calling is to *character, not task*. Flourishing together is about how we live, not what we do for a living.

Questions for Further Reflection

1. What activities outside of work sustain you? What feeds your soul? How might you make time to prioritize these activities?

2. What happens to you when you *become* your job title—in other words, when your job seems to be consuming you? What are the early warning signs and how could you act on them?

3.   What kind of flexible working practices could release greater well-being in your school?

4.   What practical steps could you take as a team to support each other's healthy life-work integration?

Knowing the seasons

The Old Testament Psalms provide us with a vision of living well through varying circumstances. Old Testament scholar Walter Brueggemann categorizes the Psalms into three broad typologies—"orientation," "dis-orientation," and "re-orientation"[6]—that can help us to identify and better understand the current season in which we find ourselves.

Using these categorizations (below), reflect on your current season with a trusted colleague—both your individual seasons and those of your team or institution. Be sure to talk about challenges *and* the hope that each season presents, as well as how you can support each other in the current season.

Songs of orientation invoke clarity in our circumstances and the sense that we are moving in the right direction, as in the well-known verses of Psalm 23:1–2—"The LORD is my shepherd; I shall not want. He makes me lie down in green pastures. He leads me beside still waters. He restores my soul"— which offers an attractive picture of a flock faithfully following the call of the shepherd's voice and direction and being led into pleasant and restorative situations from places of challenge. Other psalms (such as 8, 24, 33, 104, 133, and 145) offer celebration and gratitude for blessings. We may not find ourselves in this space often, or alternatively if we do, we might be inspired to set out for more challenging territory, while leaning on the faithfulness of God's voice.

Songs of disorientation will be familiar to leaders lying awake at night fearing a difficult decision or consumed by doubt or regret. These songs—featuring change, confusion, pain, anger, impatience, lament, and suffering—can be a comfort. For example, Psalm 13:1–2 takes us to the depths—"How long, LORD? Will you forget me forever? How long will you hide your face from me? How long must I wrestle with my thoughts and day after day have sorrow in my heart?"—and yet assures us that God is still to be found there. These psalms (such as 35, 74, 86, 95, and 137) encourage us to admit and explore our anxieties, fears, and depression, and find together some growing perspective (and patience) that God walks with us in those seasons—keeping in mind that sometimes seasons of disorientation can be just what is needed for individuals and organizations to let go of the old and allow the new to come.

Songs of reorientation can draw us toward a more hope-filled future, if we can be patient in those seasons (and avoid trying to fix everything!). Psalm 119 is an in-depth autobiographical tale—a journey of twists and turns, ups and downs—characterized by consistent return and realignment: "I have sought your face with all my heart; be gracious to me according to your promise" (verse 58); "Your word is a lamp for my feet, a light on my path" (verse 105). The calling of students, educators, leaders, and institutions is not to success, but to faithfulness. Such seasons of reorientation are more likely when we seek flourishing together.

"We share each other's wounds—we grow in the crucible of challenge."

As we have seen, Paul's second letter to the Corinthians shows Paul at his most vulnerable. He is clearly facing confusion, doubt, disappointment, pain, and uncertainty.

Since this is a highly personal letter, it is all the more remarkable that Paul's pronoun of choice is consistently "we" and not "I." There is pain, but it is shared. Flourishing schools accept and share vulnerability—literally meaning "*wound*-ability"—instinctively and regularly.

Such schools recognize that sometimes putting others first, and asking what love requires, means abiding, waiting, and sticking around together. They choose empathy over sympathy when things go wrong, and seek to stand as close together as they can in a challenge, often putting others before themselves in a sacrificial way.

Flourishing recognizes that many of these wounds are temporary and heal well through appropriate rest and attention, but some may not go away. There are scars that cannot be ignored, but they do not have to define us.

Those in flourishing schools go into battle together. They do so courageously, knowing that teams almost always need to choose to place themselves in situations where defeat is a possibility. This could be through a difficult parent meeting, exam results, a safeguarding issue, a financial proposal, or a new building project.

Great teams can grow in the moment of challenge and build resilience for the next one, but they take the risk that it will go wrong. *Without the risk, there is no chance to grow.* The battle stories motivate the next steps; the shared wounds inspire the community.

We can also see this at work in the science laboratory, where the crucible is the place of melting, burning, and changing of state—ultimately providing a safe space in which a challenge can be contained while intense heat is applied.

When a serious challenge comes, a flourishing school gathers together to plan its response, but before the spreadsheets and action plans are filled in, we ask a more important question of one another (sometimes silently, sometimes audibly): *Are you still in?* Flourishing schools name the challenges and define them accurately, but they also find a starting point and build a shared momentum to flourish together.

Finally, flourishing schools are needed everywhere there are students, and not just in the places with the most fertile or hospitable soils. Throughout nature there are plants that survive and thrive in the most intense heat, cold, rain, drought, sun, and dark. We need schools that can flourish in all these settings, by building networks of interdependence and mutual service. In these environments, leaders and teams may need to adapt to the conditions, but their best hope for flourishing is to grow together with others.

Questions for Further Reflection

1. How surprising is it that a leader like Paul reveals his vulnerability? How might that contrast with more dominant leadership paradigms?

2. When you reflect on your journey to date, what scars have you picked up? How have they shaped your thinking and practice?

3. Why do people who have been in battles together share such a strong bond?

4. When the challenge comes and your team's members ask of each other, "Are you still in?" what factors help them to answer "yes"?

"We know when and what to stop—we know
we are not without limits."

There are very few educators with a completed to-do list—there is always more to plan and implement, and every day creates new challenges to add to issues from yesterday that are still unresolved.

Additionally, our systems frequently jam us into an extremely ambitious annual planning cycle which usually overpromises and underdelivers, likely because everything seems possible in the start of the year. A start-of-year welcome speech that saw a leader outline "the five major things we are going to stop doing this year" would seem countercultural and highly unusual, but the ability to choose what to stop is one of the greatest attributes of the wise leader.

Stopping things can be one of the most powerful forces in releasing flourishing in our schools. This pruning (which may need to start with ourselves as leaders) is one of the least glamorous but most effective skills of the gardener. It is easier to say than to do, but reflecting on the things we need to ease back on will help to orient us more clearly toward our core purpose—and attain to more of the *zoē* life of abundance that God intends.

We are not taught or trained to slow down, but we need to. Patience may be one of our most important attributes—not a laissez-faire, it-will-all-be-fine approach, but rather the patience that experienced leaders have, often acquired simply by experience.

If we consider the life of Jesus for a moment, it is clear that he did a lot of things, traveled to a lot of places, and met a lot of people. And in the midst of all this activity, we see him repeatedly retreating from the crowds and his disciples to be by himself, often to pray. Jesus surely could have used that time alone to "do more"—but he did not. Jesus is an example of purposeful patience, achieving a patient purpose.

Flourishing schools also need rest.

We do not only need vacations or weekends away, but rather we need daily rhythms deliberately and strategically established, which allow flourishing to occur in good time and do not try to force it through more action. Leaders can learn from the resting of the land in agriculture. Schools that need to rapidly improve do need pace, but they also need patience if new life is to be sustained for more than the short term.

Although it is personal, knowing when and what to stop is also a corporate activity. It is fundamentally a socially negotiated decision that gives permission to pause. It can be empowering, liberating, respectful, and even lifesaving. While the pace is never likely to let up in our sector, what we often need more than "doing more" is time to rest, recharge, refine, and refuel. Life in all its fullness does not literally mean a schedule with no space, or an organization with no headroom—rather, it speaks of leaders' wisdom, perspective, planning, steadfastness, and dependability. Flourishing schools do not wait until the ground is dry and cracked before watering the plants—they irrigate well and often, keeping in mind that sometimes the most efficient irrigation systems are unseen, carefully planned beneath the surface.

The capacity in our system is not limitless, nor is it limitless in the people that work in it (however strong their sense of vocation may be). Therefore, we need to be careful gardeners. This helps us become more patient with the green shoots we are nurturing, as we realize there will often be a lot of time and a lot of water needed before seeds show any outward sign of flourishing. As counterintuitive as it may sound, the wisdom of discerning together what to stop leads to our greater flourishing.

Questions for Further Reflection

1. What kind of wisdom is needed for us to choose what to stop?

2. What does patience in leadership mean to your school, and for the well-being of your teams?

3. What could we stop for one hour per week, one day per month, or one week per year—to create the space we need to actually grow?

4. How can recognizing our limits lead to improved well-being?

SCHOOL DISCUSSION **ACTIVITY**

Walks in the garden

The Bible was written during an expansive time period in which people were significantly more acquainted with agriculture than many are today. Jesus tells numerous parables and employs metaphors related to gardening—sowing, planting, watering, harvesting, pruning. In John's gospel, Jesus says, "I am the true vine, and my Father is the gardener. He cuts off every branch in me that bears no fruit, while every branch that does bear fruit he prunes so that it will be even more fruitful."[7] And in Luke's gospel, when a frustrated landowner wants to cut down a fig tree that hasn't yet borne fruit, the gardener replies, "Leave it alone for one more year, and I'll dig around it and fertilize it. If it bears fruit next year, fine! If not, then cut it down."[8]

To think about how insights from agriculture might apply in your school, assemble a team at your school who will take regular "learning walks." Much as you would walk around a public garden and stop to note the diverse plants, landscapes, and biomes, send team members out for a set period of time (perhaps an hour) to take a walk through and around the school (perhaps once or twice a month). As you and the team walk, write down observations about places you and they observe educational flourishing in action; places where additional sunlight or water might be needed to revive growth; places where tiny green shoots are barely visible (but they're there!); places that seem to be overgrown with too much activity and are in need of pruning back; or places that are currently dormant or fallow, but that show promise for future cultivation.

Encourage yourselves not just to look for "public" displays (such as a well-polished lesson or a chapel sermon) but to seek out the quieter, subtler garden beds—such as the interaction between students during cooperative work, the layout and flow of the lunchroom, or the engagement of teachers and custodial staff. Remind yourselves (and those with whom you may come into contact while walking) that this is not a formal "observation," but rather an invitation to see in a new and different way, with a nonpunitive set of lenses—that of a gardener, who has the holistic, vibrant, bountiful flourishing of the garden in mind. Be sure to invite students to walk too!

After each walk, gather to share observations, uncover common themes, and—like wise gardeners—decide how you can best cultivate growth in your school today, as well as plan for the future. Consider:

- What evidence did you find that your school is abiding in the "vine" Jesus? How did you see your school living out a Christian vision for education?
- In what places or ways is your school bearing fruit—where or how is it flourishing well?
- In what places or ways is your school not bearing fruit—where or how is it not flourishing yet?
- Where do you think "pruning" is needed, so your school can be more fruitful—so educators and students can flourish even more?

Once you have a rhythm for these learning walks, invite new team members along so you can gain diverse perspectives. The greater the number of attentive gardeners working side by side, the more we flourish together.

Epilogue

In the foreword to this book, the Rt. Revd. Rose Hudson-Wilkin, Bishop of Dover, writes about *flourishing together*: "There is a Zulu word called *ubuntu*. It means 'I am, because you are.' In other words, we are a people together. We are interdependent. We do not exist by ourselves. No one really flourishes unless we flourish together. Black and white, young and old, rich and poor, with and without disability. We are all God's children."

I am because you are. It is a concept that eloquently underpins the Christian vision for flourishing that we have sought to outline through this book. This vision is not solely for students, nor educators, nor schools, but the three interacting together. The three need each other, in times of plenty and in times of want. They are "all parts of the same body," as the apostle Paul observed; they are the different sections of the orchestra playing as one; they are conversing guests eating together at the same table; they are fellow laborers in the same garden. They can only exist in the same place—in a school—because of one another. And each one's flourishing is dependent on their flourishing together.

We have seen how this orientation fundamentally shifts our grammar from "I" to "we" and from "me" to "us." It also calls us to think more expansively and inclusively about who we count as part of the "we"—who is called to flourish with us—perhaps more so than we have in the past, and perhaps not without discomfort. It calls us to extend our table to our community, to practice hospitality toward guests and strangers, to invite and include those on the margins, to treat all people with honor and dignity as God's image bearers, and to reflect in fuller ways the beauty and diversity of God's creation.

This orientation also leads us to reassess our priorities, change our rhythms, and reimagine our practices so they better align with a vision for flourishing. In doing so, nearly every area of school life is touched—from our school's "life in all its fullness" purpose, shared and enacted together; to our mutual relationships that, through abiding with each other, impart *shalom*; to our collective learning, not just *from* but also *with* one another; to our wise stewardship and faith-filled generosity around resources; to our holistic well-being, fostered intentionally as well as forged in challenge.

Having come this far, we have one important question left to ask and, we hope, to answer together—*why?* Why would anyone be interested in, let alone committed to, the flourishing of others, especially when our sectors and societies so frequently reward individual pursuit? Why would we include, share, pursue, and engage, when our energies could be invested elsewhere and in more directly self-enriching ways? Why would we expend the degree of prayer, thought, intentionality, humility, and commitment necessitated by a vision for flourishing together? Why would I choose to believe that "I am because you are," especially when that belief will reshape how I define and live out my purpose, relationships, learning, resources, and well-being?

At the heart of this vision for flourishing together is not simply a well-intentioned desire to build community and live well together. Rather, it is much deeper, and more transformative, because it gets to the heart of what makes such a vision for flourishing "Christian." Our answer to these "why would" questions is *love*. Love would—and therefore we should.

Love is the central message of the biblical narrative, toward which everything is drawn and about which everything turns. As the apostle John writes:

> My beloved friends, let us continue to love each other since love comes from God. Everyone who loves is born of God and experiences a relationship with God. The person who refuses to love doesn't know the first thing about God, because God is love—so you can't know him if you don't love. This is how God showed his love for us: God sent his only Son into the world so we might live through him. This is the kind of love we are talking about— not that we once upon a time loved God, but that he loved us and sent his Son as a sacrifice to clear away our sins and the damage they've done to our relationship with God. My dear, dear friends, if God loved us like this, we certainly ought to love each other. No one has seen God, ever. But if we love one another, God dwells deeply within us, and his love becomes complete in us—perfect love![1]

Love is at the core of our vision for flourishing together. Love is why teachers long to see the flourishing of students, why leaders invest in the flourishing of teachers, and why schools extend themselves in and on behalf of their communities. Love is the measure by which we will know if our Christian vision of education is achieved—as Jesus says in John's gospel, "By this everyone will know that you are my disciples, if you love one another."[2]

Love is a noun that is usually at its best as a verb; it is most compelling when seen in action versus written on a wall or a website. For these reasons, as we conclude our journey together, we humbly offer an "educator's paraphrase" of the apostle Paul's famous love passage, from his first letter to the church at Corinth. As Scripture encourages, may it help us to "think of ways to motivate one another to acts of love and good works"[3] as we pursue flourishing together in our schools.

1 Corinthians 13:1–8—An Educator's Paraphrase

If I tirelessly teach five outstanding lessons a day, and see my
students make excellent progress against their targets, but
have not love, I am only a broken window or a wall covered
in graffiti.

If I create a perfect climate for learning, have excellent meetings
with parents, and resolve all the problems of the day
through focused toil, but have not love, I am only an uneaten school lunch or a messy office.

If I give all I have to my school and work a seventy-hour week,
grading, planning, preparing, and evaluating, and have the
most perfect color-coded action plan to guide my path, but
have not love, I gain nothing.

Love is patient—showing sustaining praise, and giving students
courage to come back the next day.

Love is kind—noticing the lonely and connecting them with a
potential new friend, as well as shaping a teacher's welcome
to a student who just transferred from another school.

It does not envy what other schools, educators, or students have—
but rather practices gratefulness for the blessings it has
been given.

It does not boast—in external or superficial markers of success that most societies prioritize over a holistic education that leads to deep and abiding character.

It is not proud—refusing to label any student or vocation as "beneath" its program of study, or any family as undesirable because of their inability to pay.

It is not rude—whether by turning a blind eye to the needs of its neighbors, or by turning away those who desire to flourish within its community.

It is not self-seeking—instead giving its best resources away to other organizations, seeking their success as keenly as its own.

It is not easily angered—by differences of perspective, opinion, doctrine, or politics.

It keeps no record of wrongs—always offering wise fresh starts, and finding grace before remembering fault.

Love does not delight in evil but rejoices with the truth—whether redressing disparities and disadvantage or correcting prejudice and injustice—all of which abuse and insult fellow human beings, created in the image of God with equal value and worth.

It always protects—for example, by adapting learning plans for students who have experienced trauma, in order to prioritize belonging and safety over knowledge transfer; or by asking patient questions of a colleague struggling with mental health issues.

It always trusts—believing in and being vulnerable to others, despite the very human tendency to disappoint and fall short.

It always hopes—in the most expansive and capacious vision for education possible, reflecting the "life in all its fullness" that Jesus came to offer.

It always perseveres—no matter the level of crisis or the depth of daily challenge it may face.

Love never fails—in desiring, calling, and enabling us to flourish together.

Notes

Preface

1. John 10:10b.
2. Lynn E. Swaner, Dan Beerens, and Erik Ellefsen, eds., *MindShift: Catalyzing Change in Christian Education* (Colorado Springs: Association of Christian Schools International, 2019).
3. See "Statutory Inspection of Anglican and Methodist Schools (SIAMS): An Evaluation Schedule for Schools and Inspectors" (2018), https://www.churchof england.org/sites/default/files/2018-Evaluation%20Schedule%202018_0.pdf.
4. Lynn E. Swaner, Charlotte A. Marshall, and Sheri A. Tesar, *Flourishing Schools: Research on Christian School Culture and Community* (Colorado Springs: Association of Christian Schools International, 2019).
5. 1 Corinthians 12:25–26 (MSG).
6. Martin Luther King Jr., "Letter from a Birmingham Jail" (1963), https://king institute.stanford.edu/king-papers/documents/letter-birmingham-jail.

Introduction

1. C. S. Lewis, *Mere Christianity* (London: Macmillan, 1952), 82.
2. John 10:10b (NCV).
3. Corey L. M. Keyes, "The Mental Health Continuum: From Languishing to Flourishing in Life," *Journal of Health and Social Behavior* 43, no. 2 (2002): 207–22.
4. We are deeply indebted to Dr. David Ford, Regius Professor of Divinity at the University of Cambridge, and to Dr. Paula Gooder, Canon Chancellor of St. Paul's Cathedral, for their generosity in conversation around many of the biblical passages discussed in this book.
5. David F. Ford and Andy Wolfe, *Called, Connected, Committed: 24 Leader-*

ship Practices for Educational Leaders (London: The Church of England Education Office, 2020).

6. Genesis 1:26.

7. Psalm 139:14.

8. Acts 17:26.

9. Ephesians 2:10.

10. Job 12:7–8a (NLT).

11. Mark S. Boyce, "Wolves for Yellowstone: Dynamics in Time and Space," *Journal of Mammalogy* 99, no. 5 (2018): 1021–31.

12. BBC News, accessed October 11, 2020, https://www.bbc.com/future/article /20140128-how-wolves-saved-a-famous-park.

13. 1 Corinthians 12:25–26 (MSG).

14. John 10:10b (NCV).

15. Ecclesiastes 3:1; Psalm 1:3 (NIV).

16. Lynn E. Swaner, Charlotte A. Marshall, and Sheri A. Tesar, *Flourishing Schools: Research on Christian School Culture and Community* (Colorado Springs: Association of Christian Schools International, 2019).

17. Étienne Wenger and Beverly Wenger-Trayner, *Communities of Practice: A Brief Introduction* (2015), https://wenger-trayner.com/wp-content/uploads/2015 /04/07-Brief-introduction-to-communities-of-practice.pdf, 1; see also Étienne Wenger, *Communities of Practice: Learning, Meaning, and Identity* (Cambridge: Cambridge University Press, 2018).

18. Lee G. Bolman and Terrence E. Deal, *Reframing Organizations: Artistry, Choice, and Leadership* (New York: John Wiley & Sons, 2017), 205.

19. Richard P. Rumelt, *Good Strategy, Bad Strategy: The Difference and Why It Matters* (London: Profile Books, 2017), 6–7, emphasis in original.

20. Andy Stanley, *Visioneering: Your Guide for Discovering and Maintaining Personal Vision* (Sisters, OR: Multnomah, 2016), 18, emphases added.

Chapter 1

1. Donovan L. Graham, *Teaching Redemptively: Bringing Grace and Truth into Your Classroom* (Colorado Springs: Purposeful Design, 2009), 49; emphasis in original.

2. Angela Duckworth, *Grit: The Power of Passion and Perseverance* (New York: Scribner, 2016), 149.

3. Steven Garber, *Visions of Vocation: Common Grace for the Common Good* (Downers Grove, IL: IVP, 2014), 202.

4. Warren Cole Smith and John Stonestreet, *Restoring All Things: God's Audacious Plan to Save the World through Everyday People* (Grand Rapids: Baker, 2015), 19–20.

5. Garber, *Visions of Vocation*, 27–28, emphasis in original.

6. Ephesians 2:10 (NIV).

7. Smith and Stonestreet, *Restoring All Things*, 100–101.

8. Peter Block, *The Answer to How Is Yes: Acting on What Matters* (San Francisco: Berrett-Koehler, 2003), 4.

9. *Responsibility* is one of the thirty-five validated constructs in the Flourishing School Culture Model (FSCM). Throughout this book, FSCM constructs are italicized and referenced in the notes for each chapter.

10. Peter Greer and Chris Horst, *Mission Drift: The Unspoken Crisis Facing Leaders, Charities, and Churches* (Minneapolis: Bethany House, 2015), 156.

11. *Partnership* is a construct in the FSCM.

12. 1 Peter 4:8–9 (NIV).

13. "Integrated purpose" corresponds to the construct *Integrated Worldview* in the FSCM. It is renamed here to be inclusive of both "biblical worldview" (in North America) and "Christian vision" (in the United Kingdom).

14. Joseph Murphy, *Leading School Improvement: A Framework for Action* (West Palm Beach: Learning Sciences International, 2016), 39.

15. David F. Ford and Andy Wolfe, *Called, Connected, Committed: 24 Leadership Practices for Educational Leaders* (London: The Church of England Education Office, 2020), 7.

16. David Smith, *On Christian Teaching: Practicing Faith in the Classroom* (Grand Rapids: Eerdmans, 2018), 132.

17. Mark 2:27.

18. *Shabbat* in Hebrew.

19. Smith, *On Christian Teaching*, 133.

20. Smith, *On Christian Teaching*, 135.

21. Walter Brueggemann, *Prophetic Imagination*, 2nd ed. (Minneapolis: Fortress, 2001), 40.

22. Ephesians 3:20.

23. "Holistic learning" corresponds to the construct *Holistic Teaching* in the

FSCM. It is rephrased here to place the emphasis on students' experiences (learning) versus teachers' activity (teaching).

24. David H. Hargreaves, "A Capital Theory of School Effectiveness and Improvement," *British Educational Research Journal* 27, no. 4 (2001): 488.

25. See Joseph L. Mahoney and Roger P. Weissberg, "SEL: What the Research Says," *Educational Leadership* 76, no. 2 (2018): 34–35; Rex Miller, Bill Latham, Kevin Baird, and Michelle Kinder, *WHOLE: What Teachers Need to Help Students Thrive* (San Francisco: Jossey-Bass, 2020).

26. *Spiritual Formation* is a construct in the FSCM.

27. These findings comprise the *Questioning* construct in the FSCM.

28. *God's Story* is a construct in the FSCM.

29. Graham, *Teaching Redemptively*, 102, 105.

30. Graham, *Teaching Redemptively*, 104–5.

31. Smith and Stonestreet, *Restoring All Things*, 100–101.

Chapter 2

1. John 10:10b (NCV).

2. John 20:31 (MSG).

3. John 1:38 (NIV); from the Greek *zetein*, to seek; also a very Johannine concept, used thirty-four times in this gospel (which equates to 25 percent of all uses of the word across the whole New Testament). It has the sense of "What are you looking for?" and "What do you desire?"—both surprising first questions for the conversation between Jesus and the disciples.

4. John 2:1–12.

5. John 4:14; John 6:12–13.

6. John 21:11 (NIV).

7. John 16:33.

8. John 10:9 (NIV).

9. John 10:4 (NIV).

10. John 2:1–11.

11. John 4:4–42; John 7:53–8:11.

12. Luke 4:18–19.

13. John 3:16 (NIV).

14. John 3:16; 17:23–24; John 3:35; 5:20; 10:17; and 15:9–10.

15. John 21:15–17.

16. John 13:34–35 (NIV).

17. 1 Corinthians 13:7–8 (NIV).

18. Dan Beerens, Justin Cook, and Kathryn Wiens, "From Machine to Human," in *MindShift: Catalyzing Change in Christian Education*, ed. Lynn E. Swaner, Dan Beerens, and Erik Ellefsen (Colorado Springs: Association of Christian Schools International, 2019), 27–39.

19. Marianne Vangoor, "What Does Love Require?," *ACSI Blog*, 2019, https://blog.acsi.org/love-thy-neighbor; Bob Goff, *Everybody, Always: Becoming Love in a World Full of Setbacks and Difficult People* (Nashville: Nelson, 2018).

20. Vangoor, "What Does Love Require?"; italics in original.

21. Marianne Vangoor, email message to author, October 16, 2020.

22. Angie Bonvanie, email message to author, October 18, 2020.

23. 1 Timothy 6:19.

Chapter 3

1. Heidi Hayes Jacobs and Marie Hubley Alcock, *Bold Moves for Schools: How We Can Create Remarkable Learning Environments* (Alexandria, VA: ASCD, 2017), 7.

2. Priscilla Shirer, *One in a Million: Journey to Your Promised Land* (Nashville: B&H Publishing, 2010), ix.

3. Angela Duckworth, *Grit: The Power of Passion and Perseverance* (New York: Scribner, 2016), 149.

4. Ecclesiastes 3:11 (NIV).

5. Jeremiah 17:8 (NIV).

6. With thanks to Rex Miller for the inspiration for this activity, which he calls developing an organization's "Pixar Story," patterned on the highly successful formula developed by Disney's Pixar for animated filmmaking.

Chapter 4

1. Julie Causton and Kate MacLeod, *From Behaving to Belonging: The Inclusive Art of Supporting Students Who Challenge Us* (Alexandria, VA: ASCD, 2020), 3.

2. James Davison Hunter, *To Change the World: The Irony, Tragedy, and Possibility of Christianity Today* (New York: Oxford University Press, 2010), 244.

3. Hunter, *To Change the* World, 244.

4. "Engaging families" corresponds to the construct *Family Relationships* in the Flourishing School Culture Model (FSCM).

5. See Leonidas Kyriakides et al., "A Synthesis of Studies Searching for School Factors: Implications for Theory and Research," *British Educational Research Journal* 36, no. 5 (2010): 807–30.

6. Debbie Zacarian and Michael Silverstone, "Building Partnerships Through Classroom-Based Events," *Educational Leadership* 75, no. 1 (2017): 13.

7. See David Hopkins and David Reynolds, "The Past, Present and Future of School Improvement: Towards the Third Age," *British Educational Research Journal* 27, no. 4 (2001): 459–75.

8. Romans 12:18 (NIV).

9. *Community Engagement* is a construct in the FSCM.

10. See Joseph Murphy, *Leading School Improvement: A Framework for Action* (West Palm Beach, FL: Learning Sciences International, 2016); David Reynolds et al., "Educational Effectiveness Research (EER): A State-of-the-Art Review," *School Effectiveness and School Improvement* 25, no. 2 (2014): 197–230; G. Sue Shannon and Pete Bylsma, *Nine Characteristics of High-Performing Schools* (Olympia, WA: Office of Superintendent of Public Instruction, 2007).

11. Jeremiah 29:7 (MSG).

12. Nicholas Wolterstorff, *Educating for Shalom: Essays on Christian Higher Education*, ed. Clarence W. Joldersma and Gloria Goris Stronks (Grand Rapids: Eerdmans, 2004), 7.

13. "Removing barriers" corresponds to the construct *Insular Culture* in the FSCM. It is rephrased here to provide a sense of positive action that can be taken to remedy the tendency of school communities toward insularity.

14. Matthew 19:14 (NIV).

15. Daniel Pampuch and Darren Iselin, "From Siloed to Engaged," in *MindShift: Catalyzing Change in Christian Education*, ed. Lynn E. Swaner, Dan Beerens, and Erik Ellefsen (Colorado Springs: Association of Christian Schools International, 2019), 93–106.

16. Wolterstorff, *Educating for Shalom*, 22–23.

17. See Lynn E. Swaner and Roger C. S. Erdvig, *Bring It to Life: Christian Education and the Transformative Power of Service-Learning* (Colorado Springs: Association of Christian Schools International, 2018).

18. Hunter, *To Change the World*, 95.

19. This construct is titled *Insular Culture* in the FSCM.

20. Robert Loe, *The Relational Teacher*, 2nd ed. (Cambridge: The Relational Schools Foundation, 2016), 9.

21. "Collective leadership" encompasses the constructs *Supportive Leadership* and *Leadership Interdependence* in the FSCM.

22. See for example Kenneth Leithwood, Karen Seashore Louis, Stephen Anderson, and Kyla Wahlstrom, *How Leadership Influences Student Learning* (Saint Paul: Center for Applied Research and Educational Improvement, University of Minnesota, 2004); Hilda Borko, Shelby A. Wolf, Genet Simone, and Kay Pippin Uchiyama, "Schools in Transition: Reform Efforts and School Capacity in Washington State," *American Educational Research Association* 25, no. 2 (2003): 171–201; Karen Seashore Louis, Kenneth Leithwood, Kyla L. Wahlstrom, and Stephen E. Anderson, *Investigating the Links to Improved Student Learning: Executive Summary of Research Findings* (Saint Paul: Center for Applied Research and Educational Improvement, University of Minnesota, 2010).

23. Jonathan Eckert, *Leading Together: Teachers and Administrators Improving Student Outcomes* (Thousand Oaks, CA: Corwin, 2018), 10–11.

24. *Leadership Interdependence* is a construct in the FSCM.

25. *Supportive Leadership* is a construct in the FSCM.

26. 1 Corinthians 1:10 (NIV).

27. *Collaboration* is a construct in the FSCM.

28. See Karin Chenoweth, *"It's Being Done": Academic Success in Unexpected Schools* (Cambridge, MA: Harvard Educational Publishing Group, 2007); Karin Chenoweth, "How Do We Get There from Here?," *Educational Leadership* 75, no. 2 (2015): 16–20.

29. See Cristina Devecchi and Martyn Rouse, "An Exploration of the Features of Effective Collaboration between Teachers and Teaching Assistants in Secondary Schools," *Support for Learning* 25, no. 2 (2010): 91–99.

30. See Hopkins and Reynolds, "The Past, Present and Future of School Improvement."

31. Étienne Wenger and Beverly Wenger-Trayner, *Communities of Practice: A Brief Introduction* (2015), https://wenger-trayner.com/wp-content/uploads/2015/04/07-Brief-introduction-to-communities-of-practice.pdf, 1.

32. See Lynn E. Swaner, *Professional Development for Christian School Educa-*

tors and Leaders: Frameworks and Best Practices (Colorado Springs: Association of Christian Schools International, 2016).

33. Peter M. Senge, *The Fifth Discipline: The Art and Practice of the Learning Organization* (New York: Doubleday/Currency, 1990), 3.

34. Amanda Keddie, "School Collaborations within the Contemporary English Education System: Possibilities and Constraints," *Cambridge Journal of Education* 44, no. 2 (2014): 239.

35. Anthony S. Bryk et al., *Learning to Improve: How America's Schools Can Get Better at Getting Better* (Cambridge, MA: Harvard Education Press, 2017).

36. Andy Wolfe, "From Isolated to Networked," in *MindShift: Catalyzing Change in Christian Education*, ed. Lynn E. Swaner, Dan Beerens, and Erik Ellefsen (Colorado Springs: Association of Christian Schools International, 2019), 59.

37. Joseph Allen et al., "Observations of Effective Teacher-Student Interactions in Secondary School Classrooms: Predicting Student Achievement with the Classroom Assessment Scoring System—Secondary," *School Psychology Review* 42, no. 1 (2013): 78.

38. Loe, *The Relational Teacher*.

39. Teachers demonstrating Christ-like love, kindness, and care corresponds to the construct *Christlike Teachers* in the FSCM.

40. As the name suggests, staff mentoring of students corresponds to the construct *Mentoring Students* in the FSCM.

41. Loe, *The Relational Teacher*, 9.

42. *Caring Environment* is a construct in the FSCM.

43. Louise Michelle Bombèr, *Inside I'm Hurting: Practical Strategies for Supporting Children with Attachment Difficulties in Schools* (London: Worth, 2007).

44. Leonidas Kyriakides et al., "Improving the School Learning Environment to Reduce Bullying: An Experimental Study," *Scandinavian Journal of Educational Research* 58, no. 4 (2013): 453.

45. Loe, *The Relational Teacher*.

46. Erik W. Carter, "A Place of Belonging: Research at the Intersection of Faith and Disability," *Review & Expositor* 113, no. 2 (2016): 168.

47. Carter, "A Place of Belonging," 172.

48. Carter, "A Place of Belonging," 176.

49. Carter, "A Place of Belonging," 177.

50. Carter, "A Place of Belonging," 177–78.

51. 1 John 4:7 (NIV).

52. Karen Marie Yust, *Real Kids, Real Faith: Practices for Nurturing Children's Spiritual Lives* (Hoboken, NJ: John Wiley & Sons, 2004).

Chapter 5

1. 1 John 4:8; John 3:16; John 15:9.

2. Matthew 22:37–39.

3. See the parable of the Good Samaritan in Luke 10:25–37.

4. Colossians 3:12–13; Ephesians 4:2–3; 1 Peter 2:17.

5. John 1:38; see also John 2:12; 4:40; 11:6.

6. Jeremiah 17:7–8 (NIV).

7. John 15:4 (NIV).

8. 2 Corinthians 8:7 (NIV).

9. Matthew 8:10.

10. Matthew 9:11–13.

11. Note the response of Zacchaeus, who pledged to "restore fourfold" whatever he had defrauded, in Luke 19:8.

12. John 13:8.

13. John 13:14–15 (NIV).

14. Nicholas Wolterstorff, *Educating for Shalom: Essays on Christian Higher Education*, ed. Clarence W. Joldersma and Gloria Goris Stronks (Grand Rapids: Eerdmans, 2004), 7.

15. Jeremiah 29:7 (NIV).

16. Joel Gaines (head of The City School), interview with Lynn Swaner, October 2020; all quotes same, unless attributed otherwise.

17. A reference by the student to Deuteronomy 28:6.

18. "Mighty Writers" website, accessed October 19, 2020, https://mightywriters .org/.

19. Abigail Chang, "I've Lost Many Loved Ones Due to a Social 'Norm' in Philadelphia: Gun Violence," *The Philadelphia Inquirer*, September 8, 2020, Opinion, https://www.inquirer.com/opinion/commentary/gun-violence-philadelphia-hom icides-southwest-teens-solutions-20200904.html.

20. Michael Chen, Jenny Brady, and Joel Gaines, "From White to Mosaic," in *MindShift: Catalyzing Change in Christian Education*, ed. Lynn E. Swaner, Dan

Beerens, and Erik Ellefsen (Colorado Springs: Association of Christian Schools International, 2019), 73.

21. Wolterstorff, *Educating for Shalom*, 22.

22. Wolterstorff, *Educating for Shalom*, 75.

23. John 14:27.

24. John 20:19, 21, 26.

Chapter 6

1. Ruth Haley Barton, *Pursuing God's Will Together: A Discernment Practice for Leadership Groups* (Downers Grove, IL: IVP, 2012), 97.

2. John Hambrick, *Move toward the Mess: The Ultimate Fix for a Boring Christian Life* (Colorado Springs: David C. Cook, 2016), 151.

3. Nel Noddings, *Caring: A Relational Approach to Ethics and Moral Education* (Berkeley: University of California Press, 1984), xxii, xxi.

4. Brené Brown, *Dare to Lead: Brave Work, Tough Conversations, Whole Hearts* (New York: Random House, 2019), 13.

Chapter 7

1. Eleanor Drago-Severson, *Leading Adult Learning: Supporting Adult Development in Our Schools* (Thousand Oaks, CA: Corwin, 2009), 283.

2. James K. A. Smith, *You Are What You Love: The Spiritual Power of Habit* (Grand Rapids: Brazos, 2016), 164.

3. Warren Cole Smith and John Stonestreet, *Restoring All Things: God's Audacious Plan to Save the World through Everyday People* (Grand Rapids: Baker, 2015), 93–94; emphasis in original.

4. John E. Hull, "Aiming for Christian Education, Settling for Christians Educating: The Christian School's Replication of a Public School Paradigm," *Christian Scholar's Review* 32, no. 2 (2003): 203–223, quotations on 206–7 and 204.

5. Peter Senge, Nelda Cambron-McCabe, Timothy Lucas, Bryan Smith, Janis Dutton, and Art Kleiner, *Schools That Learn: A Fifth Discipline Fieldbook for Educators, Parents, and Everyone Who Cares about Education* (New York: Crown Business, 2012), 35.

6. Dan Beerens, Justin Cook, and Kathryn Wiens, "From Machine to Human," in *MindShift: Catalyzing Change in Christian Education*, ed. Lynn E. Swaner, Dan

Beerens, and Erik Ellefsen (Colorado Springs: Association of Christian Schools International, 2019), 39.

7. Steven Garber, *The Fabric of Faithfulness: Weaving Together Belief and Behavior* (Downers Grove, IL: IVP, 2007), 98.

8. Étienne Wenger and Beverly Wenger-Trayner, *Communities of Practice: A Brief Introduction* (2015), https://wenger-trayner.com/wp-content/uploads/2015/04/07-Brief-introduction-to-communities-of-practice.pdf, 1.

9. Joseph Murphy, *Leading School Improvement: A Framework for Action* (West Palm Beach, FL: Learning Sciences International, 2016), 45–46.

10. "Learning culture" corresponds to the construct *Culture of Improvement* in the Flourishing School Culture Model (FSCM).

11. Terrence E. Deal and Kent D. Peterson, *Shaping School Culture: Pitfalls, Paradoxes, and Promises* (San Francisco: Jossey-Bass, 2016), 9.

12. David Hopkins and David Reynolds, "The Past, Present and Future of School Improvement: Towards the Third Age," *British Educational Research Journal* 27, no. 4 (2001): 473.

13. *Outcomes Focus* is a construct in the FSCM.

14. Hopkins and Reynolds, "The Past, Present and Future of School Improvement," 473.

15. "Use of data" refers to the construct of *Data-Driven Improvement* in the FSCM.

16. Lisa Evans, Bill Thornton, and Janet Usinger, "Theoretical Frameworks to Guide School Improvement," *NASSP Bulletin* 96, no. 2 (2012): 165; *Systems Thinking* is a construct in the FSCM.

17. Chrys Dougherty and Jean Rutherford, *The NCEA Core Practice Framework: An Organizing Guide to Sustained School Improvement* (Austin, TX: Distributed by ERIC Clearinghouse, 2009), 1–2.

18. Senge et al., *Schools That Learn*, 5.

19. See David A. Garvin, *Learning in Action: A Guide to Putting the Learning Organization to Work* (Boston: Harvard Business Review Press, 2015); Donald A. Schön, *Educating the Reflective Practitioner* (San Francisco: Jossey-Bass, 2016).

20. See Laura M. Desimone, "Improving Impact Studies of Teachers' Professional Development: Toward Better Conceptualizations and Measures," *Educational Researcher* 38, no. 3 (2009): 181–99; Lynn E. Swaner, *Professional Development for Christian School Educators and Leaders: Frameworks and Best Practices* (Colorado Springs: Association of Christian Schools International, 2016).

21. The New Teacher Project, *The Mirage: Confronting the Hard Truth about Our Quest for Teacher Development* (Brooklyn: TNTP, 2015), 3.

22. *Feedback* is a construct in the FSCM.

23. Douglas B. Reeves, *Reframing Teacher Leadership to Improve Your School* (Alexandria, VA: ASCD, 2008); Douglas B. Reeves, *Transforming Professional Development into Student Results* (Alexandria, VA: ASCD, 2010), 2–3.

24. James 3:17.

25. See Karen Kearney, *Effective Principals for California Schools: Building a Coherent Leadership Development System* (San Francisco: WestEd, 2010); also, the Church of England Foundation for Educational Leadership's programs may be a helpful example of this approach, whereby leaders' knowledge and skills development and resultant performance appraisals are underpinned, shaped, and enhanced by the vision-driven leadership practices, as outlined in David F. Ford and Andy Wolfe, *Called, Connected, Committed: 24 Leadership Practices for Educational Leaders* (London: The Church of England Education Office, 2020).

26. See Andy Wolfe, "From Isolated to Networked," in *MindShift: Catalyzing Change in Christian Education*, ed. Lynn E. Swaner, Dan Beerens, and Erik Ellefsen (Colorado Springs: Association of Christian Schools International, 2019), 53–63.

27. Senge et al., *Schools That Learn*, 69.

28. *Engaged Learning* is a construct in the FSCM.

29. David J. Shernoff, Stephen M. Tonks, and Brett Anderson, "The Impact of the Learning Environment on Student Engagement in High School Classrooms," *National Society for the Study of Education* 113, no. 1 (2014): 174.

30. A "strengths-based approach to learning" corresponds to the construct *Individualized Instruction* in the FSCM.

31. Roberto D'Erizans and Tamatha Bibbo, "Time to Reflect: E-Portfolios and the Development of Growth Mindsets," *Independent School* 74, no. 2 (2015): 80.

32. See Dan Rothstein, Luz Santana, and Wendy D. Puriefoy, *Make Just One Change: Teach Students to Ask Their Own Questions* (Cambridge, MA: Harvard Education Press, 2017).

33. "Holistic learning" corresponds to the construct *Holistic Teaching* in the FSCM. It is rephrased here to place the emphasis on students' experiences (learning) versus teachers' activity (teaching).

34. Garber, *The Fabric of Faithfulness*, 89.

35. The Church of England Education Office, *"Deeply Christian, Serving the Common Good": The Church of England Vision for Education* (London, 2016).

36. Schools in the United Kingdom refer to "behaviors for learning" (BFL) systems, while in North America the term more commonly used is "classroom management." We prefer the term "BFL" because it places the emphasis on positive student behaviors as well as the goal of such a system, which is student learning.

37. Brian M. Stecher et al., *Toward a Culture of Consequences: Performance-Based Accountability Systems for Public Services* (Santa Monica, CA: RAND, 2010), 144–45.

38. 1 Corinthians 6:11 (NIV).

39. See Carol S. Dweck, *Mindset: The New Psychology of Success* (New York: Ballantine Books, 2016); Bill Murphy Jr., "Want to Train Yourself to Succeed? Science Says These 3 Things Matter Most," *Inc.*, June 7, 2017, https://www.inc.com/bill-murphy-jr/want-to-train-yourself-to-succeed-science-says-these-3-things-matter-most.html; Kong Wah Cora Chan, "Servant Leadership Cultivates Grit and Growth Mindset in Learners," *Servant Leadership: Theory and Practice* 3, no. 2 (2016): 12–22.

40. This is sometimes referred to as "beautiful work"; cf. Ron Berger, "Beautiful Work: MyPBLWorks," Beautiful Work | MyPBLWorks, 2015, https://my.pblworks.org/resource/document/beautiful_work.

Chapter 8

1. Peter Block, *The Answer to How Is Yes: Acting on What Matters* (San Francisco: Berrett-Koehler, 2003), ii.

2. Martin B. Copenhaver, *Jesus Is the Question: The 307 Questions Jesus Asked and the 3 He Answered* (Nashville: Abingdon, 2014), xix.

3. Copenhaver, *Jesus Is the Question*, xix.

4. Copenhaver, *Jesus Is the Question*, xxii.

5. Matthew 16:9 (NASB).

6. John 5:6b (NIV).

7. Mark 4:40 (NLT).

8. Luke 10:36 (NIV).

9. See World Economic Forum, *New Vision for Education: Fostering Social and Emotional Learning through Technology* (Geneva: World Economic Forum, 2016).

10. Rex Miller, Bill Latham, and Brian Cahill, *Humanizing the Education Machine: How to Create Schools That Turn Disengaged Kids into Inspired Learners* (Hoboken, NJ: John Wiley & Sons, 2017), 4.

11. Genesis 1:27.

12. Mark 10:46–52.

13. Mark 10:51 (NIV).

14. Copenhaver, *Jesus Is the Question*, 72.

15. Dan Beerens, Justin Cook, and Kathryn Wiens, "From Machine to Human," in *MindShift: Catalyzing Change in Christian Education*, ed. Lynn E. Swaner, Dan Beerens, and Erik Ellefsen (Colorado Springs: Association of Christian Schools International, 2019), 28.

16. Copenhaver, *Jesus Is the Question*, 9.

17. Lewis, *Mere Christianity* (London: Macmillan, 1952), 82.

18. Luke 8:25.

19. Luke 8:25 (KJV).

20. Matthew 14:33.

21. James K. A. Smith, *How (Not) to Be Secular: Reading Charles Taylor* (Grand Rapids: Eerdmans, 2015), 4; emphasis in original.

22. Christian D. Kettler, *The God Who Believes: Faith, Doubt, and the Vicarious Humanity of Christ* (Eugene, OR: Wipf and Stock, 2005), 50.

23. Frank D. Rees, *Wrestling with Doubt: Theological Reflections on the Journey of Faith* (Collegeville, MN: Liturgical Press, 2001), 147.

24. *Questioning* is a construct in the FSCM.

25. John 10:24–25 (NIV).

26. Matthew 16:13–16.

27. Copenhaver, *Jesus Is the Question*, xxiii.

28. Matthew 16:17 (NIV).

29. David Smith, *On Christian Teaching: Practicing Faith in the Classroom* (Grand Rapids: Eerdmans, 2018), 6.

30. The concept of the "banking" model of education is attributable to Paulo Freire; see Paulo Freire, *Pedagogy of the Oppressed* (New York: Herder and Herder, 1972).

31. Matthew 16:17.

32. Cf. Étienne Wenger and Beverly Wenger-Trayner, *Communities of Practice: A Brief Introduction* (2015), https://wenger-trayner.com/wp-content/uploads/2015/04/07-Brief-introduction-to-communities-of-practice.pdf.

33. Matthew 16:17 (NIV).

34. Ephesians 1:17.

35. James K. A. Smith, *You Are What You Love: The Spiritual Power of Habit* (Grand Rapids: Brazos, 2016), 164; emphases in original.

36. Gary Arnold, email message to Lynn Swaner, September 24, 2020; all quotes same, unless attributed otherwise. We would also like to thank the LRCA leadership, including Justin Smith (head of upper school and vice president), Ann Chami (head of lower school), Tyler Eatherton (junior high assistant principal), and Lee-Ann Murry (middle school assistant principal), for discussion with the author.

37. Justin Smith, "The Harkness Approach Brings Student-Centered, Discussion-Based Learning to LRCA," *The Warrior*, Winter 2018, 10–12.

38. Justin Smith, "Blueprinting Harkness," *The Warrior,* Winter 2020, 10.

39. Justin Smith (head of upper school and vice president), interview with Lynn Swaner, October 2020.

40. Erik Ellefsen and Justin Smith, "From Scarcity to Abundance," in *MindShift*, 47.

41. Smith, "The Harkness Approach Brings Student-Centered, Discussion-Based Learning to LRCA," 13.

Chapter 9

1. Sonia Sotomayor, *My Beloved World* (New York: Random House, 2013), 384.

2. Parker J. Palmer, "The Heart of a Teacher: Identity and Integrity in Teaching," *Change: The Magazine of Higher Learning* 29, no. 6 (1997): 15–16.

3. Bill Lucas, "A Five-Dimensional Model of Creativity and Its Assessment in Schools," *Applied Measurement in Education* 29, no. 4 (2016): 278–90.

4. Walter Brueggemann, *Prophetic Imagination*, 2nd ed. (Minneapolis: Fortress, 2001), 40.

5. Bill Lucas and Ellen Spencer, *Teaching Creative Thinking: Developing Learners Who Generate Ideas and Can Think Critically* (Bancyfelin, UK: Crown House, 2017).

6. Max Coates, "Setting Direction: Vision, Values and Culture," in *School Leadership and Education System Reform*, ed. Peter Earley and Toby Greany (London: Bloomsbury, 2017), 91.

7. The Church of England Education Office, *"Deeply Christian, Serving the Common Good": The Church of England Vision for Education* (London, 2016).

8. Proverbs 27:17 (NIV).

9. James K. A. Smith, *On the Road with Saint Augustine: A Real-World Spirituality for Restless Hearts* (Grand Rapids: Brazos, 2019), xii.

Chapter 10

1. C. S. Lewis, *Mere Christianity* (London: Macmillan, 1952), 190.

2. Anne Frank, *The Works of Anne Frank* (Westport, CT: Greenwood, 1977).

3. 2 Corinthians 9:8 (NIV); 2 Corinthians 9:11a (NIV).

4. R. Scott Rodin, *The Steward Leader: Transforming People, Organizations and Communities* (Downers Grove, IL: IVP Academic, 2010), 157.

5. Ellefsen and Smith, "From Scarcity to Abundance," in *MindShift: Catalyzing Change in Christian Education*, ed. Lynn E. Swaner, Dan Beerens, and Erik Ellefsen (Colorado Springs: Association of Christian Schools International, 2019), 42–44.

6. Ellefsen and Smith, "From Scarcity to Abundance," 42–44.

7. Carol S. Dweck, *Mindset: The New Psychology of Success* (New York: Ballantine Books, 2016).

8. *Resource Constraints* is a construct in the Flourishing School Culture Model (FSCM).

9. Rodin, *The Steward Leader*, 45; emphasis in original.

10. Rodin, *The Steward Leader*, 16.

11. *Resource Planning* is a construct in the FSCM.

12. Rodin, *The Steward Leader*, 174–75.

13. 2 Corinthians 8:7 (NIV).

14. *Qualified Staff* is a construct in the FSCM.

15. Étienne Wenger and Beverly Wenger-Trayner, *Communities of Practice: A Brief Introduction* (2015), https://wenger-trayner.com/wp-content/uploads/2015/04/07-Brief-introduction-to-communities-of-practice.pdf.

16. Thomas L. Friedman, *Thank You for Being Late: An Optimist's Guide to Thriving in the Age of Accelerations* (New York: Farrar, Straus & Giroux, 2016), 4.

17. *Resources* is a construct in the FSCM.

18. Isaiah 1:17; Micah 6:8; Proverbs 31:8–9; Psalm 82:3; Jeremiah 22:3; Zechariah 7:9–10.

19. James 1:27.

20. Donovan L. Graham, *Teaching Redemptively: Bringing Grace and Truth into Your Classroom* (Colorado Springs: Purposeful Design, 2009), 102, 105.

Chapter 11

1. Ezekiel 4:9.
2. John 3:1–21; Luke 19:1–10.
3. Acts 2:42 (NIV).
4. John 6:5 (NIV).
5. John 6:7 (NIV).
6. John 6:9 (NIV).
7. Matthew 18:4.
8. Luke 9:14–15.
9. Matthew 16:16.
10. Luke 22:19.
11. John 6:35 (NIV).
12. Romans 8:32.
13. Matthew 19:26 (NLT).
14. Erik Ellefsen and Justin Smith, "From Scarcity to Abundance," in *MindShift: Catalyzing Change in Christian Education*, ed. Lynn E. Swaner, Dan Beerens, and Erik Ellefsen (Colorado Springs: Association of Christian Schools International, 2019), 44.
15. Matthew 20:26b, 28.
16. Luke 24:30–31a.
17. Matthew 6:9–13; Luke 11:2–4.
18. Matthew 6:11.
19. Matthew 6:7–8.
20. Richard Rohr, *Just This: Prompts and Practices for Contemplation* (London: SPCK, 2017), 16.
21. Kelly Lee (headteacher, Sneinton Church of England Primary School), interview with Andy Wolfe, October 2020; all quotes from same.

Chapter 12

1. Karin Chenoweth and Christina Theokas, *Getting It Done: Leading Academic Success in Unexpected Schools* (Cambridge, MA: Harvard Education Press, 2011), 186.
2. Richard Rohr, *Just This: Prompts and Practices for Contemplation* (London: SPCK, 2017), 83–84.

3. The Church of England Foundation for Educational Leadership, *Leadership of Character Education: Developing Virtues and Celebrating Human Flourishing in Schools* (London: Church of England, 2017), 3.

4. Genesis 1:10; see also verses 12, 18, 21, 25, 31.

5. Alan Flintham, *Reservoirs of Hope: Sustaining Spirituality in School Leaders* (Newcastle upon Tyne, UK: Cambridge Scholars Publishing, 2011).

6. Christina Rossetti, "A Christmas Carol," *Scribner's Monthly* 3, no. 3 (1872): 278.

Chapter 13

1. Alex Soojung-Kim Pang, *Rest: Why You Get More Done When You Work Less* (New York: Basic Books, 2018), 242.

2. Parker J. Palmer, *Let Your Life Speak: Listening for the Voice of Vocation* (Hoboken, NJ: John Wiley & Sons, 2015), 34.

3. The Children's Society, *The Good Childhood Report* (London, 2020), 3.

4. Corey L. M. Keyes, "The Mental Health Continuum: From Languishing to Flourishing in Life," *Journal of Health and Social Behavior* 43, no. 2 (2002): 207–22.

5. "Data and Statistics on Children's Mental Health," web page, Centers for Disease Control and Prevention, June 15, 2020, https://www.cdc.gov/childrens mentalhealth/data.html.

6. The Children's Society, *The Good Childhood Report*, 3.

7. The Children's Society, *Life on Hold: Children's Well-Being and COVID-19* (London, 2020).

8. Place2Be, "Improving Children's Mental Health in Schools," Place2Be website, accessed October 11, 2020, https://www.place2be.org.uk/.

9. Nancy Lever, Erin Mathis, and Ashley Mayworm, "School Mental Health Is Not Just for Students: Why Teacher and School Staff Wellness Matter," *Report on Emotional and Behavioral Disorders in Youth* 17, no. 1 (2019): 6.

10. Rex Miller, Bill Latham, Kevin Baird, and Michelle Kinder, *WHOLE: What Teachers Need to Help Students Thrive* (San Francisco: Jossey-Bass, 2020), 32.

11. Miller, Latham, Baird, and Kinder, *WHOLE*, 136.

12. Sue Stuart-Smith, *The Well-Gardened Mind: The Restorative Power of Nature* (New York: Simon & Schuster, 2020), 39–40.

13. Pang, *Rest*, 11.

14. Exodus 20:8.

15. *Healthy Living* is a construct in the Flourishing School Culture Model (FSCM).

16. C. S. Lewis, *God in the Dock: Essays on Theology and Ethics*, ed. Walter Hooper (Grand Rapids: Eerdmans, 2014), 118.

17. Miller, Latham, Baird, and Kinder, *WHOLE*, 108–9.

18. *Stress* is a construct in the FSCM, for both teachers and leaders.

19. Miller, Latham, Baird, and Kinder, *WHOLE*, 17.

20. Lever, Mathis, and Mayworm, "School Mental Health Is Not Just for Students."

21. Peter DeWitt, "We Should Be Concerned about the Mental Health of Principals," *Education Week*, August 25, 2020, https://blogs.edweek.org/edweek/finding_common_ground/2020/08/we_should_be_concerned_about_the_mental_health_of_principals.html.

22. See Lever, Mathis, and Mayworm, "School Mental Health Is Not Just for Students," 2, 6.

23. See DeWitt, "We Should Be Concerned about the Mental Health of Principals."

24. Miller, Latham, Baird, and Kinder, *WHOLE*, 150–51.

25. Juliana Menasce Horowitz and Nikki Graf, "Most U.S. Teens See Anxiety, Depression as Major Problems," Pew Research Center's Social & Demographic Trends Project, May 30, 2020, https://www.pewsocialtrends.org/2019/02/20/most-u-s-teens-see-anxiety-and-depression-as-a-major-problem-among-their-peers/.

26. Robert Booth, "Anxiety on Rise among the Young in Social Media Age," *The Guardian*, February 5, 2019, https://www.theguardian.com/society/2019/feb/05/youth-unhappiness-uk-doubles-in-past-10-years.

27. As indicated, *Resilience* is a construct in the FSCM specific to students.

28. Nan Henderson and Mike M. Milstein, *Resiliency in Schools: Making It Happen for Students and Educators* (Thousand Oaks, CA: Corwin Press, 2003), 7.

29. Michele Kielty Briggs et al., "Assessing and Promoting Spiritual Wellness as a Protective Factor in Secondary Schools," *Counseling and Values* 55, no. 2 (2011): 171.

30. See Barbara R. Blackburn, "Five Ways to Strengthen Student Resilience," *The Education Digest* 83, no. 5 (2018): 47–50; Deepika Bali and Anita Sharma, "Art of Fostering Resilience in Adolescents," *Indian Journal of Health and Well-being* 9, no. 1 (2018): 73–75.

31. See Carol Ann Tomlinson, "One to Grow On: Growing Capable Kids," *Educational Leadership* 71, no. 1 (2013): 86.

32. Bari Walsh, "The Science of Resilience: Why Some Children Can Thrive Despite Adversity," Harvard Graduate School of Education, March 23, 2015, https://www.gse.harvard.edu/news/uk/15/03/science-resilience.

33. Louise Bombèr, *Know Me to Teach Me: Differentiated Discipline for Those Recovering from Adverse Childhood Experiences* (Duffield, UK: Worth, 2020).

34. John 16:33 (NIV).

35. Steven Garber, *The Fabric of Faithfulness: Weaving Together Belief and Behavior* (Downers Grove, IL: IVP, 2007), 18.

36. "Other-oriented" corresponds to the construct *Prosocial Orientation* in the FSCM.

37. Mary Raftopoulos and Glen Bates, "'It's That Knowing That You Are Not Alone': The Role of Spirituality in Adolescent Resilience," *International Journal of Children's Spirituality* 16, no. 2 (2011): 152.

38. See Lynn E. Swaner and Roger C. S. Erdvig, *Bring It to Life: Christian Education and the Transformative Power of Service-Learning* (Colorado Springs: Association of Christian Schools International, 2018).

39. Miller, Latham, Baird, and Kinder, *WHOLE*, 249–50.

Chapter 14

1. Jeremiah 17:7–8 (NIV).

2. Parker J. Palmer, *The Courage to Teach: Exploring the Inner Landscape of a Teacher's Life* (San Francisco: Jossey-Bass, 1998), 17.

3. 2 Corinthians 4:7–9 (NIV).

4. See, for example, Matthew 19:21; Mark 10:21; Luke 12:33; Luke 18:22.

5. Matthew 6:19.

6. Galatians 6:2.

7. Luke 2:52 (NIV).

8. Joshua 1:5.

9. Matthew 1:23.

10. Philippians 4:11b–13.

11. Alan Hardie, chief executive of the Northumberland Church of England Academy Trust, interview with Andy Wolfe, October 2020; all quotes from same.

12. 2 Corinthians 4:1 (NIV).

Chapter 15

1. Martin Luther King Jr., *I Have a Dream: Writings and Speeches That Changed the World* (New York: HarperCollins, 1992), 23.
2. Brené Brown, *Dare to Lead: Brave Work, Tough Conversations, Whole Hearts* (New York: Random House, 2019), 17.
3. 1 Corinthians 12:25–26 (MSG).
4. Gillian Schofield and Mary Beek, *The Secure Base Model: Promoting Attachment and Resilience in Foster Care and Adoption* (London: British Association of Adoption and Fostering, 2014).
5. Walter Brueggemann, *Spirituality of the Psalms* (Minneapolis: Fortress, 2002).
6. Brueggemann, *Spirituality of the Psalms.*
7. John 15:1–2 (NIV).
8. Luke 13:8–9 (NIV).

Epilogue

1. 1 John 4:7–12 (MSG).
2. John 13:35 (NIV).
3. Hebrews 10:24 (NLT).

Index

Index